Early Families of Lancaster, Lebanon and Dauphin Counties Pennsylvania

Keith A. Dull

HERITAGE BOOKS
2006

HERITAGE BOOKS
AN IMPRINT OF HERITAGE BOOKS, INC.

Books, CDs, and more—Worldwide

For our listing of thousands of titles see our website
at
www.HeritageBooks.com

Published 2006 by
HERITAGE BOOKS, INC.
Publishing Division
65 East Main Street
Westminster, Maryland 21157-5026

Copyright © 1997 Keith A. Dull

Other books by the author:
Early Families of York County, Pennsylvania, Volume 1
Early Families of York County, Pennsylvania, Volume 2
Early Families of Somerset and Fayette Counties, Pennsylvania
Early Families of Berks, Bucks and Montgomery Counties, Pennsylvania
Early German Settlers of York County, Pennsylvania

All rights reserved. No part of this book may be reproduced or transmitted in any form or by any means, electronic or mechanical, including photocopying, recording or by any information storage and retrieval system without written permission from the author, except for the inclusion of brief quotations in a review.

International Standard Book Number: 978-1-58549-420-8

Contents

Sources and Abbreviations	v
Biehlmajer	1
Ehrhardt	6
Friesner	20
Fuesser	40
Griffith	46
Grimm	47
Horauff/Harruff	52
Haushalter	64
Hess	68
Houtz	69
Kern	71
Maurer	87
Miller	90
Moser	91
Mueller	94
Neff	95
Schaack/Schock	111
Schwingel	122
Shope	130
Stein	134
Dester/Tester	136
Weidman	142
Index	147

Sources

These genealogies were compiled from research conducted at the Allen County Public Library, Fort Wayne, Indiana; the Huntington County Public Library, Huntington, Indiana; the Indiana State Library, Indianapolis, Indiana; and the York County, Historical Society, York, Pennsylvania.

The following court records were consulted:

Adams County, Pennsylvania wills, tax lists, and deeds.
Bedford County, Pennsylvania deeds and tax lists.
Dauphin County, Pennsylvania wills, tax lists, and deeds.
Lancaster County, Pennsylvania wills, tax lists, and deeds.
Lebanon County, Pennsylvania wills, tax lists, and deeds.
Somerset County, Pennsylvania tax lists and wills.
York County, Pennsylvania wills, tax lists, and deeds.
Fairfield County, Ohio tax lists and wills.
Madison County, Ohio tax lists and wills.
Ross County, Ohio tax lists and wills.
Hardy County, Virginia/West Virginia wills, tax lists, and deeds.
Hampshire County, Virginia/West Virginia wills, tax lists, and deeds.
Frederick County, Virginia wills tax lists, and deeds.
Monongalia County, Virginia wills, tax lists and deeds.
Rockingham County, Virginia wills tax lists, and deeds.
Shenandoah County, Virginia wills, tax lists, and deeds.
Frederick County, Maryland wills, tax lists, and deeds.

The following church records were consulted:

Salem Church (Dauphin County).
Reformed Church at Hummelstown (Dauphin County).
Fredericktown Church (Dauphin County).
St. Paul's Church (Dauphin County).
St. Jacob's (Kimmerlin's) (Lebanon County).
Quitophallia Church (Lebanon County).
Zion (Lebanon County).
Trinity Church (Lebanon County).
Bindnagel Church (Lebanon County).
Trinity Church (Lancaster County).
First Reformed Church (Lancaster County).

Cocalico Church (Lancaster County).
Manheim Church (Lancaster County).
Maytown Church (Lancaster County).
Muddy Creek Church (Lancaster County).
Seltenreich Church (Lancaster County).
Christ's Church (Littlestown, Adams County).
Christ's Lutheran (York County).
Trinity (York County).
Berlin Church (Somerset County).
Salisbury Church (Somerset County).
Records of Johan Wilhelm Weber.
Records of Johan Casper Stoever.
Records of Johan Conrad Bucher.

The following census records were consulted:

Adams County, Pennsylvania.
Dauphin County, Pennsylvania.
Lancaster County, Pennsylvania.
Lebanon County, Pennsylvania.
Somerset County, Pennsylvania.
York County, Pennsylvania.
Allen County, Ohio.
Darke County, Ohio.
Fairfield County, Ohio.
Franklin County, Ohio.
Madison County, Ohio.
Marion County, Ohio.
Mercer County, Ohio.
Montgomery County, Ohio.
Pickaway County, Ohio.
Scioto County, Ohio.
Warren County, Ohio.
Delaware County, Indiana.
St. Joseph County, Indiana.
Rockingham County, Virginia.
Shenandoah County, Virginia.
Frederick County, Maryland.

The following books were consulted:

Schenck, Shenk, Shank; History of the Descendants of Andreas Schenck in America by Thomas L. Shank.
18th Century Emigrants from German Speaking Lands to North America, Vol. I & II by Annette K. Burgert.
18th Century Emigrants From Northern Alsace to America by Annette K. Burgert.

Information from the following researchers contributed to portions of this book:

Roger Sims
June Beason
Wilmer Kerns
David Sprinkle

Abbreviations

b. - born
d. - died
m. - married

LANCASTER, LEBANON & DAUPHIN COUNTIES

Michael Biehlmajer

Michael[1a] was b. in 1650. He was a subject of the Deutschen Orden, and farmer at Weidelsbach, Bavaria, Germany. He m. Margaretha. She was b. in 1644, and d. in Weidelbach on Nov. 23, 1700. Michael d. there on Apr. 22, 1714. They were the parents of the following children:

Johann Andreas[1.1a], b. on Dec. 11, 1676.

Michael[1.2a], b. about 1680. In 1701, he resided in Bernhardsweiler, and was a subject of the Deutschen Orden at Weidelbach. In 1726, he was a farmer, subject of Lord Schell, and village major at Bernhardsweiler. He m. Jacobina, daughter of Georg Hasel, at Weidelbach on May 17, 1701, and Maria Anna Dorothea, daughter of Hanss Leonhart Rietmuller, at Weidelbach on Nov. 5, 1726.

Melchior[1.3a], b. about 1683, and m. Ursula Lintermayer at Weidelbach on Apr. 16, 1703. In 1703 and 1705, he was a courtman, clerist, and subject of the Deutschen Orden of Weidelbach. In 1709, he was a subject of Lord Schell at Ketschenweiler, Germany.

Peter[1.4a], b. about 1693, and m. Margaretha, daughter of Leonhardt Hauckler, at Weidelbach on Aug. 27, 1714. He was a farmer, and subject of the Deutschen Orden at Weidelbach.

Johann Andreas Biehlmajer

Johann Andreas[1.1a] m. Catharina. He was a shepherd and subject of Lord Schell living in Ketschenweiler, Bavaria in 1709, and in 1714, he was residing in Schonbronn, Baden-Wurtemberg. He d. at Schonbronn on Mar. 26, 1744 from "stitches in the side." Catharina was b. in Dec. 1675, and d. from "stitches in the side" at Schonbronn in June 1743. They were the parents of the following children:

Johann Leonhardt[1.1.1a], b. in 1706.

Rosina[1.1.2a], b. at Ketschenweiler, and baptized at Weidelbach on Jan. 15, 1709. She m. Andreas Schenck.

Christina[1.1.3a], b. at Ketschenweiler, and baptized at Weidelbach on Oct. 4, 1711.

Johann Jacob[1.1.4a], b. in 1714.

Anna Sybilla[1.1.5a], m. Georg Michael, son of Casper Schmidt, at Marktlustenau on Mar. 18, 1732. They arrived at Philadelphia on the ship *Loyal Judith* on Sep. 25, 1732, with Andreas Schenck, and Jacob Biehlmajer.

Johann Leonhardt Biehlmajer

Johann Leonhardt$^{1.1.1a}$ arrived at Philadelphia in the ship *Britannia* on Sep. 21, 1731. He m. Anna Barth at Trinity Evangelical Lutheran Church of Lancaster, Pennsylvania, on Nov. 9, 1736. He wrote his will in Lancaster County, Manheim Township, Pennsylvania, on Oct. 14, 1772, and it was probated on Dec. 15, 1772. Anna d. sometime after 1772. They baptized the following children at Trinity Lutheran Church (except Martin):

Johann Michael$^{1.1.1.1a}$, b. on Sep. 10, 1738, and baptized on Sep. 24, 1738.

Anna Maria$^{1.1.1.2a}$, b. on Oct. 23, 1739, and baptized on Nov. 18, 1739. She m. Jacob Schoch/Shock.

Anna Barbara$^{1.1.1.3a}$, b. on Feb. 2, 1741, and baptized on Mar. 29, 1741. She m. Peter Longacre.

Catharina$^{1.1.1.4a}$, b. on Dec. 28, 1742, and baptized on Jan. 16, 1743. She m. Jacob Mayer.

John Martin$^{1.1.1.5a}$, b. on July 13, 1746, and baptized on Sep. 9, 1746 at Swatara. He m. Catherine, daughter of Gabriel and Anna Margaret Thomas, on Mar. 8, 1767. She was b. on July 25, 1747. Martin d. in Washington County, Maryland, on Apr. 12, 1812/19.

Johann Leonhardt$^{1.1.1.6a}$, b. on Mar. 7, 1749, and baptized on Mar. 9, 1749. He m. Anna Margaretha Shreiner at Trinity Lutheran in Feb. 1770.

Johann Michael$^{1.1.1.7a}$, b. on Oct. 20, 1751, and baptized on Oct. 20, 1751. He m. Maria, and received a plantation in Frederick County, Virginia, from his father.

Johann Georg$^{1.1.1.8a}$, b. on Mar. 21, 1755, and baptized on Mar. 23, 1755.

Andrew$^{1.1.1.9a}$, b. on Sep. 22, 1756, and d. in Montour County, Liberty Township, Pennsylvania, on Feb. 2, 1825. He m. Veronica Schellenberger. She was b. on Aug. 22, 1757, and d. on Feb. 8, 1823. They are both buried in Billmeyer cemetery. Andrew received his father's plantation in Manheim Township.

Rosina Biehlmajer

Rosina$^{1.1.2a}$, m. Andreas Schenck, at Crailsheim, Baden, Wurtemburg, Germany, on Sep. 14, 1731. They met while Rosina served at Rothendorf, and Andreas lived on his father's farm at Veitschwind. They were m. dishonorably, because Rosina was six months pregnant. At the birth of their son, Hanns Georg, Andreas was a weaver living with his father, and Rosina was living with her father.

They later showed repentance and paid the charge at the local ministry. Andreas arrived at Philadelphia in the ship *Loyal Judith* with his brothers-in-law, Jacob Biehlmajer and Georg Michael Schmidt, on Sep. 25, 1732. Andreas and Rosina resided in Lancaster County, Pennsylvania, from 1733 to 1739, and moved to York County by 1744. On Jan. 8, 1749/50, Frederick Stroll sold Andreas land in Hellam Township, a lot, and house in the town of York, situated at the cross street by the court house. After a short illness, Andreas had been cutting during the afternoon harvest, and on July 9, 1762, he relapsed and d. in York Township on July 10, 1762, about 5:00 am. He was buried in our God's acre in the town of York at 3:00 pm. on July 11, accompanied by a large funeral procession. Rosina d. sometime after Feb. 24, 1769, when her son Jacob released a lot to her in the town of York. Andreas and Rosina's son, John petitioned the court for a division of Andreas' 150 acres on Aug. 31, 1762. On Sep. 2, 1762, the court declined the request, and ordered John to pay the widow, Rosina, and other heirs. Andreas and Rosina had the following children:

Hannss Georg$^{1.1.2.1a}$, b. at Schonbronn on Dec. 13, 1731, baptized at Marktlustenau on Dec. 14, 1731, and d. sometime before 1739. His godfather was Georg Langohr.

Johannes$^{1.1.2.2a}$, b. on Oct. 16, 1733. He was baptized at Trinity Evangelical Church of Lancaster, Pennsylvania, on Oct. 23, 1733, and sponsored by Johannes Vogel and wife. He m. Magdalena, daughter of Johan Georg and Anna Maria Hertzog. She d. on Jan. 19, 1804. Johannes resided in Shenandoah County, Virginia, in Mar. 1773, and d. sometime before May 1774.

Andreas$^{1.1.2.3a}$, b. on Sep. 7, 1735, and d. sometime before 1745. He was baptized at Trinity Evangelical Lutheran Church of Lancaster, Pennsylvania, on Oct. 10, 1735. He was sponsored by Johannes Vogel and wife.

Johannes Martin$^{1.1.2.4a}$, b. on Aug. 12, 1737, and baptized at Trinity Evangelical Lutheran Church of Lancaster on Oct. 23, 1737. He was sponsored by Johan Martin Weybrecht. He m. Carolina Dorothea, daughter of Johann Georg and Anna Maria Hertzog. She d. in Page County, Virginia, on Dec. 24, 1814, and Martin d. there in Mar. 1804. They resided in Shenandoah County, Virginia, in Dec. 1772.

Johannes Georg$^{1.1.2.5a}$, b. on Aug. 13, 1739. He was baptized at Trinity Evangelical Lutheran Church of Lancaster on Nov. 25, 1739, and sponsored by Martin Weybrecht. He m. Catherina Christina, and moved to Frederick County, Woodsboro, Maryland, where he d. in July 1837.

Johannes Jacob[1.1.2.6a], b. in 1742. He m. Anna Maria, daughter of Johannes and Anna Wolf in Christ's Lutheran Church of York on Aug. 4, 1767. She was baptized by Reverend Jacob Lischy on Apr. 8, 1750.

Rosina[1.1.2.7a], b. on Apr. 4, 1744, and baptized at Christ's Lutheran Church of York on Apr. 15, 1744. She was sponsored by her uncle and aunt, Jacob and Helena Biehlmajer. She was alive in Sep. 1762.

Helena[1.1.2.8a], b. on Sep. 22, 1745, and m. Johannes Ruhl at Christ's Lutheran Church of York on Aug. 14, 1764. She was b. in York Township on Sep. 22, 1745, baptized at Christ's Lutheran Church of York on Feb. 9, 1746, sponsored by her uncle and aunt, Jacob and Helena Biehlmajer, and d. in Codorus Township on Aug. 27, 1826. Johannes served during the Revolutionary War as a Private in Captain George Hoover's Company of Associators of Codorus Township, and a Private in Captain John Sherer's Company (the Eighth), Seventh Battalion, York County Militia from about 1778 to 1782. He was a member of the second class of inhabitants of Codorus Township, classified under an act of assembly passed in 1780, entitled "An Act to Complete the Quota of the Federal Army"; each class was "required to provide, in fifteen days from Jan. 30, 1781, one able-bod. recruit for the Continental Army, to serve during the war," under penalty of a fine of 15 pounds specie; the class proved delinquent. John was a yeoman in Codorus Township. In 1779, John owned 100 acres, two horses and four cattle; in 1780, 80 acres, two horses, and two cattle; in 1781, 235 acres; in 1782, 225 acres, two horses and four cattle, and in 1783 had 225 acres, one house, one outhouse, three horses, three horned cattle, and eight sheep. John had a 94 acre 149 perch tract called *Square Compas* patented to him by the Commonwealth of Pennsylvania on May 6, 1790. On Jan. 18, 1812, John purchased 130 acres 111 perches called *George Town* and 11 acres and 12 perches in Codorus Township from Georg Philip and Loveis DeHoff. Johannes d. in Codorus Township on Jan. 23, 1825, and was buried in Steltz Union (Bethlehem) Church cemetery beside his wife.

Andreas[1.1.2.9a], b. on Sep. 22, 1745, and baptized at Christ's Lutheran Church of York on Feb. 9, 1746. He was sponsored by his uncle and aunt, Jacob and Helena Biehlmajer. He was a wheelwright, m. Elizabeth, daughter of Martin Capler, at Christ's Lutheran Church of York on Aug. 21, 1759, and d. d. in Berks County, Reading, Pennsylvania, in Nov. 1777.

LANCASTER, LEBANON & DAUPHIN COUNTIES 5

Hans Michael$^{1.1.2.10a}$, b. on Sep. 1, 1747, and d. sometime before 1749. He was baptized at Christ's Lutheran Church of York on Oct. 21, 1747, and sponsored by his uncle, Jacob Biehlmajer.

Mathias$^{1.1.2.11a}$, b. on Sep. 1, 1747, and baptized at Christ's Lutheran Church of York on Oct. 21, 1747. He was alive in Sep. 1762.

Johannes Michael$^{1.1.2.12a}$, b. on Sep. 7, 1749. He was baptized at Christ's Lutheran Church of York on Oct. 22, 1749. He moved to Frederick County, Woodsboro, Maryland, where he d. sometime after 1810.

Anna Maria$^{1.1.2.13a}$, b. about 1751. Her uncle, Jacob Biehlmajer, was appointed her guardian.

Johann Jacob Biehlmajer

Johan Jacob$^{1.1.4a}$ was baptized at Schonbronn on Nov. 6, 1714. He arrived at Philadelphia on the ship *Loyal Judith* on Sep. 25, 1732 with Andreas Schenck and Georg Michael Schmidt. He m. Helena Holtzender/Holtzdorn. She was b. in 1717, and d. in York County, Pennsylvania, on Nov. 14, 1803. Jacob d. in York County, York, Pennsylvania, on Feb. 16, 1777. They are both buried beneath the floor of Christ's Lutheran Church of York. They had the following children baptized at Christ's Lutheran Church:

Johann Jacob$^{1.1.4.1a}$, b. on Feb. 21, 1743, and baptized in 1743. He was sponsored by Gerhardt Brenner and wife. He d. in York on Oct. 1782.

Susanna$^{1.1.4.2a}$, b. on Nov. 2, 1746, and baptized on Nov. 16, 1746. She was sponsored by Johannes and Susanna Schreck.

Rosina$^{1.1.4.3a}$, b. on Mar. 21, 1749, and baptized on Apr. 9, 1749. She was sponsored by her uncle and aunt, Andreas and Rosina Schenck. She m. Johan Leonhard, son of Martin Weigel. He was b. on Apr. 2, 1743.

Michael$^{1.1.4.4a}$, b. on Jan. 1, 1752, baptized on Jan. 4, 1752, and sponsored by Michael and Eva Margaret Ebert. He was a printer, and resided in Montgomery County, Germantown, Pennsylvania.

Andrew$^{1.1.4.5a}$, b. on May 21, 1754, baptized on May 26, 1754, and m. Barbara. He d. at York on Mar. 8, 1835, and she d. on Feb. 16, 1816, at age 55.

Elisabeth$^{1.1.4.6a}$, b. on Feb. 21, 1757, baptized on Feb. 27, 1757, and sponsored by Michael and Eva Margaret Ebert. She d. in York, on Feb. 13, 1824.

Anna Maria$^{1.1.4.7a}$, b. on Dec. 15, 1759, and sponsored by Michael and Eva Margaret Ebert. She m. Henry Shafer.

Maria Juliana[1.1.4.8a], b. on Feb. 18, 1763, and sponsored by John and Juliana Hay.

Jacob[1.1.4.9a], b. on Sep. 17, 1763, and baptized on Sep. 25, 1763, and sponsored by Jacob and Catherine Kern.

****

Christian Ehrhardt

Christian[1b] was the son of Daniel Ehrhardt, and confirmed at Hunspach, Northern Alsace, France, in 1730. Daniel d. sometime after 1730 in Retschwiller, Soultz-Sous-Forets, France. Christian m. Anna Barbara, daughter of Jacob Clor, at Hunspach on Oct. 1, 1734, and Susanna, daughter of Jacob and Susanna Muller of Oberkutzenhausen, at Rittershoffen on May 5, 1738. Anna Barbara was b. at Hunspach, and d. at Rittershofen in 1738. Christian arrived at Philadelphia on the ship *Robert and Alice* in 1739, and settled in Lancaster County, Rapho Township, Pennsylvania. He was taxed in Rapho Township in 1757. He had 100 acres in 1758/59, and 150 acres in 1771. He d. about 1783, and Susanna d. sometime after 1750. They had the following children:

Daniel[1.1b], b. about 1735.

Georg[1.2b], b. about 1736.

Nicholas[1.3b], b. about 1737, and d. in Lancaster County, Hanover Township in 1776(?). He took the Oath of Allegiance at Hanover on July 12, 1777. He was taxed in Rapho Township in 1758 and 1759, and he was taxed in East Hanover Township in 1769 and 1771.

Martin[1.4b], b. about 1738.

Susanna[1.5b], b. on May 17, 1741.

Anna Eva[1.6b], b. on Dec. 25, 1744.

Jacob[1.7b], b. about 1746. He was taxed as a freeman in Rapho Township in 1769. He m. Susanna. Jacob d. Rapho Township in July 1804, and his will was probated on July 31, 1804.

Christian[1.7b], b. on May 18, 1748, and d. in Lancaster County, Rapho Township in Nov. 1793.

Anna Catharina[1.8b], b. on Apr. 17, 1750.

Daniel Ehrhardt

Daniel[1.1b] m. Margaret Grau in Lancaster County on Sep. 30, 1757. He was taxed in Rapho Township in 1777-1783. He was a laborer paying rent to John Miller in Manor Township, Millerstown in 1770 and 1771. He took the Oath of Allegiance at Donegal on Nov. 22, 1777.

LANCASTER, LEBANON & DAUPHIN COUNTIES

He d. in Lancaster County, Rapho Township in Nov. 1810 (his will was probated on Nov. 30, 1810). Daniel had the following children:
Jacob$^{1.1.1b}$, b. about 1760.
Elizabeth$^{1.1.2b}$, b. on Apr. 5, 1767, and m. Abraham Gerber.

Georg Ehrhardt

Georg$^{1.2b}$ was taxed in Lancaster County, Rapho Township, Pennsylvania, in 1756-59 (in 1759, he had 50 acres). He m. Elisabetha about 1762. Georg moved to Frederick County, Woodsboro, Maryland, about 1766, and Rockingham County, Timberville, Virginia, in 1782. George sold his 200 acres in Woodsboro to George Murdoch for 2, 050 pounds in 1781. He had one dwelling and two other buildings in 1784. He was taxed for six horses, and paid taxed for his son John in 1788 (Captain Trumboe's Company number 10). In 1792, he and his sons, Jacob and John were taxed (George with seven people) in Captain Ezekiel Harrison's Company, East Plains District/West Portion of Plains District that included the area of Timberville (aka Rader's Church, The Plains, The Forest). Georg d. in Feb. 1801. His estate was administered on Feb. 8, 1801 by his executers, Jacob Ehrhardt, John Ehrhardt, and Philip Brenner, and valued at 6, 000 pounds. Georg's son, Philip, chose Mathias Miller as his guardian. Georg and Elisabetha gave consent for their daughter, Magdalena's, marriage in June 1796, and sponsored her daughter's baptism in Aug. 1798. Elisabetha may have been m. to a (Georg Michael) Kips (from Germany and Pennsylvania (a Michael Kipp immigrated to America on Oct. 10, 1749)) before she m. Georg Ehrhardt. This is indicated because she appears as a sponsor, and grandmother to Michael and Catharina Kip's daughter. Georg and Elisabetha Ehrhardt's daughter Catharina m. George Springer, so this would show that Michael was her son. If Elisabetha m. (Georg Michael) Kips, she had the following children:
Michael$^{1.1kip}$, b. in 1759 (age 75 on Feb. 19, 1834 (some sources say he was b. in 1760)).
Jacob$^{1.2kip}$, b. on Nov. 11, 1760.
Georg$^{1.3kip}$, b. about 1762.

Michael Kips

Michael$^{1.1kip}$ m. Catharina Mullenbarger in Rockingham County, Virginia, on Apr. 26, 1782, and d. in Montgomery County, Virginia, in July (June), 1835. He enlisted in the Revolutionary War in Apr. 1778 (in Rockingham County?), and in the Spring of 1780/81. He was pensioned in 1834 (his brother, Jacob, says that his brother in

Montgomery County, Virginia, has the family bible (this could refer to Michael Kips, or John Ehrhardt)). He resided in Rockingham County, Timberville District in 1788, and purchased 205 acres there in 1789. He had land in 1782, and purchased 58 acres on Mar. 14, 1786. They lived next to Georg and Elisabetha Ehrhardt. Michael's will was probated in Montgomery County in July 1835. Michael and Catharina had the following children baptized at Rader's Lutheran Church in Rockingham County, Virginia (in 1788, he is listed with a tithable, George Kips, and in 1792, he is listed with a son?brother, George Kips age 21 (b. in 1771)):

Maria$^{1.1.1kip}$, b. on Sep. 27, 1783, baptized on Apr. 4, 1784, and m. Jacob Miller in Rockingham County in 1802. He was b. in 1780. After Jacob's death, she m. John Hinsgardner (before 1835).

John$^{1.1.2kip}$, b. on Apr. 27, 1786, baptized on Aug. 27, 1786, and sponsored by John and Maria Pelz.

Sarah$^{1.1.3kip}$, b. on July 27, 1789, and baptized in May 1790. She m. Peter Knop in Rockingham County in 1807, and d. before 1835.

Elisabeth$^{1.1.4kip}$, b. on Feb. 20, 1793, and sponsored by Margaretha Dacherta. She m. Philip Olinger in Rockingham County on Nov. 3, 1810.

Catharina$^{1.1.5kip}$, b. on Mar. 12, 1797, baptized on Oct. 7, 1797, and sponsored by John and Catharina Roller. She m. Philip Bowers in Rockingham County on Sep. 26, 1811.

Margaret$^{1.1.6kip}$, b. on Mar. 19, 1801, baptized on May 24, 1801, and sponsored by her grandmother, Elisabetha Ehrhard. She m. Samuel Cook in Montgomery County on Mar. 10, 1819.

Hannah$^{1.1.7kip}$, b. on Jan. 8, 1804, baptized on May 6, 1804, and sponsored by Valentine and Christina Voland. She m. Christian Price in Montgomery County on Oct. 23, 1819.

Jacob Kips

Jacob$^{1.2kip}$, b. on Nov. 11, 1760, m. Elizabeth, daughter of Georg Adam and Elisabeth (Ridenouer) Zerckel, on Jan. 24, 1786, and d. in Shenandoah County, New Market, Virginia, on Apr. 20, 1849. She was b. on May 19, 1766, and d. on June 21, 1857. They are buried in Zirkle cemetery. He served in the Revolutionary War from Rockingham County, Virginia, and was pensioned for his service. He enlisted in Apr. 1778 (in Rockingham County?), and was drafted in Sep. 1781. In 1786, he moved to Shenandoah County. They had the following children baptized at Davidsburg Lutheran Church in Shenandoah County, New Market, Virginia:

Georg$^{1.2.1kip}$, b. on Feb. 14, 1787, baptized at Rader's Lutheran Church on July 19, 1787, and sponsored by Georg Adam and Elisabetha Zirkel. He m. Eve, daughter of Nicholas Tussing, and d. on Feb. 26, 1879. She was b. on Sep. 19, 1786, and d. on Nov. 25, 1850. They are buried in Zirkle cemetery.

Michael$^{1.2.2kip}$, b. on Mar. 3, 1789, baptized at Rader's on July 19, 1789, and sponsored by his parents. He d. on Jan. 8, 1815, and is buried in Zirkle cemetery.

Eva$^{1.2.3kip}$, b. on Apr. 16, 1792, and sponsored by Eva Zirkel. She d. on Feb. 16, 1879, and is buried in Zirkle cemetery.

Jacob$^{1.2.4kip}$, b. on Mar. 25, 1794, and sponsored by Jacob and Elisabetha Ohlinger. He m. Elizabeth Barb, and d. on Sep. 4, 1886. She was b. in 1807, and d. on June 15, 1858. They are buried in Zirkle cemetery.

Elisabet$^{1.2.5kip}$, b. on Sep. 15, 1798, baptized on Oct. 21, 1798, and sponsored by Paul and Elisabeth Henkel. She m. Benjamin Landis, and d. in 1885.

Heinrich$^{1.2.6kip}$, b. on Oct. 25, 1801, baptized on Mar. 4, 1802, and sponsored by his parents. He d. on Aug. 10, 1854, and is buried in Zirkle cemetery.

Catharina$^{1.2.7kip}$, b. on Nov. 3, 1803, baptized on Mar. 6, 1804, and sponsored by her parents. She m. John Cline in Shenandoah County on May 8, 1822, and d. in 1841.

Anna Maria$^{1.2.8kip}$, b. on Aug. 11, 1807, baptized on Nov. 15, 1807, and sponsored by her parents. She m. Samuel Hupp, and d. in 1867.

Moses$^{1.2.9kip}$, b. on Mar. 5, 1809, baptized on May 11, 1809, and sponsored by his parents. He d. on Feb. 16, 1893, and is buried in Zirkle cemetery.

Georg Kips

Georg$^{1.3kip}$ m. Maria (she may have d. before 1822), and had the following children baptized at Davidsburg Lutheran Church in Shenandoah County, New Market, Virginia (the parents are the sponsors for all the children's baptisms):

Johannes$^{1.3.1kip}$, b. on Oct. 1, 1792, and baptized on June 5, 1803.

Georg$^{1.3.2kip}$, b. about 1793, and m. Margaretha about 1813.

Sara$^{1.3.3kip}$, b. on Jan. 2, 1796, and baptized on June 5, 1803.

Jacob$^{1.3.4kip}$, b. on Mar. 21, 1798, and baptized on June 5, 1803.

Elisabetha$^{1.3.5kip}$, b. on May 29, 1800, and baptized on June 5, 1803.

Serina$^{1.3.6kip}$, b. on Feb. 2, 1803, and baptized on June 5, 1803.

Lucinda$^{1.3.7kip}$, b. on Mar. 24, 1805, and baptized on Feb. 8, 1807.

Michael$^{1.3.8kip}$, b. on Nov. 30, 1819, and baptized on June 18, 1820.

Elisabetha Ehrhardt was alive as of Apr. 14, 1811, when she sponsored the baptism of a granddaughter. Georg and Elisabetha had the following children:

Andrew$^{1.2.1b}$, b. about 1763, and taxed in Rockingham County, Virginia, in 1787 and for one horse in 1788 (Captain George Chrisman's Company number 12).

Anna Catharina$^{1.2.2b}$, b. about 1765.

Christian$^{1.2.3b}$, b. about 1767.

Johan$^{1.2.4b}$, baptized at Rocky Hill (Grace) Lutheran Church on June 4, 1769.

Anna Elisabetha$^{1.2.5b}$, baptized at Rocky Hill (Grace) Lutheran Church on Jan. 25, 1772.

Georg Jacob$^{1.2.6b}$, baptized at Rocky Hill (Grace) Lutheran Church on Apr. 30, 1775.

Magdalena$^{1.2.7b}$, b. on Mar. 1, 1776, baptized at Rocky Hill (Grace) Lutheran Church on May 26, 1776, and confirmed in Rader's Lutheran Church on Oct. 23, 1801. She m. Johan Frederick Friesner$^{1.2c}$.

Henrich$^{1.2.8b}$, baptized at Rocky Hill (Grace) Lutheran Church on Sep. 13, 1778.

Mary$^{1.2.9b}$, b. in Maryland in 1782.

Philip$^{1.2.10b}$, b. on Feb. 16, 1788.

Anna Catharina Ehrhardt

Anna Catharina$^{1.2.2b}$ m. George, son of George Springer, in Rockingham County on Nov. 11, 1786, and d. in Fairfield County, Rush Creek Township, Ohio, between 1830 and 1840. George's will was filed in Fairfield County, Rush Creek Township, Ohio, in 1812. They had the following children, baptized at Rader's Lutheran Church in Rockingham County:

Johan Jacob$^{1.2.2.1b}$, b. on May 30, 1788, baptized on June 29, 1788, and sponsored by Henry Gut. He m. Kasiah Fast in Fairfield County on May 2, 1811.

Georg$^{1.2.2.2b}$, b. on Nov. 3, 1789, baptized on Apr. 4, 1790, and sponsored by his father. He m. Elizabeth Hidlebough in Fairfield County, Ohio, on June 11, 1812, and resided in Hocking County, Ohio.

Susanna$^{1.2.2.3b}$, b. about 1791, and m. Jool G. McNamee in Fairfield County on Aug. 1, 1811.

Catherine Elisabeth$^{1.2.2.4b}$, b. on Feb. 17, 1793, and sponsored by Elisabeth Ehrhardt at her baptism. She m. Jacob Fast in Fairfield County on Nov. 24, 1814.

Henrich$^{1.2.2.5b}$, b. on Mar. 2, 1795, baptized on Oct. 11, 1795, and sponsored by Henry Gut and wife. He m. Margaret Fast in Fairfield County on Feb. 13, 1817, and Comfort Reynolds in Fairfield County on May 13, 1823.

Magdalena$^{1.2.2.6b}$, b. on Jan. 29, 1797, baptized on Easter Sunday, 1798, and sponsored by her parents. She m. John Miller in Fairfield County on May 14, 1818.

John$^{1.2.2.7b}$, b. about 1799, and m. Ann Fast in Fairfield County on Feb. 4, 1819.

Peter$^{1.2.2.8b}$, b. about 1801.

Sally$^{1.2.2.9b}$, b. about 1803.

Barbara$^{1.2.2.10b}$, b. about 1805.

Christian Ehrhardt

Christian$^{1.2.3b}$ had his taxed paid for by his father in Rockingham County in 1787. He is probably the Christian Ehrhardt in Augusta County, Virginia, in 1810 (2 sons & 1 daughter b. before 1790 and 2 daughters b. between 1800 and 1810) and 1820. A Peter Ehrhardt (10010-10100) is residing beside this Christopher (Christian) in 1810, and a John is residing beside Christian in 1820. In 1830, Christian, John, and Peter resided in Augusta County, Southern District. Christian m. Elizabeth, and had the following daughter in Shenandoah County, Virginia.

Eva$^{1.2.3.1b}$, b. on Apr. 7, 1793, baptized at the Old Pine Church in Shenandoah County on July 7, 1793, and sponsored by her grandmother, Elisabeth Ehrhardt, at her baptism.

Johann Ehrhardt

Johann$^{1.2.4b}$ m. Margaret, daughter of Adam Painter, in Rockingham County, Virginia, in 1790. Margaret was b. on May 1,

1769. He moved to Montgomery County, Christianburg, Virginia, between 1792 and 1797. John's will was probated in Montgomery County in Apr. 1804. They had the following children:

John$^{1.2.4.1b}$, b. on Sep. 24, 1791, baptized at Rader's on Apr. 15, 1792, and sponsored by Christian and Elizabeth Ehrhardt.

George$^{1.2.4.2b}$, b. on Apr. 5, 1793, baptized at Rader's on Oct. 13, 1793, and sponsored by Peter and Maria Schmidt.

Henry$^{1.2.4.3b}$, b. on May 13, 1797.

Adam$^{1.2.4.4b}$, b. on Sep. 30, 1801.

Abraham$^{1.2.4.5b}$, b. about 1803, m. Sarah, daughter of John Shufflebarger, in Montgomery County on Sep. 27, 1824, and had his estate settled there in Feb. 1834.

Margaret$^{1.2.4.6b}$, b. on Apr. 12, 1806, and m. Eli Davis in Montgomery County on Jan. 2, 1833.

Mary$^{1.2.4.7b}$, b. on July 17, 1814, and m. Andrew Hutsell in Montgomery County on May 16, 1832.

George Ehrhardt

George$^{1.2.4.2b}$ m. Nancy, daughter of William Taylor, in Montgomery County on Mar. 28, 1825. She was b. in Virginia in 1801, and d. in Montgomery County on Dec. 9, 1862. They had the following children:

John$^{1.2.4.2.1b}$, b. in 1826.

William$^{1.2.4.2.2b}$, b. in 1828.

Joseph P.$^{1.2.4.2.3b}$, b. on May 21, 1829, and d. in Montgomery County on Apr. 13, 1852.

David$^{1.2.4.2.4b}$, b. in 1834, and was killed in the Civil War at the Battle of Chancellorsville, on May 2, 1864 (Norfolk, Roanoke). He m. Mary.

Henry$^{1.2.4.2.5b}$, b. in 1836.

Margaret J.$^{1.2.4.2.6b}$, b. in 1838.

Elizabeth$^{1.2.4.2.7b}$, b. in 1841.

Henry Ehrhardt

Henry$^{1.2.4.3b}$ m. Mary Kerby, and had the following children in Montgomery County, Virginia:

Rhoda Emily Frances$^{1.2.4.3.1b}$, b. on July 8, 1834, and m. William Davis in Wythe County, Virginia, on Oct. 9, 1852.

Adam Ehrhardt

Adam$^{1.2.4.4b}$ m. Sarah Lendum Wright (b. in Ireland in 1808), and had the following children in Montgomery County, 41st District Virginia:

Margaret E.$^{1.2.4.4.1b}$, b. in 1834.
Eliza Anne$^{1.2.4.4.2b}$, b. in 1836.
Mary J.$^{1.2.4.4.3b}$, b. in 1838.
Robert B.$^{1.2.4.4.4b}$, b. in 1840.
Emeline$^{1.2.4.4.5b}$, b. in 1843.
Henry J.$^{1.2.4.4.6b}$, b. in 1845.
John$^{1.2.4.4.7b}$, b. in 1846, and d. before 1850.

Anna Elisabetha Ehrhardt

Anna Elisabetha$^{1.2.5b}$ m. Philip, son of John and Catharina (Herbine) Brenner, in Shenandoah County, Virginia, on Oct. 22, 1794. He was b. in Rockingham County, Virginia, on Apr. 15, 1775, baptized at Rader's in 1775, and sponsored by Phillip Herrbein and wife. Philip's estate was administered in Rockingham County on Aug. 4, 1828. They had the following children in Rockingham County, Virginia:

Catharina$^{1.2.5.1b}$, b. on Jan. 15, 1794, and may be the Catherine that m. Adam May in Rockingham County on Oct. 5, 1815.

Sarah$^{1.2.5.2b}$, b. on Dec. 21, 1795, and m. John Bille/Bible in Rockingham County on Aug. 8, 1815.

Philip$^{1.2.5.3b}$, b. about 1797, helped to administer his father's estate, and resided in Rockingham County in 1830.

John$^{1.2.5.4b}$, b. on Aug. 4, 1799.
Magdalene$^{1.2.5.5b}$, b. in 1801.
Elizabeth$^{1.2.5.6b}$, b. on Feb. 2, 1803.
Mary$^{1.2.5.7b}$, b. on Oct. 2, 1804.
Jonathan$^{1.2.5.8b}$, b. on Feb. 2, 1806, and m. Margaret Showalter in Rockingham County on Apr. 5, 1830.
Michael$^{1.2.5.9b}$, b. on Sep. 8, 1807.

Georg Jacob Ehrhardt

Jacob$^{1.2.6b}$ m. Catherine, daughter of John Coole, in Rockingham County, Virginia, on Feb. 16, 1802. They resided in Rockingham County in 1830. They had the following children in Rockingham County:

Maria$^{1.2.6.1b}$, b. about 1803.

John[1.2.6.2b], b. on Apr. 5, 1805, baptized at Rader's on Apr. 10, 1811, and sponsored by his parents. He m. Mary Ridenouer in Rockingham County on Jan. 26, 1826.

Margaretha[1.2.6.3b], b. on Aug. 5, 1809, baptized at Rader's on Apr. 10, 1811, and sponsored by her parents.

Solomon[1.2.6.4b], b. on Nov. 1, 1811, baptized at Rader's on Oct. 25, 1812, and sponsored by his parents.

Jacob[1.2.6.5b], b. on Jan. 9, 1813, baptized at Rader's on Nov. 8, 1817, and sponsored by his parents.

Heinrich Ehrhardt

Henrich[1.2.8b] d. in Rockingham County, Virginia, on May 6, 1851. He m. Elisabeth, daughter of Jacob and Maria Dorothea Stoutmire/Staudemeyer, in Rockingham County on June 9, 1801. She was b. in York County, Dover Township, Pennsylvania, on Feb. 16, 1776, baptized at Strayer's on Feb. 25, 1776, and sponsored by Bernhardt and Ursula Mueller. They had the following son:

John[1.2.8.1b], b. on Mar. 9, 1802, baptized at Rader's on May 30, 1802, and sponsored by Michael and Catharine Gibs.

John Ehrhardt

John[1.2.8.1b] m. Mary, daughter of Casper Branner, and d. on Dec. 13, 1873. She was b. on Aug. 14, 1807, and d. on May 1, 1877. They had the following children baptized at Rader's Lutheran Church in Rockingham County:

George[1.2.8.1.1b], b. on Feb. 19, 1831, baptized at Rader's, and sponsored by Henry and Elizabeth Ehrhardt. He m. Sarah Bowman on Aug. 11, 1859.

Catharina[1.2.8.1.2b], b. on Apr. 29, 1832, baptized at Rader's in 1832, and sponsored by her parents. She m. S. H. Myers on Dec. 7, 1854.

Isaac[1.2.8.1.3b], b. on Apr. 14, 1834, baptized on July 13, 1834, and sponsored by his parents. He m. Elizabeth Orebaugh on Dec. 2, 1869.

William Harvey[1.2.8.1.4b], b. on Oct. 23, 1836, baptized in Oct. 1837, and sponsored by his parents. He m. Margaret Jane, daughter of Emanuel and Elizabeth Roller on Dec. 12, 1872, and Eliza Jane, daughter of John D. and Sarah (Plecker) Wise, on Feb. 5, 1884. Margaret was b. on Oct. 25, 1845, and d. on Nov. 7, 1876. Eliza was b. on June 14, 1845. He served as a Sergeant in the Civil War, and fought in the battles of Winchester, Cross Keys, Front Royal, Sharpsburg,

LANCASTER, LEBANON & DAUPHIN COUNTIES 15

Brandy Station, Upperville, Second Manassas, Culpeper, Cedar Mountain, the Wilderness, the fighting around Richmond, Trevilian, etc.

Elizabeth$^{1.2.8.1.5b}$, b. on June 9, 1838, and m. Josiah Braner on Mar. 30, 1865.

Sarah$^{1.2.8.1.6b}$, b. on Feb. 18, 1840, and m. Michael Fitzmoyer on Nov. 23, 1866. He d. on May 4, 1883.

Casper H.$^{1.2.8.1.7b}$, b. on Jan. 8, 1842, and killed during the Civil War at Ashland on June 1, 1864.

Nason B.$^{1.2.8.1.8b}$, b. on Mar. 30, 1844, and d. on Mar. 2, 1865. He served in the Civil War.

Mary V.$^{1.2.8.1.9b}$, b. on May 13, 1846, and m. Solon M. Bowman on Feb. 19, 1871.

Mary Ehrhardt

Mary$^{1.2.9b}$ m. Barrett Stoutmire/Bernhardt Stauedemeyer, son of Jacob and Maria Dorothea Stauedemeyer, in Rockingham County in 1798. He was b. in York County, Dover Township, Pennsylvania, on Aug. 19, 1774, baptized at Strayer's Lutheran Church on Oct. 23, 1774, and sponsored by Bernhardt and Ursula Mueller. Barrett and Mary were residing in Rockingham County in 1810, Shenandoah County in 1830, and Miami County, Bethel Township, Ohio, in 1840. Barrett's will was probated in Miami County in 1845. Mary was residing in Bethel Township in 1850. They had the following children:

Lydia$^{1.2.9.1b}$, b. about 1800, and m. Joshua Scarff in Shenandoah County on Dec. 13, 1819.

Son$^{1.2.9.2b}$, b. about 1802. This is possibly the Christian that m. Mary Cook in Shenandoah County on Feb. 2, 1824.

Daughter$^{1.2.9.3b}$, b. about 1804.

Mary$^{1.2.9.4b}$, b. about 1806, and m. John Buswell in Shenandoah County on Feb. 21, 1826.

Isaac$^{1.2.9.5b}$, b. in 1822, and resided in Miami County, Bethel Township, Ohio, in 1850. His wife d. before 1850.

Philip Ehrhardt

Philip$^{1.2.10b}$ m. Rebecca, daughter of Jacob Mueller, in Rockingham County, Virginia, on Apr. 10, 1810, and Sarah Collins in Augusta County, Virginia, on June 8, 1843. Sarah was b. in Virginia in 1797. Philip resided in Rockingham County, Virginia, in 1810, Augusta County in 1840, and in 1850, resided in Augusta County, Second District, Virginia. He d. in Augusta County, Virginia, on Apr. 18, 1860.

Philip and Rebecca had the following children in Rockingham County, Virginia:

Lidia[1.2.10.1b], b. on Mar. 7, 1811, baptized at Rader's on Apr. 14, 1811, and sponsored by her grandmother, Elisabeth Ehrhardt.

Sarah[1.2.10.2b], b. on June 15, 1812, baptized at Rader's on Oct. 14, 1813, and sponsored by Jacob Weller and wife.

Michael[1.2.10.3b], b. on Feb. 20, 1814, baptized at Rader's on Mar. 7, 1814, and sponsored by his parents.

John[1.2.10.4b], b. on Nov. 12, 1816, baptized at Rader's on May 4, 1817, and sponsored by his parents.

Polly[1.2.10.5b], b. in 1818.

Katherine[1.2.10.6b], b. in 1820.

Philip[1.2.10.7b], b. in Dec. 1821.

Rebecca[1.2.10.8b], b. in 1825, and m. Joseph Andrew. He was b. in Virginia in 1822.

Leah Ann[1.2.10.9b], b. in 1826.

Abraham[1.2.10.10b], b. in 1828, and resided in Augusta County, Second District, Virginia, in 1850.

John Ehrhardt

John[1.2.10.4b] m. Elizabeth Staubus in Augusta County on Dec. 25, 1839. She was b. in Virginia in 1821. They resided in Augusta County, Second District, Virginia, in 1850, and had the following children:

Elizabeth[1.2.10.4.1b], b. in 1841.

Clement M.(H.)[1.2.10.4.2b], b. in 1846, and d. in Augusta County, Virginia, on Dec. 16, 1896.

Christine[1.2.10.4.3b], b. in Apr. 1850.

Martin Ehrhardt

Martin[1.4b] m. Anna Maria Kolb in Lancaster County, Lancaster, Pennsylvania, on Dec. 13, 1757. He resided in Rapho Township in 1770, and took the Oath of Allegiance in Lancaster County, Donegal on Nov. 22, 1777. He moved to Frederick County, Woodsboro, Maryland, sometime before 1786, and was taxed in Rockingham County, Virginia, in 1787. He was taxed at Keezeltown (Captain Richard Ragan's Company East District, East Portion of Central District and Linville) with his son, Martin in 1792, and he was residing there on Dec. 7, 1791. He moved to Warren County, Franklin Township, Ohio, sometime between Feb. 1797, and 1800, and d. there, intestate, on Feb. 5, 1817 (at age 96 ?b. 1721?). His estate was administered by Nicholas and George Ehrhardt on Nov. 7, 1817. They were the parents of the following children:

Martin$^{1.4.1b}$, b. about 1758.

Nicholas$^{1.4.2b}$, b. about 1761. He was taxed in Frederick County, Virginia, in 1787, and helped to administer his father's estate in 1817. He was taxed in Frederick County, Virginia, in 1782.

Elisabeth$^{1.4.3b}$, b. about 1771, and m. Alpert Eger in Rockingham County, Virginia, in 1792.

Georg W.$^{1.4.4b}$, b. in 1774.

Susanna$^{1.4.5b}$, b. about 1780, and m. Edward Thompson in Rockingham County, Virginia, on Aug. 15, 1801.

Martin Ehrhardt

Martin$^{1.4.1b}$ m. Eva about 1785, and Catherine, daughter of Henry Sipe, in Shenandoah County, Virginia, on Jan. 22, 1789. He was residing in Warren County, Turtle Creek Township in 1806-19, and Darke County, Ohio, on Feb. 28, 1822. They had the following children:

Johan Jacob$^{1.4.1.1b}$, baptized at Frederick County, Woodsboro, Rocky Hill (Grace) Lutheran Church on Aug. 2, 1786. This may be the Jacob Earhart that had a will probated in Montgomery County, Ohio, on Aug. 14, 1837, naming wife Elizabeth, and children Mary, Margaret, Abraham, Elizabeth, and Catherine.

Polly$^{1.4.1.2b}$, b. about 1788, and m. Aaron Richardson in Warren County, Ohio, on Apr. 17, 1808.

Peter$^{1.4.1.3b}$, b. about 1788, and m. Prudence Leviston in Warren County on June 30, 1808.

Henry$^{1.4.1.4b}$, b. about 1790, and m. Amy Allen in Warren County on Oct. 20, 1814, and Elizabeth Tapscot in Warren County on June 12, 1823.

Christina$^{1.4.1.5b}$, b. on May 1, 1792, baptized at Glade Reformed Church at Frederick County, Maryland/Virginia, on Aug. 5, 1792, and sponsored by Andrew and Christina Hedge.

Elizabeth$^{1.4.1.6b}$, b. about 1794, and m. John C. Fenney in Warren County on May 15, 1815.

Martin W.$^{1.4.1.7b}$, b. in 1810.

Martin W. Ehrhardt

Martin W.$^{1.4.1.7b}$ m. Mary Ann Baird in Warren County on June 9, 1828, Rachel Stickles on Oct. 4, 1832 (this record for Martin W.), and Elizabeth (b. OH 1818), and had the following children in Warren County, Turtle Creek Township:

Aminda$^{1.4.1.7.1b}$, b. in 1833.
S. M.$^{1.4.1.7.2b}$, b. in 1835.
Mary$^{1.4.1.7.3b}$, b. in 1837.
William$^{1.4.1.7.4b}$, b. in 1839.
C. E.$^{1.4.1.7.5b}$, b. in 1841.
M. J.$^{1.4.1.7.6b}$, b. in 1843.
Franklin$^{1.4.1.7.7b}$, b. in 1845.

Georg W. Ehrhardt

Georg$^{1.4.4b}$ m. Molly/Mary, daughter of David Smith, in Rockingham County in 1798. Mary was b. in Virginia on Sep. 11, 1778, and d. on Jan. 17, 1858. George helped administer the estate of his father in Warren County, Ohio, in 1817. He moved to Darke County in 1818, and settled in the area of Richland Township, that became Greeneville Township. His will was written on Apr. 23, 1850, and probated in Darke County, Greeneville Township, Ohio, on July 7, 1851. He d. on June 17, 1851. Georg and Molly had the following children (a George L., b. in 1842, was residing with George and Molly in 1850):

Martin D.$^{1.4.4.1b}$, b. in Rockingham County, Keezeltown District, Virginia, in 1799.

Samuel E.$^{1.4.4.2b}$, b. in Rockingham County, Virginia, in 1801.

Elizabeth$^{1.4.4.3b}$, b. in Rockingham County, Virginia, on Apr. 14, 1802 (1804), and m. William T(F.). Hunter in Darke County on Oct. 27, 1825. She d. in Greeneville Township on May 11, 1853. William was b. in Warren County, Ohio, on Jan. 2, 1801, and d. on Sep. 26, 1840.

Polly$^{1.4.4.4b}$, b. about 1804, and m. Abraham Scribner in Darke County on Jan. 18, 1825.

George Washington$^{1.4.4.5b}$, b. in Ohio in 1811.

William S.$^{1.4.4.6b}$, b. in 1813.

Nancy$^{1.4.4.7b}$, b. about 1815, and m. John McGlaughlin in Darke County on June 18, 1835.

Mahala$^{1.4.4.8b}$, b. in 1817, and m. Samuel Shaffer in Darke County on May 3, 1849. He was b. in Ohio in 1824. She resided in Greeneville Township in 1850.

Julia Ann$^{1.4.4.9b}$, b. in 1818, and was unmarried and residing with her parents in 1850.

Henry J.$^{1.4.4.10b}$, b. in 1820. He was residing with his father in 1850. His will was probated in Darke County, Ohio, on June 20, 1866.

Martin D. Ehrhardt

Martin D.[1.4.4.1b] m. Mary Studabaker in Darke County on Dec. 8, 1825. His will was written on June 18, 1841, and probated in Darke County, Greeneville Township, Ohio, on Nov. 9, 1852. She was b. in Ohio in 1809. They had the following children:
George[1.4.4.1.1b], b. in 1827.
Mahala[1.4.4.1.2b], b. in 1829.
Martin[1.4.4.1.3b], b. in 1831.
Mary[1.4.4.1.4b], b. in 1835.
Elizabeth[1.4.4.1.5b], b. in 1838.
William[1.4.4.1.6b], b. in 1843.
Maria[1.4.4.1.7b], b. in 1847.

Samuel E. Ehrhardt

Samuel[1.4.4.2b] m. Elizabeth, daughter of Azor Scribner, in Darke County on Dec. 15, 1825. She was b. in Ohio in 1806, and d. in Mar. 1873. Samuel d. in Jan. 1854. They resided in Darke County, Greeneville Township, Ohio, in 1850, and had the following children:
Marcella[1.4.4.2.1b], b. on Jan. 10, 1827, and m. James B. Avery in Darke County, Ohio, on Nov. 14, 1848. He was b. in New London County, Connecticut on Aug. 27, 1826. She d. in 1873.
George F.[1.4.4.2.2b], b. in 1837.
Samuel M.[1.4.4.2.3b], b. on July 22, 1839, m. Rosan, and d. in Darke County on Aug. 27, 1911. She was b. on Aug. 21, 1843, and d. on Feb. 12, 1903. They are buried in Beamsville cemetery.
Elizabeth[1.4.4.2.4b], b. in 1842.
Stephen[1.4.4.2.5b], b. in 1844.
Isaac S.[1.4.4.2.6b], b. in 1846.
David S.[1.4.4.2.7b], b. in 1849.

George Washington Ehrhardt

George Washington[1.4.4.5b] m. Louisa. She was b. in Ohio in 1822. They resided in Darke County, Richland Township, Ohio, in 1850, and had the following children:
Phebe[1.4.4.5.1b], b. in 1845.
Sarah A.[1.4.4.5.2b], b. in 1847.
Sophronia[1.4.4.5.3b], b. in 1849.

William S. Ehrhardt

William S.[1.4.4.6b] m. Margaret, daughter of Thomas and Nancy (Riffle) Hathaway, in 1838. She was b. in Ohio on Oct. 5, 1822, and d.

on Mar. 25, 1874. She is buried in Beamsville cemetery, in Richland Township. William was alive in 1874. They resided in Darke County, Richland Township, Ohio, in 1850, and had the following children:
Nancy J.$^{1.4.4.6.1b}$, b. in 1841.
Ann Eliza$^{1.4.4.6.2b}$, b. in 1844, m. Milo Orlan, son of Charles and Martha (Oliver) Smith in Darke County on Apr. 27, 1864, and d. in Racine, Wisconsin in 1927. He was b. in Darke County on Mar. 3, 1845, and d. there on Mar. 31, 1903.
Thomas J.$^{1.4.4.6.3b}$, b. in 1845.

Christian Ehrhardt

Christian$^{1.7b}$ m. Barbara. He was taxed in Rapho Township in 1770, and in Londonderry Township, as a freeman in 1775. He took the Oath of Allegiance in Lancaster County on June 13, 1777. Christian d. in Rapho Township in Feb. 1809, and his will was probated on Feb. 14, 1809. They had the following children in Rapho Township:
Christian$^{1.7.1b}$; Jacob$^{1.7.2b}$; John$^{1.7.3b}$; Mary$^{1.7.4b}$; Ann$^{1.7.5b}$.

****

Johannes Friesner

Johannes^{1c} m. Susanna Margaretha$^{1.4f}$, daughter of Johann Peter and Anna Mariae Grimm, at Lancaster County, Lancaster, First Reformed Church, Pennsylvania, on Apr. 13, 1773. Johannes may have been the Johannes that arrived at Philadelphia on the ship *Brothers* on Aug. 24, 1750, or it may have been his father. Johannes was a freeman in Lancaster County, Earl Township, Pennsylvania, in 1770, and a tailor in 1772. In 1782, he resided in Lancaster County, Warwick Township. In 1783, he was residing in York, Pennsylvania, as a tailor, with 5 people, and in 1790 he was residing in Rockingham County, Linneville District, Virginia. In 1792, he was taxed at Linneville Creek, the west portion of Linneville District (Captain Jacob Lincoln's Company). He d. in July 1801. Susanna was a communicant at Rader's Lutheran Church on Oct. 25, 1801, and in Mar. 1807. Susanna d. in Fairfield County, Pleasant Township, Ohio, on Oct. 15, 1823, and is buried in Colfax cemetery. Johannes estate was administered on July 21, 1801 by his executers, Henry Friesner and Henry Stolp, and valued at 4,000 pounds. Johannes son, Johan, chose Peter Krim as his guardian. Johannes and Susanna were the parents of the following children:
Johan Henrich$^{1.1c}$, b. on Mar. 12, 1774.

Johan Frederick[1.2c], b. on Dec. 1, 1775.
Marie[1.3c], b. in 1780, and m. James Cahon in Rockingham County, Virginia, on Aug. 18, 1807. She was confirmed at Rader's Lutheran Church on Oct. 23, 1801.
Jacob[1.4c], b. about 1782 (it has not been proven that his is a Friesner, his name appears as Fries, Friener, and Friesner).
Johan Michael[1.5c], b. on Sep. 29, 1785.

Johan Henrich Friesner

Johan Henrich[1.1c] was baptized at Seltenreich Reformed Lutheran Church on Dec. 18, 1774, and sponsored by his uncle and aunt, Johan Henrich and Christina Grimm. He was confirmed at Rader's Lutheran Church on Oct. 23, 1801. He m. Barbara, daughter of Jacob and Catharina Elisabetha (Rein) Koch, in Rockingham County on Mar. 20, 1803. Henrich moved to Fairfield County, Ohio, about 1806, and d. on Sep. 15, 1845. She was b. on Sep. 7, 1782, and d. on Mar. 8, 1847. They are buried in Colfax cemetery. Henrich and Barbara had the following children:

Andrew[1.1.1c], b. on July 7, 1803.
John[1.1.2c], b. on Oct. (Aug.) 8, 1805.
Jacob[1.1.3c], b. on July 3, 1807.
Susanna[1.1.4c], b. on Aug. 9, 1809, and d. in Hancock County, Illinois. She m. Isaac Swigert.
Samuel[1.1.5c], b. on May 4 (14), 1812.
Elizabeth[1.1.6c], b. on Sep. 1, 1814.
Henry[1.1.7c], b. on Sep. 3, 1817.
Lewis[1.1.8c], b. on July 13, 1819.
Anna Elizabeth[1.1.9c], b. on Jan. 6, 1822, and m. George W. Warner in Fairfield County in 1843.
Levi[1.1.10c], b. on Oct. 6, 1824, and m. Catherine Friesner[1.5.7c] in Fairfield County on May 17, 1846, and Lucy Ann Macklin in Fairfield County on Aug. 17, 1856 (b. in Ohio in 1836). He resided in Pleasant Township in 1850. Catherine d. on Dec. 29, 1855. He d. on Sep. 3, 1880.

Andrew Friesner

Andrew[1.1.1c] d. in Fairfield County on Jan. 9, 1895, and is buried in Colfax cemetery. He m. an unknown woman about 1824, Elizabeth Musser in Fairfield County on Oct. 31, 1834, and Sarah Rugh in Fairfield County on Jan. 25, 1849. Elizabeth was b. on Jan. 6, 1801, d. on Nov. 7, 1847, and is buried in Colfax cemetery. Sarah was b. in

Ohio on July 15, 1820 (1824), d. on Nov. 25, 1899, and is buried in Colfax cemetery. Andrew had the following children in Berne Township:

Mary Ann$^{1.1.1.1c}$, b. on Oct. 10, 1825.

Sarah$^{1.1.1.2c}$, b. about 1826, and m. Joseph Hish in Fairfield County, Lancaster on Aug. 3, 1848.

Mary (Polly)$^{1.1.1.3c}$, b. in 1828, and m. David Engle in Fairfield County on Sep. 12 (10), 1850.

Lydia$^{1.1.1.4c}$, b. about 1829, and m. James H. Patton in Fairfield County on Oct. 21, 1849.

Isabell$^{1.1.1.5c}$, b. on Jan. 9, 1831, m. Peter J. Harmon in Fairfield County on Aug. (Oct.) 7, 1855, and d. there on Feb. 5, 1896. He was b. on June 8, 1827, and d. on Mar. 29, 1900. They are buried in Pleasant Hill cemetery.

Martha M.$^{1.1.1.6c}$, b. on Sep. 24, 1834 (1832), m. Lewis Friesner$^{1.2.4.4.c}$, and d. on Jan. 4, 1852. She is buried in Colfax cemetery.

Andrew Jackson$^{1.1.1.7c}$, b. in 1837, and m. Sarah Elizabeth Bowman in Perry County, Ohio, on Mar. 6, 1856. In 1868, they resided in Coffey County, Leroy, Kansas.

Mary Ann Friesner

Mary Ann$^{1.1.1.1c}$ m. John Stuckey in Fairfield County, Lancaster on Aug. 27, 1844, and d. in Ohio on May 27, 1910. She is buried in Stuckey cemetery. They had the following children in Fairfield County:

Elizabeth$^{1.1.1.1.1c}$, b. on Jan. 30, 1847.

John H.$^{1.1.1.1.2c}$, b. on May 10, 1865.

Emma$^{1.1.1.1.3c}$, b. in Greenfield Township on Aug. 16, 1867.

John Friesner

John$^{1.1.2c}$ d. in Fairfield County on Jan. 12, 1876. He m. Emily Dean in Fairfield County on Mar. 4, 1829. She was b. in Philadelphia County, Philadelphia, Pennsylvania, on Nov. (June) 3, 1807, and d. on Feb. 10, 1895. They are buried in Zeigler cemetery, and had the following children in Pleasant Township:

Samuel Edward$^{1.1.2.1c}$, b. on Mar. 13, 1831, and m. Hannah Hamilton in Fairfield County on Feb. 27, 1853, and Elizabeth Brown in Fairfield County, Lancaster on July 14, 1859. Samuel d. in Fairfield County on Apr. 27 (6), 1908. Hannah was b. on July 29, 1829, and d.

LANCASTER, LEBANON & DAUPHIN COUNTIES 23

on May 12, 1856. Elizabeth was b. on July 28, 1840, and d. on Dec. 19, 1926. They are buried in Zeigler cemetery.

Barbara Jane[1.1.2.2c], b. on Feb. 7, 1834, m. Elias H. Cupp in Fairfield County on May 13, 1855, and d. in Fairfield County on Mar. 1, 1899.

John D.[1.1.2.3f], b. on Dec. 27, 1836, and m. Mary Arnold in Fairfield County, Lancaster on Feb. 14, 1861, and d. in Fairfield County on Dec. 24, 1920.

Allen Dean[1.1.2.4c], b. Dec. 6, 1838. He m. Mary Ann Weaver in Fairfield County on June 5, 1864, and d. in Fairfield County, Baltimore, Ohio, on Apr. 7, 1924. She was b. in 1845, and d. in 1924. They are buried in New St. Peter's cemetery.

Emily[1.1.2.5c], b. on Feb. 9, 1841, m. Isaac W. Keller in Fairfield County on Mar. 19, 1861, and d. in Fairfield County, Lancaster on May 20, 1920. She is buried in Forest Rose cemetery.

Richard Henry[1.1.2.6c], b. on Feb. 8, 1844, m. Nancy Ann Kiger in Fairfield County on Jan. 19 (18), 1871, and d. there on Jan. 17, 1882. He is buried in Zeigler cemetery.

Emanuel D.[1.1.2.7c], b. on Feb. 17, 1847, m. Sadie J. Miller in Fairfield County on Mar. 19, 1876. Emanuel d. in Fairfield County on Jan. (Mar.) 13, 1891, and is buried in Zeigler cemetery.

Benavel D.[1.1.2.8c], b. on July 20, 1849, m. Sarah Elizabeth Miesse in Fairfield County on Jan. 1, 1874, and d. in Fairfield County, Greenfield Township on Apr. 5, 1930. He is buried in Forest Rose cemetery.

Jacob Friesner

Jacob[1.1.3c] d. in Coles County, Charleston, Illinois, on Jan. 24, 1857. He m. Mary, daughter of Henry and Barbary Weil. She was b. on May 14, 1806, and d. in Effingham County, Mocassin Creek Township, Illinois, on Nov. 5 (6), 1878. She is buried in Pleasant Grove cemetery. They had the following children:

Henry[1.1.3.1c], b. in Fairfield County, Ohio, on Jan. 15, 1830. He m. Martha, daughter of Samuel and Hester (Fleming) Swisher, in Coles County, Illinois, on Mar. 7, 1857, and d. in Sac County, Iowa, on Apr. 18, 1915. She was b. in Franklin County, Ohio, on Aug. 16, 1837, and d. in Sac County, Iowa, on June 14, 1895.

Barbara[1.1.3.2c], b. in Fairfield County, Ohio, in 1831, and m. Lewis Letner in Coles County, Illinois, on Nov. 26, 1851.

Mary[1.1.3.3c], b. in Fairfield County in 1833, and m. John Moore in Coles County, Illinois, on Oct. 13, 1859.

Levi[1.1.3.4c], b. in Fairfield County in 1836, m. Martha J. Stull in Cook County, Chicago, Illinois, on Mar. 2, 1855, and d. in Johnson County, Olathe, Kansas, on Apr. 6, 1892.

Lewis[1.1.3.5c], b. in Fairfield County on July 1, 1838, m. Mary Reemer in Coles County, Illinois, on Aug. 28, 1858, and d. in Calhoun County, Rockwell City, Iowa, on Jan. 21, 1915.

Noah[1.1.3.6c], b. in Fairfield County on Mar. 1, 1840, m. Emeline Kirkpatrick in Coles County, Illinois, on Aug. 15, 1861, and d. in Linn County, Meadville, Missouri, on Nov. 11, 1899.

Leah Grace[1.1.3.7c], b. in 1843 at Coles County, Illinois, and m. William Ezekiel Ensign in Effingham County, Illinois, on Nov. 25, 1861. She d. in Effingham County, Effingham, Illinois, on Oct. 23, 1881

Nancy[1.1.3.8c], b. in Coles County about 1845, m. John Ensign in Effingham County, Illinois, on Nov. 28, 1861, and d. in Effingham County on Dec. 10, 1864. She is buried in Pleasant Grove cemetery.

Ann Elizabeth[1.1.3.9c], b. in Coles County about 1847, and was buried in Coles County, Charleston Township, Illinois, on Dec. 22, 1854. She is buried in Yocum cemetery.

Elizabeth[1.1.3.10c], b. about 1855, and m. ____ Bader.

Samuel Friesner

Samuel[1.1.5c] d. in Champaign County, Thomasboro, Illinois, on Oct. 24, 1891. He m. Mary, daughter of David and Catherine (Spitler) Kauffman, in Fairfield County on Jan. 28, 1836. She was b. in Fairfield County, Ohio, on May 3, 1818, and d. in Story County, Nevada, Iowa, on Sep. 24, 1900. Samuel moved to Pratt County, Illinois, in 1852. They had the following children:

David K.[1.1.5.1c], b. in Fairfield County, Lancaster, Ohio, on Nov. 28, 1837, m. Elsie Ann Burriff in Fairfield County on Dec. 23, 1858, and Cal Wilson. He d. in Feb. 1910.

Henry C.[1.1.5.2c], b. on Feb. 9, 1840, m. Sarah C. (E.) Morain in Champaign County, Illinois, on Feb. 21, 1866, and d. in Thomasboro on Mar. 18, 1900.

Anna Elizabeth[1.1.5.3c], b. on June 25, 1847, m. Thomas Asbery Morain on Jan. 28, 1869, and d. in Thomasboro on Oct. 18, 1928.

Susan Catherine[1.1.5.4c], b. on Mar. 27, 1849, m. Thomas J. Matheny on July 22, 1879, and d. in Story County, Nevada, Iowa, in 1930.

LANCASTER, LEBANON & DAUPHIN COUNTIES

Mary Jane$^{1.1.5.5c}$, b. in Lancaster, Ohio, on July 19, 1852, m. Robert A. Frazier in Urbana, Illinois, on Sep. 23, 1874, and d. in Story County, Nevada, Iowa, on July 31, 1926.

Elizabeth Friesner

Elizabeth$^{1.1.6c}$ m. Samuel Barr in Fairfield County on Mar. 8, 1835, and had the following children in Fairfield County:

Henry$^{1.1.6.1c}$, b. in 1837, and m. Mary Ann Macklin in Fairfield County on Feb. 17, 1859.
Ann E.$^{1.1.6.2c}$, b. in 1840, and m. Adam Kemerer in Fairfield County on Dec. 31, 1857.
Lewis$^{1.1.6.3c}$, b. in 1840.
Wilson$^{1.1.6.4c}$, b. in 1852.

Henry Friesner

Henry$^{1.1.7c}$ probably m. Lavina Kemper in Fairfield County on Mar. 9, 1846. He is unmarried and residing with his brother, Andrew, in 1850. He m. Jane Farier (b. in Pennsylvania in 1840) in Fairfield County on Aug. 28, 1859, and had the following children in Pleasant Township:

Sarah E.$^{1.1.7.1c}$, b. in 1860.
Emma$^{1.1.7.2c}$, b. in 1861.
Andrew$^{1.1.7.3c}$, b. in 1863.
Margaret$^{1.1.7.4c}$, b. in 1867.
John$^{1.1.7.5c}$, b. in 1870.

Lewis Friesner

Lewis$^{1.1.8c}$ m. Martha Ann Warner in Fairfield County on Apr. 1, 1847, and d. on Oct. 23, 1893. She was b. in Ohio in 1829, and d. on Dec. 22, 1882. They had the following son in Pleasant Township:

Thomas Jefferson$^{1.1.8.1c}$, b. on Aug. 15, 1851, m. Elizabeth Jane Allmon on Oct. 19, 1874, and d. on Oct. 23, 1893.

Johan Frederick Friesner

Johan Frederick$^{1.2c}$ was baptized at Seltenreich Reformed Lutheran Church on Mar. 10, 1776, and sponsored by his uncle and aunt, Johan Frederick and Eva Schuetz. He was confirmed at Rader's Lutheran Church on Oct. 23, 1801. He m. Magdalena, daughter of Georg and Elisabetha Ehrhardt, in Rockingham County, Rader's Lutheran Church, Virginia, on June 21, 1796. She was b. in Frederick County, Woodsboro, Maryland, on Mar. 1, 1776, and d. in Fairfield

County, Rush Creek Township, Ohio, on Aug. 23, 1843. Frederick purchased land in Rush Creek Township, Fairfield County, Ohio, on Nov. 6, 1805, and in 1827, he had 91 acres in section 29 of Rush Creek Township. Frederick resided with his son, Noah, in Auburn Township in 1850, and d. on Dec. 28, 1857. Frederick and Magdalena are buried in Friesner cemetery. They had the following children:

Elizabeth$^{1.2.1c}$, b. on June 22, 1797, baptized at Rader's Lutheran Church on Aug. 26, 1798, and sponsored by her grandparents, Georg and Elisabetha Ehrhardt. She m. James McFadden in Fairfield County on Apr. 27, 1817.

John$^{1.2.2c}$, b. on Apr. 5, 1799, baptized at Rader's Lutheran Church on June 9, 1799, and sponsored by Jacob and Dorothea Stautenmayer.

Frederick$^{1.2.3c}$, b. on Jan. 12, 1801.
Henry$^{1.2.4c}$, b. on Feb. 22, 1803 (1804).
David $^{1.2.5c}$, b. on Oct. 26, 1805.
Susanna$^{1.2.6c}$, b. on Oct. 10, 1808, and m. Daniel Swartz.
Lydia$^{1.2.7c}$, b. about 1812, and m. Isaac Blosser in Fairfield County on Jan. 28, 1836.
Noah$^{1.2.8c}$, b. on Oct. 10, 1813.
Rebecca$^{1.2.9c}$, b. about 1815, and m. George Lutz in Fairfield County on Jan. 26(28), 1836.
Polly$^{1.2.10c}$, b. on Feb. 26, 1823.

John Friesner

John$^{1.2.2c}$ m. Anna Maria, daughter of John Fought, and d. in Hocking County, Marion Township, Ohio, on Apr. 22, 1845. Anna Maria was b. in Pennsylvania in 1806, and d. in Hocking County on June 15, 1894. She resided in Marion Township in 1850. They had the following children:

Anna$^{1.2.2.1c}$, b. on July 5, 1825.
Lucinda$^{1.2.2.2c}$, b. in 1827.
Peter$^{1.2.2.3c}$, b. about 1830, and m. Matilda Miller in Fairfield County, Lancaster on Feb. 6, 1851. He has not been proven as a son.
Sarah$^{1.2.2.4c}$, b. in 1832.
Isabel$^{1.2.2.5c}$, b. in 1835.
Joshua$^{1.2.2.6c}$, b. in 1838, and d. in Hocking County on Sep. 9, 1849.
William $^{1.2.2.7c}$, b. in Ohio in 1840, and d. in Hocking County on Sep. 3, 1865.

Susanna[1.2.2.8c], b. in 1842.
Mary Magdalene[1.2.2.9c], b. in 1845.

Anna Friesner

Anna[1.2.2.1c] m. Joseph Logan Beery in Hocking County on Oct. 20, 1842, and d. in Adams County, Decatur, Indiana, on June 25, 1860. She is buried in Beery cemetery. He was b. in 1821, and d. in 1887. They had the following children:

William Francis[1.2.2.1.1c], b. about 1843.
Benjamin Franklin[1.2.2.1.2c], b. about 1845.
Solomon Forest[1.2.2.1.3c], b. about 1847.
Mahala[1.2.2.1.4c], b. about 1849, and m. Henry Konkel.
Mary Elizabeth[1.2.2.1.5c], b. about 1851, and m. ___ Hammer.
James Daniel[1.2.2.1.6c], b. about 1853.
Caleb F.[1.2.2.1.7c], b. in Adams County, Decatur, Indiana, on Oct. 11, 1855.
Sarah F.[1.2.2.1.8c], b. about 1857, and m. H. H. Thomas.
Jesse[1.2.2.1.9c], b. in 1860.
Jonas[1.2.2.1.10c], b. in 1860.

Lucinda Friesner

Lucinda[1.2.2.2c] m. Abraham Good (b. in 1822) in Hocking County on May 11, 1845, and had the following children:

Mahala[1.2.2.2.1c], b. in 1847, and m. ___ Stewart.
Diana[1.2.2.2.3c], b. in 1848, and m. John William Adelsperger.
Lorenzo D.[1.2.2.2.4c], b. about 1850.
Anna Mary[1.2.2.2.5c], b. about 1852.
Obediah[1.2.2.2.6c], b. about 1854.

Sarah Friesner

Sarah[1.2.2.4c] m. John R. Kerwood (b. in 1830) in Fairfield County on Nov. 2, 1854, and had the following children:

Flavias[1.2.2.4.1c], b. in 1856.
Asenath[1.2.2.4.2c], b. in 1858, and m. ___ Wright.
Frances[1.2.2.4.3c], b. in 1859, and m. ___ Welty.

Isabel Friesner

Isabel[1.2.2.5c] m. Isaac Miller (b. in 1835) in Hocking County on May 4, 1854, and had the following children:

Mary[1.2.2.5.1c], b. in 1855.
Harriet[1.2.2.5.2c], b. in 1856.

28   EARLY FAMILIES OF PENNSYLVANIA

Sarah$^{1.2.2.5.3c}$, b. in 1858.
Isabel$^{1.2.2.5.4c}$, b. in 1860.

Mary Magdalene Friesner

Mary Magdalene$^{1.2.2.9c}$ m. John Palmer in Hocking County on Feb. 5, 1863, and d. in Hocking County in June 1869. They had the following children:
Aaron$^{1.2.2.9.1c}$.
Anderson/Andrew$^{1.2.2.9.2c}$.

Frederick Friesner

Frederick$^{1.2.3c}$ d. in Hocking County, Falls Creek Township, Ohio, on Feb. 25, 1861. He is buried in Fairview cemetery. He m. Leah, daughter of John Fought (b. in Pennsylvania on Feb. 23, 1801, and d. in Falls Township on Oct. 17, 1877), and had the following children in Falls Creek Township:
Simeon$^{1.2.3.1c}$, b. on Oct. 4, 1823.
Mary$^{1.2.3.2c}$, b. in 1825.
Susannah$^{1.2.3.3c}$, b. in 1827.
Magdalena$^{1.2.3.4c}$, b. in 1828.
Leah$^{1.2.3.7c}$, b. in 1831.
Elizabeth$^{1.2.3.8c}$, b. in 1834.
Solomon$^{1.2.3.9c}$, b. in 1835, and m. Christina Weaver on Jan. 3, 1861.

Simeon Friesner

Simeon$^{1.2.3.1c}$ m. Elizabeth A. Zellers (b. in Ohio in 1828, and d. in 1865) in Hocking County, Ohio, on Sep. 16, 1847, and Sarah Zeller in Hocking County on May 8, 1866, and d. in Falls Creek Township on Apr. 11 (Mar. 22), 1867. Simeon had the following children:
Lydia C.$^{1.2.3.1.1c}$, b. in 1848, and m. William A. Knight in Hocking County on Aug. 29, 1868. She d. in 1873.
Jacob F.$^{1.2.3.1.2c}$, b. in 1850, and d. in 1880.
Mary E.$^{1.2.3.1.3c}$, b. about 1852, and m. Joseph Klinger.
Henry F.$^{1.2.3.1.4c}$, b. about 1854.
Almedia$^{1.2.3.1.5c}$, b. in 1858, and d. in 1864.
William E.$^{1.2.3.1.6c}$, b. in 1860, and d. in 1887.
Simeon E.$^{1.2.3.1.7c}$, b. in 1863, and d. in 1864.
John W.$^{1.2.3.1.8c}$, b. in 1864, and d. in 1882.
Simeon L.$^{1.2.3.1.9c}$, b. in 1866.

LANCASTER, LEBANON & DAUPHIN COUNTIES

Mary Friesner

Mary$^{1.2.3.3c}$ m. Elias Fink in Hocking County, Ohio, on Aug. 17, 1843, and William Murphy about 1851, and had the following children (she was residing with her father, unmarried in 1850):

William$^{1.2.3.3.1c}$, b. in 1845, and m. Philia R. Crooks (?) and Susanna Strohl.
Leah$^{1.2.3.3.2c}$, b. in 1852.
Alfred$^{1.2.3.3.3c}$, b. in 1854.
Allen$^{1.2.3.3.4c}$, b. in 1858.
Susan A.$^{1.2.3.3.5c}$, b. in 1860.
Albert$^{1.2.3.3.6c}$, b. in 1863.
William$^{1.2.3.3.7c}$, b. in 1866.

Susannah Friesner

Susannah$^{1.2.3.4c}$ m. Samuel B. Stivison in Hocking County, Ohio, on Apr. 26, 1849, and had the following children:

Solomon$^{1.2.3.4.1c}$, b. in 1850.
Leah$^{1.2.3.4.2c}$, b. in 1852.
Lewis$^{1.2.3.4.3c}$, b. in 1854.
Simeon$^{1.2.3.4.4c}$, b. in 1855.
Elizabeth$^{1.2.3.4.5c}$, b. in 1857.
David$^{1.2.3.4.6c}$, b. in 1858.
Edward$^{1.2.3.4.7c}$, b. in 1864.
Ida$^{1.2.3.4.8c}$, b. in 1867.

Magdalena Friesner

Magdalena$^{1.2.3.5c}$ m. David Gross in Hocking County on Apr. 8, 1846, and had the following children:

Martin$^{1.2.3.5.1c}$, b. in 1847, and m. Lucinda.
Simeon$^{1.2.3.5.2c}$, b. in 1849.
Frederick$^{1.2.3.5.3c}$, b. in 1852.
Ellen$^{1.2.3.5.4c}$, b. in 1857.
Emma$^{1.2.3.5.5c}$, b. in 1859.
Effie$^{1.2.3.5.6c}$, b. in 1861.
Edward$^{1.2.3.5.7c}$, b. in 1864.
Ida$^{1.2.3.5.8c}$, b. in 1867.

Leah Friesner

Leah$^{1.2.3.7c}$ m. Michael Kreig/King in Hocking County on Feb. 4, 1855, and had the following children:

John F.$^{1.2.3.7.1c}$, b. in 1856.

Marcelles A.$^{1.2.3.7.2c}$, b. in 1857.
Lafayette C.$^{1.2.3.7.3c}$, b. in 1859.
Homer D.$^{1.2.3.7.4c}$, b. in 1860.
Ida V.$^{1.2.3.7.5c}$, b. in 1864.
Michael$^{1.2.3.7.6c}$, b. in 1866.
Archibald$^{1.2.3.7.7c}$, b. in 1869.

Elizabeth Friesner

Elizabeth$^{1.2.3.8c}$ m. Jacob N. Zeller in Hocking County on Aug. 2 (22), 1855, and had the following children:
Emily T.$^{1.2.3.8.1c}$, b. in 1856.
Naoma$^{1.2.3.8.2c}$, b. in 1858.
David$^{1.2.3.8.3c}$, b. in 1860.
Leah C.$^{1.2.3.8.4c}$, b. in 1864.

Henry Friesner

Henry$^{1.2.4c}$ m. Rebecca, daughter of Ludwig and Anna (Beery) Seitz, in Fairfield County, Ohio, on Mar. 6, 1825. She d. in Shelby County, Illinois, on Sep. 28, 1887. Henry d. in Fairfield County, Rush Creek Township, Ohio, on Sep. 26, 1855. He is buried in Beery-Miller cemetery. They had the following children in Rush Creek Township:
Abraham Seitz$^{1.2.4.1c}$, b. on Jan. 9, 1826.
Elizabeth$^{1.2.4.2c}$, b. on July 1 (21), 1827.
Frederick$^{1.2.4.3c}$, b. on Oct. 4 (July 28) (Sep. 28), 1828.
Lewis$^{1.2.4.4c}$, b. on Nov. 4, 1829, m. Martha M. Friesner$^{1.1.1.4c}$ in Fairfield County on Sep. 4, 1851, and d. on Oct. 1, 1855. He is buried in Beery-Miller cemetery.
Catherine$^{1.2.4.5c}$, b. on Dec. 12, 1831.
Noah$^{1.2.4.6c}$, b. on Aug. 18, 1833, and d. on Apr. 5, 1859. He is buried in Beery Miller cemetery.
Anna$^{1.2.4.7c}$, b. on Dec. 31, 1834, m. William Jefferson Miller in Fairfield County on May 20, 1858, and d. on Dec. 3, 1859.
Leah$^{1.2.4.8c}$, b. on Nov. 15, 1836.
Rachel$^{1.2.4.9c}$, b. on Feb. 20, 1838, and m. John Swartz in Fairfield County on Feb. 16 (18), 1858.
Daniel$^{1.2.4.10c}$, b. on June 3, 1839, and d. on Apr. 2, 1855.
Henry$^{1.2.4.11c}$, b. on Apr. 11, 1841, m. Maria Stuckey in Fairfield County on Aug. 25, 1860, and d. in Allen County, Ohio, on Mar. 24, 1917.
Jacob$^{1.2.4.12c}$, b. on Feb. 12, 1843.

LANCASTER, LEBANON & DAUPHIN COUNTIES 31

Rebecca[1.2.4.13c], b. on Feb. 10, 1846, and d. on Sep. 21, 1855. She is buried in Beery-Miller cemetery.

John Seitz[1.2.4.14c], b. on Aug. 30, 1847.

George W.[1.2.4.15c], b. on Feb. 16, 1849, and d. on June 19, 1866. He is buried in Beery Miller cemetery.

Abraham Seitz Friesner

Abraham Seitz[1.2.4.1c] m. Eliza Jane Miller (b. in 1829) in Fairfield County, Lancaster on Mar. 9, 1848 (Apr. 15, 1849), and Catherine Brenneman (b. in 1838) about 1861. They resided in Fairfield County, Rush Creek Township in 1850, and later in Allen County, Elida, Ohio, and Shelby County, Illinois. Abraham d. on Dec. 31, 1870, and Eliza d. in 1860. Abraham had the following children:

Harvey[1.2.4.1.1c], b. in 1849. He m. Catherine Beery, and d. in 1926. She was b. in 1846.

William Miller[1.2.4.1.2c], b. in 1851. He m. Charlotte Emma Fant (1850- 1883), and Addie Belle Towell before 1887. Addie was b. in 1860. William d. in 1894.

Nancy Jane[1.2.4.1.3c], b. in 1853. She m. Elisha Hadley Colwell (b. in 1844).

Henry[1.2.4.1.4c], b. in Elida on May 8, 1855. He m. Rachel Jane, daughter of Henry and Rebecca (Hufford) Swartz, in Shelby County, Pickaway Township, Illinois, on Apr. 18, 1878. She was b. in Fairfield County, Berne Station, Ohio, on Dec. 26, 1856, and d. in Shelby County, Illinois, on Jan. 25, 1937. Henry d. in Shelby County, Strassburg, Illinois, on Jan. 27, 1938.

Rebecca Amerretta[1.2.4.1.5c], b. in 1857. She m. Nicholas Westenbarger (b. in 1855).

John Lutz[1.2.4.1.6c], b. in 1859. He m. Ella Catherine Heft, and d. in 1909. She was b. in 1868, and d. in 1928.

Caroline[1.2.4.1.7c], b. in 1862.

Jacob Brenneman[1.2.4.1.8c], b. in 1864. He m. Mary Inhoff (b. in 1868).

Daniel[1.2.4.1.9c], b. in 1867.

Lydia Ann[1.2.4.1.10c], b. in 1869.

Elizabeth Friesner

Elizabeth[1.2.4.2c] m. Henry Syfert on Aug. 20, 1848, and d. on Dec. 21, 1878. They had the following children:

Rebecca[1.2.4.2.1c], b. in 1849, and m. Oliver Scott Carr. He was b. in 1847.

Mary Ann[1.2.4.2.2c], b. in 1854, and m. Francis Marion Forest. He was b. in 1853.
Eliza Ellen[1.2.4.2.3c], b. in 1858, and d. in 1886.
Stephen Douglas[1.2.4.2.4c] b. in 1860, and m. Sarah Ann Pritchard. She was b. in 1872, and d. in 1887.
William Sherman[1.2.4.2.5c], b. in 1864.

Frederick Friesner

Frederick[1.2.4.3c] m. Elizabeth Geil in Fairfield County on Aug. 1 (10), 1850, and d. on Feb. 16 (10), 1862. He is buried in Beery-Miller cemetery. She was b. in 1832, and d. in 1865. They had the following children in Fairfield County:

John H.[1.2.4.3.1c], b. on Sep. 14, 1851, and d. on Sep. 26, 1862. He is buried in Beery-Miller cemetery.
Abraham Allen[1.2.4.3.2c], b. in 1854.
Fannie Fern[1.2.4.3.3c], b. on June 7, 1856. She m. Eli Wolf (b. in 1856).
Mary Alice[1.2.4.3.4c], b. in 1857. She m. Elijah Hamilton (b. in 1851).
Emma Frances (Florence)[1.2.4.3.5c], b. on June 22, 1862. She m. Frederick Gustavus Jones (b. in 1859).

Catherine Friesner

Catherine[1.2.4.5c] m. Noah Syphert in Fairfield County on Aug. 4, 1849. They resided in Allen County, Lima, Ohio, in 1852, and Shelby County, Shelbyville, Illinois, in 1867. They had the following children:

John Wesley[1.2.4.5.1c], b. on June 7, 1850, and m. Emma Askins. She was b. in 1853.
Elizabeth Ann[1.2.4.5.2c], b. on Feb. 29, 1852, and m. Edward McDonald. He was b. in 1852.
Franklin Pierce[1.2.4.5.3c], b. in 1853, and m. Anna Maria Shumaker. She was b. in 1858.
George Henry[1.2.4.5.4c], b. on Dec. 11, 1854, and d. in 1855.
William Benjamin[1.2.4.5.5c], b. on Dec. 16, 1856, and m. Winnie Elizabeth Yantis. She was b. in 1863.
Andrew Jackson[1.2.4.5.6c], b. in 1858, and m. Emma Molica Stevson. She was b. in 1863.
Sarah Amanda[1.2.4.5.7c], b. on Sep. 1, 1860, and m. William Henry Fritz. He was b. in 1849.
Emily Jane[1.2.4.5.8c], b. on Oct. 6, 1861, and d. in 1862.

LANCASTER, LEBANON & DAUPHIN COUNTIES 33

Lodema Ellen$^{1.2.4.5.9c}$, b. on Dec. 4, 1862, and m. John William Turner. He was b. in 1858.
Catherine Rosella$^{1.2.4.5.10c}$, b. on Sep. 25, 1864.
Lillie Belle$^{1.2.4.5.11c}$, b. on June 4, 1867.
Lulu Charity$^{1.2.4.5.12c}$, b. on Sep. 10, 1868.
Ida Rebecca$^{1.2.4.5.13c}$, b. on Apr. 14, 1870.
Edward Monroe$^{1.2.4.5.14c}$, b. on Sep. 11, 1871.
Oliver Simon$^{1.2.4.5.15c}$, b. on Aug. 2, 1873.

Henry Friesner

Henry$^{1.2.4.11c}$ m. Maria Stuckey in Fairfield County on Aug. 25, 1860, and d. in Allen County, Ohio, on Mar. 24, 1917. She was b. in 1841, and d. in 1929. They had the following children:

Wilson$^{1.2.4.11.1c}$, b. in 1861. He m. Ida Lizzie, daughter of John and Rachel (Friesner) Swartz.

Cynthia Ann$^{1.2.4.11.2c}$, b. in 1863. She m. Christian Steeman Ireland, and d. in 1938. He was b. in 1859.

Samuel Sherman$^{1.2.4.11.3c}$, b. in 1865. He m. Barbara Ellen Thomas, and d. in 1956. She was b. in 1869, and d. in 1956.

Elizabeth Eureka$^{1.2.4.11.4c}$, b. in 1867, m. John W. Clapper, and d. in 1911.

Jesse Tay/Lay$^{1.2.4.11.5c}$, b. in 1871. He m. Lulu L. Whyman, Hattie Russell, and Alice Nunniviller, and d. in 1951. Lulu was b. in 1881, and d. in 1923.

Eva May$^{1.2.4.11.6c}$, b. in 1871. She m. John Conrad (1860-1929), ___ Baker, John Hanby, and Frank Willoughby.

Charles Linn$^{1.2.4.11.7c}$, b. in 1873, and d. in 1908.

Lily Belle$^{1.2.4.11.8c}$, b. in 1885. She m. Harvey Oscar Conrad, and d. in 1917. He was b. in 1883.

Jacob Friesner

Jacob$^{1.2.4.12c}$ m. Lydia Hendricks on Mar. 5, 1868, and d. on Aug. 8, 1885. She was b. in 1847. They had the following children:
Mary Ellen$^{1.2.4.12.1c}$, b. in 1868.
Catherine May$^{1.2.4.12.2c}$, b. in 1873.
John Jefferson$^{1.2.4.12.3c}$, b. in 1876.
Clara Maria$^{1.2.4.12.4c}$, b. in 1879.

John Seitz Friesner

John Seitz$^{1.2.4.14c}$ m. Isabella Marie Freshwater (b. in 1847) on Sep. 15, 1872, and had the following children:

Golda May[1.2.4.14.1c], b. in 1873.
William Edward[1.2.4.14.2c], b. in 1874.
Walter David[1.2.4.14.3c], b. in 1876.
John Henry[1.2.4.14.4c], b. in 1878.
Norma Belle[1.2.4.14.5c], b. in 1880.

David Friesner

David[1.2.5c] m. Elizabeth Spear in Fairfield County on Dec. 13, 1826, and Rebecca, daughter of Daniel and Elizabeth (Hite) Seitz, in Fairfield County on Dec. 22, 1844. Elizabeth was b. on Jan. 14, 1800, and d. on July 14, 1844. David d. in Fairfield County, Rush Creek/Auburn Township on July 31, 1889. They are buried in Friesner cemetery. In 1850, David resided in Auburn Township, and in 1860, he resided in Rush Creek Township. He had the following children:

Eli[1.2.5.1c], b. on Aug. 22, 1827 (1829).
Ephraim[1.2.5.2c], b. in 1828.
Catherine[1.2.5.3c], b. on Dec. 15, 1830.
David J.[1.2.5.4c], b. in 1833, and m. Rebecca Hoffert in Fairfield County on Oct. 27, 1859.
Samuel[1.2.5.5c], b. in 1835.
Lydia[1.2.5.6c], b. in 1837.
Isaac[1.2.5.7c], b. in 1839, and m. Mary Stoneburner in Hocking County on Sep. 22, 1861.
Joseph[1.2.5.8c], b. in 1843, and m. Emma/Emily Barnes in Hocking County, Ohio, on Nov. 1, 1860.
Eliza[1.2.5.9c], b. on Apr. 25, 1846, and d. in 1854. She was buried in Colfax cemetery on Mar. 2, 1854.
Lewis[1.2.5.10c], b. on Nov. 8, 1847, and d. on Mar. 14 (3), 1849. He is buried in Friesner (Colfax) cemetery.
Absalom[1.2.5.11c], b. on July 11, 1849.
Daniel[1.2.5.12c], b. on Aug. 1, 1852 (1853), and d. on Sep. 8, 1870. He is buried in Friesner cemetery.
Bartlett[1.2.5.13c], b. on Dec. 27, 1853 in Auburn Township, and m. Mary Hoffert in Fairfield County on Apr. 14, 1877. She was b. on Feb. 4, 1853, and d. on Oct. 1, 1943. Bartlett d. on Apr. 18, 1942. They are buried in Friesner cemetery.
Mary A.[1.2.5.14c], b. in 1856 in Auburn Township.
Aaron[1.2.5.15c], b. on June 20, 1865, and buried in Colfax cemetery on Apr. 15, 1870.

Eli Friesner

Eli$^{1.2.5.1c}$ m. Christina Hoffert in Fairfield County on Dec. 11, 1851, and d. in Chatham County, Savannah, Georgia on Jan. 19, 1864. She was b. in 1831. They had the following children:

Sarah Ann$^{1.2.5.1.1c}$, b. in 1852, and m. David Ruff.
Elizabeth$^{1.2.5.1.2c}$, b. in 1854, m. Jacob Palmer, and d. in 1880.
Margaret$^{1.2.5.1.3c}$, b. in 1856.
Solomon$^{1.2.5.1.4c}$, b. in 1858.
Mary$^{1.2.5.1.5c}$, b. in 1861.
Rebecca$^{1.2.5.1.6c}$, b. in 1864.

Ephraim Friesner

Ephraim$^{1.2.5.2c}$ m. Diana (b. in Ohio in 1826) on Sep. 20, 1849, and had the following son in Rush Creek Township:

Simeon$^{1.2.5.2.1c}$, b. in 1850.

Catherine Friesner

Catherine$^{1.2.5.3c}$ m. John Keckler in Fairfield County on Aug. 7, 1851, and d. in Fairfield County on June 25, 1856. He was b. in 1826, and d. in 1897. They had the following children:

Ephraim$^{1.2.5.3.1c}$, b. in 1852.
Elizabeth$^{1.2.5.3.2c}$, b. in 1854.
Maria A.$^{1.2.5.3.3c}$, b. in 1856.

Samuel Friesner

Samuel$^{1.2.5.5c}$ m. Catherine Rhinehart in Fairfield County on Mar. 23, 1856. She was b. in 1836, and d. in Rush Creek Township on Nov. 28, 1874. She is buried in the Old Olive Branch cemetery. They had the following children:

Anna Mary$^{1.2.5.5.1c}$, b. in 1858.
Lydia$^{1.2.5.5.2c}$, b. in 1860.
Joseph$^{1.2.5.5.3c}$, b. in 1863.
William$^{1.2.5.5.4c}$, b. in 1866.
Sarah$^{1.2.5.5.5c}$, b. in 1869.

Absalom Friesner

Absalom$^{1.2.5.11c}$ m. Mahala Beery in Hocking County on Sep. 27, 1870 (1871). They resided in Randolph County, Union City, Indiana, in 1872. Absalom d. in Union City, Indiana, on Dec. 14, 1920. Mahala was b. in 1846, and d. in 1917. They had the following children:

Louis W.$^{1.2.5.11.1c}$, b. in 1872, and d. in 1928.
Bert C.$^{1.2.5.11.2c}$, b. in 1875, m. Jennie Snell, and d. in 1959.
Pearl S.$^{1.2.5.11.3c}$, b. in 1877. He m. Maude Morgan (b. in 1876), d. in 1946.
Charles V.$^{1.2.5.11.4c}$, b. in 1882. He m. Bessie Hartman (b. in 1882).
Ray Jones$^{1.2.5.11.5c}$, b. in 1885. He m. Cara Ellen Boyer (b. in 1881).
Marion Winfield$^{1.2.5.11.6c}$, b. in 1888, m. Melba Beatrice Williams (b. in 1889), and d. in 1953.

Daniel Swartz

Susanna$^{1.2.6c}$ m. Daniel, son of Georg Heinrich and Elnora (Seitz) Swartz, at Fairfield County, Lancaster, Ohio, on Sep. 20, 1827. Daniel was a farmer and an Evangelical Lutheran minister (for 60 years) in Berne Township. Susanna d. in Berne Township on July 19, 1884, and Daniel on Mar. 7, 1891. They are buried in Mt. Tabor cemetery. Daniel had 204 acres in Section 36 of Berne Township, near Sugar Grove, Ohio, which was his father's old homestead on Rush Creek. After Susanna's death, Daniel m. Susan Rife. Daniel and Susanna had the following children in Berne Township:

Louis$^{1.2.6.1a}$, b. on May 6, 1829. He m. Priscilla, daughter of Samuel and Catharina Engel, in Hocking County, Ohio, on Apr. 10, 1853, and d. in Fairfield County, Greenfield Township, Ohio, in 1891. She was b. in Ohio on Dec. 24, 1834, baptized at St. Jacobus Lutheran Church in Hocking County, Ohio, on May 12, 1838, and d. on Sep. 9, 1922. They are buried in Greenfield Township cemetery.

Benjamin$^{1.2.6.2a}$, b. in 1832. He was a blacksmith. He m. Rebecca Engel in Hocking County, Ohio, on Feb. 8, 1858, and Sophia (b. in 1836), daughter of Sarah Engel about 1859.

Lydia$^{1.2.6.3a}$, b. on Apr. 2, 1834, and m. Christoph Friedrich, son of Andreas and Magdalena (Roth) Kull. He was b. on May 9, 1837, baptized at St. Jacobus Lutheran Church in Hocking County, Marion Township, Ohio, on June 11, 1837, and sponsored by Friedrich and Catharina Scholl. Lydia and Friedrich were m. in Fairfield County, on Nov. 20, 1862 (Daniel Swartz officiated), and Laura LaMunyon, widow of William Rider, and Saul Friesner, in Mercer County on Apr. 28, 1902. Laura was b. in Kentucky in 1837, and d. in Mendon in Jan. 1923. Frederich was a farmer and wagonmaker. He was a wagonmaker until 1877, when he began farming in Fairfield County, and in 1897, moved to Mercer County. He resided in Fairfield County, Berne

LANCASTER, LEBANON & DAUPHIN COUNTIES 37

Township, in 1860 (he is listed with his father, and as an assistant carriage maker living with Anthony Zeick); Greenfield Township, in 1880; Mercer County, Black Creek Township, Ohio, in 1900; and Mercer County, Union Township, Mendon, Ohio, in 1920. In the fall of 1902, he moved to Mendon. Lydia d. in Fairfield County, Greenfield Township, Ohio, on Aug. 24, 1892, and is buried in Mt. Tabor cemetery. Frederich d. at the home of his daughter, Sarah, in Dublin Township on Apr. 29, 1931. He was buried in Fairfield County, in Mount Tabor cemetery. He was a member of the Evangelical Lutheran Church until he moved to Mercer County, and became a member of the M. E. Church.

Magdalene$^{1.2.6.4a}$, b. in 1835. She m. Henry Hite/Heyd in Fairfield County, Ohio, on Mar. 23, 1851, and S. J. Carpenter about 1863.

David$^{1.2.6.5a}$, b. in Nov. 1836. He m. Esther Engel in Fairfield County, Ohio, on Nov. 5, 1857. They were residing in Berne Township in 1900.

Mary$^{1.2.6.6a}$, b. in 1838, and m. Eduard, son of Andreas and Magdalena (Roth) Kull. He was b. on Mar. 31, 1839, baptized at St. Jacobus Lutheran Church on May 19, 1839, and sponsored by Friedrich and Catharina Scholl. They were m. in Fairfield County, Ohio, on Dec. 18, 1862. Eduard was a farmer in Greenfield Township in 1880. He d. in 1919, and she d. in 1898. They are buried in Mt. Tabor cemetery.

Samuel$^{1.2.6.7a}$, b. in 1840. He m. Katie (Catherine) Brown.

Lear (Leah)$^{1.2.6.8a}$, b. in 1843, and m. George Louck in Fairfield County on Feb. 27, 1862, and D. Miesse.

Susanna$^{1.2.6.9a}$, b. in 1845. She m. George Stroll.

Noah$^{1.2.6.10a}$, b. in Fairfield County, Swartz Post Office, on July 16, 1847. He m. Mary Jane Roby on Sep. 1, 1869, and d. in Jay County, Portland, Indiana, on Jan. 28, 1928 (services were held at Portland Evangelical Church, and was reported in the Ohio City Progress). He is buried in the family plot in Maple Crest cemetery in Lancaster, Ohio. All of his siblings predeceased him except for three sisters, who resided in Fairfield, County.

Elenora$^{1.2.6.11a}$, b. in June 1850, and m. Amos Miller. They resided in Fairfield County, Liberty Township in 1900.

Elizabeth$^{1.2.6.12a}$, b. in 1853, and m. _____ Friesner.

Noah Friesner

Noah$^{1.2.8c}$ m. Lydia Meucle in Fairfield County on Apr. 10, 1834. She was b. in Ohio on Jan. 1, 1816, and d. on Nov. 7, 1862. In

1850, he resided in Auburn Township, and in 1860, he resided in Rush Creek Township. Noah d. on Apr. 17, 1869. They are buried in Friesner cemetery. They had the following children in Auburn Township:

Melinda[1.2.8.1c], b. in 1835, and m. Thomas J. Derr in Fairfield County on Aug. 25, 1853.

John[1.2.8.2c], b. on Sep. 30, 1838.

Diana[1.2.8.3c], b. on Mar. 19, 1847.

William A.[1.2.8.4c], b. on Aug. 16, 1849, and d. on Sep. 22, 1854. He is buried in Friesner cemetery.

Sarah Salome[1.2.8.5c], b. in 1858.

John Friesner

John[1.2.8.2c] m. Catherine and later m. Lucretia Harmon in Fairfield County on Apr. 12, 1861, and d. on Oct. 24, 1873. He is buried in Friesner cemetery. John and Catherine had the following children:

I.[1.2.8.2.1c], b. in 1866.

Emanuel[1.2.8.2.2c], b. in 1868.

Frederick[1.2.8.2.3c], b. in 1869.

Diana Friesner

Diana[1.2.8.3c] m. Abraham Huddle (b. in 1845) in Fairfield County on Apr. 26, 1866, and had the following children:

Charles M.[1.2.8.3.1c], b. in 1867, and m. Emma A. Fox.

Cora E.[1.2.8.3.2c], b. in 1870, and m. I. M. Studabaker.

Polly Friesner

Polly[1.2.10c] m. John Shoemaker in Fairfield County on Feb. 23, 1839, and d. there on Apr. 20, 1845. She is buried in Friesner cemetery. They had the following children:

Malinda[1.2.10.1c], b. in 1842, and m. Daniel Everett in Fairfield County on Oct. 7, 1858.

David[1.2.10.2c], b. in 1844, m. Sarah Ann Seitz (d. in 1874) on Oct. 4, 1866, and Maria Smith, and d. in Effingham County, Illinois, on May 17, 1910.

Jacob Friesner

Jacob[1.4c], m. Catherine, daughter of Martin Snider, in Rockingham County, Virginia, in 1802. They had the following son in Rockingham County, McGaheysville, Virginia:

Joseph[1.4.1c], b. on Oct. 1, 1803, baptized at Peaked Mountain Lutheran Church on Dec. 23, 1803, and sponsored by Jacob and Maria Ergebrecht.

Johan Michael Friesner

Johan[1.5c] was baptized at the First Reformed Church of York on Jan. 23, 1786, sponsored by his parents, and confirmed at Rader's Lutheran Church on Oct. 23, 1801. He m. Catherine, daughter of Casper and Catherine (Stihli) Hufford, in Fairfield County, Ohio, on Feb. 11, 1812. She was b. in Frederick County, Woodsboro, Maryland, on Oct. 7, 1792, and d. in Fairfield County, Pleasant Township on Jan. 4, 1853. Johan d. in Fairfield County sometime on June 1, 1850. They are buried in Friesner cemetery, and had the following children:

Sarah[1.5.1c], b. on Dec. 19, 1812 (Jan. 20, 1813), m. Isaac Hunsaker in Fairfield County, Lancaster on Oct. 22, 1835, and d. in Fairfield County on Aug. 12 (13), 1852. She is buried in Friesner cemetery.

Daniel[1.5.2c], b. in 1815.

Barbara[1.5.3c], b. on Nov. 16, 1817.

Benjamin[1.5.4c], b. on Sep. 19, 1819 (1820).

Casper[1.5.5c], b. in 1823, and m. Sarah Graves in Fairfield County, Lancaster on Mar. 29, 1846 (1847). She d. before 1850. He was unmarried and in Pleasant Township in 1860, and d. in Jan. 1862.

Michael[1.5.6c], b. on Oct. 6 (10), 1824, and d. in Fairfield County on Feb. 14 (Oct. 5), 1850.

Catherine[1.5.7c], b. on Oct. 13, 1828, and m. Levi Friesner[1.1.10f]. She was residing in Pleasant Township in 1850, and d. on Dec. 29, 1855. She is buried in Friesner cemetery.

Daniel Friesner

Daniel[1.5.2c] d. in Hocking County, Logan, Ohio, on Nov. 24, 1859. He m. Elizabeth Shields (b. in Maryland in 1815) in Fairfield County on Sep. 7, 1837, and had the following children in Hocking County, Logan Township, Ohio:

William S.[1.5.2.1c], b. on Aug. 19, 1838, m. Philia R. Crooks on June 23, 1864, and was a lawyer and teacher.

Catherine A.[1.5.2.2c], b. in 1840, and m. Charles A. Barker in Hocking County, Logan Township on Oct. 27, 1859.

Joseph Simpson[1.5.2.3c], b. in 1842, and m. Jennie.

Sarah[1.5.2.4c], b. in 1845, and m. ___ Cutler.

John Shields$^{1.5.2.5c}$, b. on May 13, 1848, and m. Harriette Gallagher in Sep. 1879. He was a lawyer and judge.

Barbara Friesner

Barbara$^{1.5.3c}$ m. Joseph Simpson in Fairfield County on Dec. 7, 1834, and d. in Fairfield County, Rush Creek Township on Oct. 20, 1895. She resided in Fairfield County, Bremen, Ohio, and is buried in Mt. Zwingli cemetery. He was b. in England on Jan. 24, 1812, and d. on Mar. 19, 1891. They had the following children:
Lica Helen$^{1.5.3.1c}$.
Mary$^{1.5.3.2c}$, b. about 1851, and m. Emmanuel Hufford.

Benjamin Friesner

Benjamin$^{1.5.4c}$ m. Lydia Stemen (b. in Fairfield County, Ohio, on May 21, 1827) in Fairfield County on Aug. 29 (20), 1844, and d. there on Mar. 11, 1864. He is buried in Friesner cemetery. They had the following children in Pleasant Township:
Benton B.$^{1.5.4.1c}$, b. on Dec. 3, 1845, and d. about 1933. He is buried in W. Rushville cemetery in Fairfield County.
Ellen$^{1.5.4.2c}$, b. on Oct. 16, 1847, and m. George Wolfinger.
Allen Jefferson$^{1.5.4.3c}$, b. on Mar. 28, 1850, m. Lynda J. Yost, and d. in Fairfield County on Jan. 2, 1938. He is buried in W. Rushville cemetery.
Franklin P.$^{1.5.4.4c}$, b. on June 2, 1852.
Mary$^{1.5.4.5c}$, b. in Sep. 1853, and m. Charles Hodgson.
Emma E.$^{1.5.4.6c}$, b. on June 1, 1855, and m. George Hilton.
Sarah A.$^{1.5.4.7c}$, b. on Feb. 4, 1859, m. Freeman Reuben Sedwell on July 23, 1881, and d. on Apr. 27, 1902.

****

Fuesser

Unknown^{1d} had the following children:
Hans Wendel$^{1.1d}$, b. in 1670.
Johann Friedrich$^{1.2d}$, b. about 1673, and m. Anna Catharina.
Christoph$^{1.3d}$, b. about 1675, and m. Anna Margaretha.

Hans Wendel Fuesser

Hans Wendel$^{1.1d}$ m. Anna Barbara about 1699, and Anna Maria Sara Bruchbach in 1708. Wendel had the following children at Hassloch, Pfalz, Bayern, Germany:

LANCASTER, LEBANON & DAUPHIN COUNTIES 41

Philipps Jacob$^{1.1.1d}$, b. in 1697.
Johann Wendel$^{1.1.2d}$, b. on Feb. 14, 1700.
Johann Nikolaus$^{1.1.3d}$, b. on July 17, 1701.
Hans Wendel$^{1.1.4d}$, b. on Oct. 11, 1703.
Johann Conradt$^{1.1.5d}$, b. on Nov. 29, 1705.
Johann Georg$^{1.1.6d}$, b. on Oct. 9, 1707.
Maria Magdalena$^{1.1.7d}$, b. on Dec. 23, 1708.
Johannes$^{1.1.8d}$, b. on Jan. 2, 1711.
Johann Conradt$^{1.1.9d}$, b. on Apr. 1, 1713, and baptized on Apr. 9, 1713.
Johann Jacob$^{1.1.10d}$, b. on Oct. 2, 1715.
Johann Jacob$^{1.1.11d}$, b. on July 17, 1717, and baptized on July 22, 1717.
Anna Magdalena$^{1.1.12d}$, b. on June 24, 1720.
Anna Maria$^{1.1.13d}$, b. on Feb. 3, 1723.
Johann Christoph$^{1.1.14d}$, b. on July 18, 1725.
Johann Wendel$^{1.1.15d}$, b. on Mar. 25, 1727.

Philipss Jacob Fuesser

Philipss Jacob$^{1.1.1d}$ m. Margaretha Philippena, and had the following children at Hassloch:
Maria Magdalena$^{1.1.1.1d}$, b. on Aug. 4, 1720.
Johann Christoph$^{1.1.1.2d}$, b. on Oct. 21, 1722.
Philipss Lorentz$^{1.1.1.3d}$, b. on Mar. 7, 1725.
Anna Margaretha$^{1.1.1.4d}$, b. on May 6, 1728.

Johann Nikolaus Fuesser

Johann Nikolaus$^{1.1.3d}$ m. Juliana Sophia, daughter of Johann Wendel and Anna Catharina Hautz, in Hassloch on Apr. 7, 1722. They immigrated to America in 1730. Nicholas received a warrant for 100 acres on Oct. 12, 1737 (a Wendle Feezer received a warrant for 100 acres on the same day (this may be Nicholas' father). Juliana was alive on July 12, 1748, when she was a sponsor at Muddy Creek. He was taxed in Cocalico Township in 1751, and 1756. Nikolaus appeared on a deed in Cocalico Township on July 27, 1765. Johan Nicholas and Juliana Sophia had the following children (at Hassloch before 1731):
Maria Catharina$^{1.1.3.1d}$, b. on Dec. 26, 1722.
Philip Jacob$^{1.1.3.2d}$, b. on Mar. 3, 1724.
Anna Catharina$^{1.1.3.3d}$, b. on Dec. 26, 1725.
Anna Maria (Susanna)$^{1.1.3.4d}$, b. about 1727 (Susanna m. Andrew Rheim/Ream).

Johann Jacob[1.1.3.5d], b. on Apr. 16, 1728.
Philip Peter[1.1.3.6d], b. on Apr. 5, 1730.
Christina[1.1.3.7d], b. about 1732, and was a sponsor to a child's baptism at Muddy Creek in 1751.
(Anna) Maria Margaretha[1.1.3.8d], b. about 1733, and m. Philip Gruenwald on Apr. 16, 1754.
Georg[1.1.3.9d], b. about 1735.
Johan Peter[1.1.3.10d], b. about 1737.

Philip Jacob Fuesser

Philip Jacob[1.1.3.2d] m. Anna Eva about 1745. He was taxed in Cocalico Township in 1751 and 1756. They had the following children in Lancaster County, East Cocalico Township, Pennsylvania:

Anna Maria[1.1.3.2.1d], baptized at Muddy Creek on Sep. 21, 1746, and sponsored by Anna Maria Fuesser.

Maria Christina[1.1.3.2.2d], baptized at Muddy Creek on July 31, 1751, and sponsored by Philip Fritz and Maria Christina Stein.

Johann Jacob Fuesser

Johann Jacob[1.1.3.5d] m. Anna Maria about 1751, and was a communicant at Christ's Church, York (now Adams) County, Germany Township, Littlestown, Pennsylvania, on Apr. 21, 1776. He was taxed in Lancaster County, Cocalico Township, Pennsylvania, in 1756. He was a yeoman in York County, Germany Township, Pennsylvania, when he purchased 200 acres of land there on July 2, 1762. His will was probated on Nov. 3, 1777, and executed by his widow, and his son, Nicholas. Jacob willed that his elder children should take care of his younger children, and as they came of age, they were to receive £100, and their share of his estate. Anna Maria was on the 1790 census of York County, and her probate inventory was taken in 1796. Jacob and Anna Maria had the following children in Lancaster County, East Cocalico Township, Pennsylvania:

Johan Nicholas[1.1.3.5.1d], b. about 1750.

Maria Barbara[1.1.3.5.2d], b. about 1752. She was given her father's large house for £100 in her father's will.

Catharina[1.1.3.5.3d], b. about 1754, and was given her father's small house in Petersburg in his will.

Christina[1.1.3.5.4d], b. about 1755. She was a communicant in 1776, and a sponsor to Adam Sell's baptism in 1778. She was given a house in her father's will.

Anna Maria$^{1.1.3.5.5d}$, b. about 1756. She was a communicant in 1776, and was a sponsor to the baptism of her niece in 1782. She may have m. Joseph, son of Georg and Maria Margaretha Lohr, about 1783, but this has not been proven. Joseph Lohr's wife, Anna Maria was b. in 1756, and d. in Frederick County, Emmitsburg, Maryland, in Aug. 1822.

Johan Adam$^{1.1.3.5.6d}$, b. on Sep. 3, 1761, baptized at Muddy Creek on Oct. 4, 1761, and sponsored by Adam Krill and wife.

Johan Jacob$^{1.1.3.5.7d}$, b. on Sep. 20, 1763, and m. Christina before Nov. 1787. He moved to Frederick (now Carroll) County, Westminster District, Maryland, before 1800. He resided there in 1810, and 1820, and d. there on Jan. 10, 1834. Christina was b. on Dec. 12, 1766, and d. on Jan. 26, 1830. They are buried in Saint Mary's Lutheran cemetery at Silver Run.

Juliana$^{1.1.3.5.8d}$, b. about 1765, and was a sponsor to the baptism of Elisabeth Sell in 1787.

Johannes$^{1.1.3.5.9d}$, b. about 1767.

Johan Nicholas Fuesser

Johan Nicholas$^{1.1.3.5.1d}$ m. Elisabeth about 1775. They were communicants in 1776. He was on the 1800 census of Adam's County, Germany Township. He received his father's plantation for £100 in his father's will. His will was written in Adams County, Germany Township, Pennsylvania, on Nov. 4, 1815, and probated on Dec. 1, 1815. They had the following children baptized at Christ's Church of Littlestown:

Magdalene$^{1.1.3.5.1.1d}$, b. on Aug. 2, 1777, and sponsored by Ludwig and Margaret Engelman. She m. Peter Shilt.

Anna Maria$^{1.1.3.5.1.2d}$, b. on Feb. 4, 1780, baptized on Feb. 12, 1780, and sponsored by Anna Maria Fuesser, widow.

Elisabeth$^{1.1.3.5.1.3d}$, b. on Feb. 25, 1782, baptized on Dec. 25, 1782, and sponsored by Anna Maria Fuesser, single.

Catharina$^{1.1.3.5.1.4d}$, b. on Mar. 19, 1785, baptized on Apr. 5, 1785, and sponsored by Johan Adam and Elisabeth Fuesser.

Johan Jacob$^{1.1.3.5.1.5d}$, b. on Nov. 10, 1787, and sponsored by Johan Jacob and Christina Fuesser.

Barbara$^{1.1.3.5.1.6d}$, b. on Dec. 12, 1790, and sponsored by Abraham and Barbara Kuntz.

Rachel$^{1.1.3.5.1.7d}$, b. on Aug. 5, 1795, baptized on Oct. 11, 1795, and sponsored by John and Magdalene Fuesser.

Maria Barbara Fuesser

Maria Barbara[1.1.3.5.2d], m. Adam Sell before 1776, and had the following children baptized at Christ's Church of Littlestown (they were communicants at Littlestown in 1776):

Hannah[1.1.3.5.2.1d], b. on Jan. 4, 1777, baptized on Jan. 9 (19), 1777, and sponsored by Abraham and Hannah Sell.

Adam[1.1.3.5.2.2d], b. on Nov. 9, 1778, baptized on Nov. 25, 1778, and sponsored by the child's father, and Christina Fuesser.

Maria Elisabeth[1.1.3.5.2.3d], b. on Sep. 27, 1780, baptized on Oct. 15, 1780, and sponsored by Anna Maria Fuesser, widow.

Abraham[1.1.3.5.2.4d], b. on June 15, 1782, baptized on July 28, 1782, and sponsored by Abraham and Hannah Sell.

Anna Maria[1.1.3.5.2.5d], b. on Apr. 16, 1785, baptized on May 16, 1785, and sponsored by Anna Maria Fuesser, widow.

Elisabeth[1.1.3.5.2.6d], b. on Apr. 15, 1787, and sponsored by Juliana Fuesser, single.

John[1.1.3.5.2.7d], b. on May 12, 1790, baptized on June 20, 1790, and sponsored by his parents.

Jacob[1.1.3.5.2.8d], b. on May 17, 1792, and sponsored by his parents.

Catharina[1.1.3.5.2.9d], b. on Jan. 3, 1795, baptized on Feb. 8, 1795, and sponsored by Catharina Fuesser.

Catharina Fuesser

Catharina[1.1.3.5.3d] was a communicant in 1776, and was a sponsor to Catharina Sell in 1795. She had the following son with Jacob Bayer (they do not appear to have been m.):

Jacob[1.1.3.5.3.1d], b. on Apr. 1, 1787, baptized at Littlestown, and sponsored by Nicholas and Elisabeth Fuesser.

Johan Adam Fuesser

Johan Adam[1.1.3.5.6d] m. Elisabeth before Apr. 1785, and moved to Frederick (now Carroll) County, Silver Run, Maryland, before 1792. He resided there in 1820, and d. there on Jan. 6, 1834. Elisabeth was b. on Mar. 30, 1765, and d. on Feb. 18, 1837. They had the following children:

Maria Catharina[1.1.3.5.6.1d], b. on Feb. 24, 1788, baptized at Christ's Church of Littlestown on Feb. 30, 1788, and sponsored by Anna Maria Fuesser.

Adam[1.1.3.5.6.2d], b. about 1790.

Elisabeth[1.1.3.5.6.3d], baptized at St. Mary's Lutheran Church at Silver Run on Apr. 8, 1792.
Anna Maria[1.1.3.5.6.4d], baptized at St. Mary's on May 10, 1795.
Salome[1.1.3.5.6.5d], baptized at St. Mary's on Apr. 9, 1797.
Rachel[1.1.3.5.6.6d], baptized at St. Mary's on July 8, 1798.

Adam Fuesser

Adam[1.1.3.5.6.2d] m. Susanna (Oct. 2, 1795-Oct. 30, 1843, buried St. Mary's), and had the following children in Carroll County, Silver Run (baptized at St. Mary's Lutheran Church):
Adam[1.1.3.5.6.2.1d], baptized at St. Mary's on Dec. 11, 1813 (?to Adam and Elizabeth).
Jacob[1.1.3.5.6.2.2d], baptized on Feb. 13, 1814.
Elisabeth[1.1.3.5.6.2.3d], baptized on Jan. 15, 1815.
Johann Georg[1.1.3.5.6.2.4d], baptized on May 11, 1817.
Daniel[1.1.3.5.6.2.5d], baptized on May 7, 1820.
Johannes[1.1.3.5.6.2.6d], baptized on Dec. 14, 1823.
Michael[1.1.3.5.6.2.7d], baptized on Sep. 18, 1825.

Johannes Fuesser

Johannes[1.1.3.5.9d] m. Magdalene, and moved to Frederick County, 5th District, Maryland, about 1799/1800. He appeared on the 1820 census there, and d. between 1820, and 1830. Magdalene resided in 7th District in 1830. They had the following children baptized at Christ's Church of Littlestown:
Georg[1.1.3.5.9.1d], b. on Oct. 17, 1793, baptized on Dec. 24, 1793, and sponsored by Georg and Veronica Koenig. He m. Mary, and d. in Frederick County, Thurmont, Maryland, on June 28, 1841. She d. on Jan. 24, 1887, aged 93 years. They are buried in Apples cemetery.
John[1.1.3.5.9.2d], b. on May 12, 1795, baptized on July 12, 1795, and sponsored by Nicholas and Elisabeth Fuesser.
Jacob[1.1.3.5.9.3d], b. on Nov. 17, 1796, baptized on Jan. 29, 1797, and sponsored by his parents. He m. Sarah and Lydia, and d. in Frederick County, Emmitsburg, Maryland, on Nov. 11, 1851. Sarah d. at Emmitsburg on Apr. 20, 1839, aged 39 years and 3 months. Lydia d. on Oct. 29, 1894, aged 74 years, 7 months, and 14 days. They are buried in Emmitsburg Lutheran cemetery.
Daughter[1.1.3.5.9.4d], b. about 1809.
Daughter[1.1.3.5.9.5d], b. about 1811.
Daughter[1.1.3.5.9.6d], b. about 1813.

Georg Fuesser

Georg[1.1.3.9d] m. Anna Barbara, daughter of Daniel and Mary Shuy, about 1759. He took the Oath of Allegiance in Lancaster County on May 29, 1777. He was taxed in Cocalico Township in 1769, and 1770. They had the following children in Lancaster County, East Cocalico Township, Pennsylvania:

Son[1.1.3.9.1d], baptized at Muddy Creek on July 13, 1760, and sponsored by Peter Fuesser and wife.

Johan Peter Fuesser

Johan Peter[1.1.3.10d] m. Anna Catharina Ditzler about 1760. He had land in Adamsburg on Aug. 24, 1761, and took the Oath of Allegiance on Nov. 3, 1778. He was taxed in Cocalico Township in 1756, 1758, 1769, 1770, 1771. His will was written in Cocalico Township on Jan. 13, 1791, and probated on Dec. 16, 1791. They had the following children in Lancaster County, East Cocalico Township, Pennsylvania:

Daughter[1.1.3.10.1d], baptized at Muddy Creek on Mar. 1, 1761, and sponsored by Georg and Catarina Ache (the daughter that m. Rudolph Bear?).

Elizabeth[1.1.3.10.2d], m. Georg Rup.

Anna[1.1.3.10.3d], (the daughter that m. Jacob Leib?).

Susanna[1.1.3.10.4d], (the daughter that m. Peter Smith?).

****

Samuel Griffith

Samuel[1e] resided in Marion County, Claridon Township, Ohio, from 1832-1834. He had 5 cattle in 1832, 1 house and 4 cattle in 1833, and 5 cattle in 1834. His widow may have been Sarah, who resided in Marion County, Scott Township, Ohio, in 1840, with one male aged 15-20, one male 20-30, and one female 50-60 and Robert Griffith (resided in Marion County, Scott Township in 1840, with 1 male under 5 years old, 1 male aged 5-10, 1 male 30-40, 1 female under 5, 1 female 5-10, 1 female 20-30). In 1835, Robert was taxed in Scott Township with 40 acres in RTS 16/4/12 (?in the North East corner of the Township, that became Crawford County). Samuel was probably the father of the following children:

William[1.1e], taxed in Claridon Township in 1833 with 1 house and 3 cattle.

Nancy[1.2e], b. about 1812, and m. Bella Collins in Claridon Township on Aug. 21, 1835.

Marian[1.3e], b. about 1816, and m. Daniel Haley in Claridon Township on Jan. 8, 1837. They resided in Claridon Township in 1840. Son[1.4e], m. Nancy Neff about July 1843, and d. before Feb. 1845. After his death, his widow m. Samuel Harruff (presumably-see entry on Harruff family (speculation based on marriage record and death certificate)).

****

Johann Peter Grimm

Johann Peter[1f] m. Annae Mariae about 1740. He immigrated to America from Unkenbach, Pfalz Bayern, Germany, in the ship *Forest* on Oct. 11, 1752, with a wife and six children. Peter was a freeman in Lancaster County, Earl Township, New Holland, Pennsylvania, in 1771/72. Peter and Annae Mariae had the following children (the first 7 baptized in Evangelisch, Obermoschel, Pfalz, Bayern):

Anna Magdalena[1.1f], baptized on June 23, 1741.
Johanna Catharina[1.2f], baptized on Jan. 1, 1742.
Johann Jacob[1.3f], baptized on Jan. 3, 1743.
Susanna Margaretha[1.4f], b. in 1744, baptized on Oct. 2, 1744, and m. Johannes Friesner[1c]. A Margreta Grimin took communion at Seltenreich on May 25, 1765, and this is probably her.
Johann Heinrich[1.5f], baptized on Aug. 28, 1746.
Johann Peter[1.6f], b. on Dec. 2, 1748, and baptized on Dec. 13, 1748.
Maria Elisabetha[1.7f], baptized on Apr. 12, 1751.
Johannes[1.8f], b. about 1753.
Eva[1.9f'], b. in 1755, and confirmed at Cocalico Reformed Church on Apr. 28, 1771.

Anna Magdalena Grimm

Anna Magdalena[1.1f] m. Johan Heinrich, son of Heinrich and Christina Margaretha (Fink) Walther, in the First Reformed Church of Lancaster on Feb. 17, 1760. He was baptized at the First Reformed Church of Lancaster on Oct. 28, 1739, and sponsored by Johan Henry Klein. They moved to York, Pennsylvania, and had the following children:

Maria Elisabetha[1.1.1f], b. on July 1, 1760, and baptized at Christ's Lutheran Church of York, York County, Pennsylvania, on July 12, 1761.

Susanna$^{1.1.2f}$, b. on Feb. 17, 1763, baptized at Trinity Lutheran on Apr. 25, 1763, and sponsored by her parents.

Anna Margaretta$^{1.1.3f}$, b. on July 15, 1767, and baptized at Trinity Lutheran on Oct. 18, 1767.

John Heinrich$^{1.1.4f}$, b. on July 8, 1769, baptized at Trinity Lutheran on July 23, 1769.

Magdalena$^{1.1.5f}$, b. on Nov. 16, 1772, baptized at Trinity Lutheran Church of York, York County, Pennsylvania, on Nov. 22, 1772, and sponsored by Catharina Baecker.

Johann Jacob Grimm

Johann Jacob$^{1.3f}$ m. Christine, and had the following daughter in Earl Township:

Anna Maria$^{1.7.1f}$, b. on June 2, 1776, baptized at Seltenreich on July 28, 1776, and sponsored by Leonard and Anna Maria Stein.

Johann Heinrich Grimm

Johann Heinrich$^{1.5f}$ m. Anna Christina, daughter of Johan Leonhard and Catharina Mueller, at Lancaster County, Seltenreich Lutheran Church on Nov. 16, 1773, and Maria Sophia, daughter of Johann Leonhardt (1712-1785) and Anna Maria (Lang) Stein, on May 3, 1778. Anna Christina was b. on Sep. 10, 1753, and d. in Earl Township on Dec. 22, 1776. Maria Sophia was b. in 1752. Johan Heinrich was a freeman in Earl Township in 1771, and a mason in 1770. In 1769, he was a freeman at George Schyker's in Earl Township. Johan Heinrich had the following children in Earl Township:

Johan Leonhard$^{1.5.1f}$, b. on Nov. 21, 1774, baptized at Seltenreich on Dec. 18, 1774, and sponsored by his grandparents, Johan Leonhard and Maria Sophia Mueller.

Maria Christina$^{1.5.2f}$, b. on Dec. 22, 1776, baptized at Seltenreich on Dec. 30, 1776, and sponsored by Leonard and Sophia Mueller.

Anna Maria$^{1.5.3f}$, b. on Jan. 29, 1779, baptized at Seltenreich on May 2, 1779, and sponsored by Leonard and Anna Maria Stein.

Henry$^{1.5.4f}$, b. on Nov. 13, 1784, baptized at Seltenreich in 1785, and sponsored by Peter and Sophia Grimm.

Peter$^{1.5.5f}$, b. on Aug. 21, 1785, baptized at Seltenreich on Dec. 15, 1785, and sponsored by David and Margaret Diefendoerfer.

John$^{1.5.6f}$, b. on Apr. 6, 1788, and baptized at Seltenreich on May 1, 1788.

LANCASTER, LEBANON & DAUPHIN COUNTIES 49

Elizabeth[1.5.7f], b. on Dec. 6, 1789, and baptized at Seltenreich on Jan. 1, 1790.

Catherine[1.5.6f], b. on July 16, 1792, baptized at Seltenreich on Aug. 5, 1792, and sponsored by her parents.

Maria Margaret[1.5.7f], b. on Oct. 5, 1794, baptized at Seltenreich on Nov. 9, and sponsored by her parents.

Johann Peter Grimm

Johann Peter[1.6f] m. Anna Maria Sophia, daughter of Johan Leonhard and Catharina Mueller, at Lancaster County, Seltenreich Lutheran Church on Jan. 5, 1773. He resided in Rockingham County, Timberville, (Captain Ezekiel Harrison's Company, East District) Virginia, in 1792, with five people in his household (Peter Crim). Peter d. in Rockingham County on Sep. 6, 1825 (aged 76 years, 8 (3)months, and 14 days), and is buried in Rader's Lutheran Church cemetery. Sophia d. there on Jan. 14, 1836, aged 84 (81) years, 9 months, and 27 days. Peter and Sophia had the following children in Earl Township:

Adam[1.6.1f], b. about 1773, and m. Elizabeth, daughter of John Croy/Gray, in Rockingham County in 1792. He has not been proven as a son.

Johan Peter[1.6.2f], b. on June 29, 1777, baptized at Seltenreich on Aug. 10, 1777, and sponsored by Michael and Eleonore Schnoeder.

Sophia[1.6.3f], b. on July 15, 1779, baptized at Seltenreich on Aug. 22, 1779, and sponsored by Henry and Sophia Grimm. She m. John Leonard in Rockingham County on Jan. 29, 1798.

Catharina[1.6.4f], b. on July 15, 1779, baptized at Seltenreich on Aug. 22, 1779, and sponsored by Henry and Sophia Grimm. She m. Jacob Groff in Rockingham County on Mar. 25, 1799. He was b. in 1774. Catharina and Jacob were confirmed at Rader's on Oct. 25, 1801.

John[1.6.5f], b. on Nov. 10, 1780, baptized at Seltenreich on Dec. 4, sponsored by Michael Schneder and wife, and confirmed at Rader's Lutheran Church on Oct. 25, 1801.

Peter[1.6.6f], b. on Oct. 3, 1784, baptized at Seltenreich on May 1, 1788, and confirmed at Rader's on Oct. 25, 1801.

Salome[1.6.7f], b. on Jan. 25, 1787, baptized at Seltenreich on May 1, 1788, and confirmed at Rader's on Oct. 25, 1801.

Maria Magdalena[1.6.8f], b. on Dec. 9, 1789, baptized at Rader's on Apr. 19, 1790, and m. Abraham Heed in Rockingham County on Aug. 27, 1808.

Michael$^{1.6.9f}$, b. on June (July) 15, 1793, baptized at Rader's on Oct. 22, 1794, and sponsored by his parents. He d. on Jan. 16, 1827, and is buried in Rader's Lutheran Church cemetery.

Peter Grimm

Peter$^{1.6.6f}$ m. Elizabeth Shaver in Rockingham County in 1805, and d. on Aug. 19, 1836. She d. on Nov. 30, 1850 at 65 years, 11 months and 10 days. They are buried in Rader's Lutheran Church cemetery, and had the following children baptized at Rader's Lutheran Church:

Jacob$^{1.6.6.1f}$, b. on Feb. 13, 1806, baptized on May 25, 1806, and sponsored by his parents.

Anna Maria$^{1.6.6.2f}$, b. on Mar. 30, 1808, baptized on July 24, 1808, and sponsored by Maria Grim.

Solomon$^{1.6.6.3f}$, b. on Nov. 28, 1812, baptized on Apr. 16, 1813, and sponsored by his parents.

Catharina$^{1.6.6.4f}$, b. on Mar. 9, 1816, baptized on June 7, 1816, and sponsored by her parents.

Johannes Grimm

Johannes$^{1.8f}$ resided in Rockingham County, Timberville, (Captain Ezekiel Harrison's Company, East District) Virginia, in 1792, as Jno. Crim. He had two people in his household. He assessed the estate of Johannes Friesner, as John Krim. He m. Juliana. They were sponsors for the baptism of George, son of George and Elizabeth Gehr at Cocalico Lutheran Church in Lancaster County, Pennsylvania, on Aug. 20, 1783. John and Juliana had the following children:

Jacob$^{1.8.1f}$, b. about 1776 (it has not been established if he was a son of Peter or John).

John$^{1.8.2f}$, b. about 1778.

Elizabeth$^{1.8.3f}$, b. about 1781, and m. Daniel Hoof/Hooft in Rockingham County on Nov. 28, 1802.

Salome$^{1.8.4f}$, b. on Jan. 12, 1790, and buried at Rader's on Jan. 4, 1793.

Magdalena$^{1.8.5f}$, b. on June 11, 1795, baptized at Davidsburg Lutheran Church in Shenandoah County, New Market, Virginia, on Sep. 21, 1795, and sponsored by Frederick and Sabina Schoster.

Salome$^{1.8.6f}$, b. on May 12, 1797, baptized at Davidsburg Lutheran on Sep. 28, 1797, and sponsored by Heinrich and Margaretha Spitzer.

Jacob Grimm

Jacob$^{1.8.1f}$ m. Margaretha, and had the following children baptized at Rader's Lutheran Church:

Isaac$^{1.8.1.1f}$, b. on May 3, (about 1806), and sponsored by Samual Hat and wife.

Solome$^{1.8.1.2f}$, b. on Nov. 24, 1808, and sponsored by Samuel and Elizabeth Hat.

John Lee$^{1.8.1.3f}$, b. on Jan. 26, 1810, baptized on Apr. 14, 1811, and sponsored by his parents.

John Grimm

John$^{1.8.2f}$ had the following children baptized at Rader's Lutheran Church:

John George$^{1.8.2.1f}$, b. on July 20, 1810, baptized on Apr. 14, 1811, and sponsored by his parents.

Soloma$^{1.8.2.2f}$, b. about 1812.

William Booten$^{1.8.2.3f}$, b. on May 29, 1831, baptized on Sep. 10, 1836, and sponsored by his parents.

Eva Grimm

Eva$^{1.9f}$ m. Johan Frederick Schuetz in Lancaster County, Seltenreich Lutheran Church on May 7, 1775. He m. Catharina about 1769. Frederick baptized the following children at the White Oaks Congregation in Lancaster County:

Sophia Catharina, b. on May 15, 1770, baptized on July 25, 1770, and sponsored by Sophia Catharina Miller.

Johann Friedrich, b. on Nov. 23, 1771, baptized on Jan. 12, 1772, and sponsored by Friederich and Catharina Koehler.

Elisabeth, b. on Feb. 10, 1774, baptized on Apr. 3, 1774, and sponsored by Elisabeth Kiber.

Susanna$^{1.9.1f}$, b. on Feb. 7, 1779, baptized on Apr. 18, 1779, and sponsored by her parents.

Catharina$^{1.9.2f}$, b. on May 14, 1780, baptized on Aug. 14, 1780, and sponsored by her parents.

Eva$^{1.9.3f}$, b. on Apr. 25, 1783, baptized on July 13, 1783, and sponsored by her parents.

Anna Maria$^{1.9.4f}$, b. on Aug. 31, 1784, baptized on June 10, 1785, and sponsored by her parents.

****

52   EARLY FAMILIES OF PENNSYLVANIA

Andreas Horauff

Andreas[1g] arrived at Philadelphia on the ship *Phoenix* in 1752, and settled in Bucks County, Bedminster Township, Pennsylvania, where they sponsored Elisabeth, daughter of Philip Jacob and Christine Wolf at Keller's Lutheran Church on Aug. 13, 1758. Later they moved to the area of Lancaster County, Pennsylvania, which later became Dauphin County, Derry Township, Hummelstown. He d. at Hummelstown in Feb. 1777, and his will was probated in Lancaster County on Feb. 26, 1777 (written on Dec. 16, 1776). His widow, Maria Elisabetha, m. Frederick Evers after 1780. She d. at Hummelstown in June 1805. Her will was written on Nov. 12, 1801, and probated on June 10, 1805. Andreas and Maria Elisabetha had the following children:

Jacob[1.1g], b. on Dec. 12, 1753.
Ludwic[1.2g], b. on Dec. 12, 1753.
Andreas[1.3g], b. about 1756.
Peter[1.4g], b. about 1759.
Nicholas[1.5g], b. about 1762.
Johan Henrich[1.6g], b. on Sep. 1, 1765, baptized at Swatara on Sep. 15, 1765, and sponsored by Johannes and Regina Oehrle.
Antony[1.7g], b. on Feb. 2, 1768, baptized by Reverend Conrad Bucher at Frederickstown/Hummelstown on Apr. 4, 1768, and sponsored by Johan Antony and Margaretha Emrick. He d. sometime before 1805.

Jacob Harruff

Jacob[1.1g] m. Elizabeth about 1783, and Katherine Kline (1771-1845) about 1790. Jacob enlisted in the Revolutionary War in Middletown, Lancaster County, Pennsylvania, in the Spring of 1776/77. He served 4 to 6 months as a Private in Captain Cowden's and Captain Church's Company. In 1777/78, he enlisted in Captain Riegor's and Brook's Company for 12 months, where he was engaged in driving teams at Valley Forge. He later served 3 months as a Private in Captain McCullaugh's Company. After the War, he resided in Cumberland County, Carlisle, Pennsylvania, and 10 years after the war, he resided in Mahoning County, Boardman Township, Ohio. In 1806, he moved to Canfield, Ohio. He then moved to Franklin County, Pennsylvania, for 7 years, and then moved to Trumbull County, Austintown Township, Ohio, in 1816. He was allowed pension on Aug. 24, 1832. He d. in Trumbull County, Canfield, Ohio, on Mar. 22, 1838. Jacob had the following children:

John$^{1.1.1g}$, b. in 1786 in Dauphin County, West Hanover Township, Pennsylvania.

Anna Eva$^{1.1.2g}$, b. on Apr. 19, 1786 in West Hanover Township, baptized on June 25, 1786, and sponsored by Valentine and Anna Eva Hummel.

Catherine Elisabeth$^{1.1.3g}$, b. Dec. 12, 1788, baptized on Jan. 18, 1789 in Cumberland County, Carlisle, Pennsylvania (First Evangelical Lutheran Church), and sponsored by George and Catharina Klein. She d. in Portage County, Ohio.

Susan$^{1.1.4g}$, b. at Carlisle on July 2, 1791, and d. on June 25, 1862.

Jacob$^{1.1.5g}$, b. at Carlisle in 1793.

William$^{1.1.6g}$, b. at Carlisle on Sep. 22, 1799.

Andrew$^{1.1.7g}$, b. in 1802.

Lewis$^{1.1.8g}$, b. at Carlisle in 1805, and d. in Mahoning County, Ohio, in 1875.

Leah$^{1.1.9g}$, b. at Carlisle about 1807.

Rachel$^{1.1.19g}$, b. at Carlisle about 1809.

Mary$^{1.1.11g}$, b. at Carlisle about 1811.

John Harruff

John$^{1.1.1g}$ m. Susanna (1786-1850), moved to Portage County, Rootstown Township, Ohio, in 1805, and d. there in 1850. They had the following children:

John$^{1.1.1.1g}$, b. about 1812, and m. Sarah Decoursey in Medina County, Ohio, on Dec. 24, 1833. He has not been confirmed as a son.

William H.$^{1.1.1.2g}$, b. about 1815, and m. Mary M. Flick in Cuyahoga County, Ohio, on Apr. 15, 1841. He has not been proven as a son.

Valentine$^{1.1.1.3g}$, b. about 1817, and m. Malvina Case in Trumbull County on Nov. 5, 1838. He has not been proven as a son.

Samuel$^{1.1.1.4g}$, b. about 1820.

Josiah$^{1.1.1.5g}$, b. about 1823, and m. Hannah Beeman in Trumbull County on Feb. 15, 1844. He has not been proven as a son.

Samuel Harruff

Samuel$^{1.1.1.4g}$ m. Lydia (b.1820), daughter of Lawrence and Elizabeth Hartleroad, on June 5, 1844, and had the following children:

Ora L.$^{1.1.1.4.1g}$; Ezra$^{1.1.1.4.2g}$; Everet$^{1.1.1.4.3g}$; Emma$^{1.1.1.4.4g}$; John E.$^{1.1.1.4.5g}$; Celia E.$^{1.1.1.4.6g}$, m. Edward Atchison.

Susan Harruff

Susan$^{1.1.4g}$ m. John, son of Ludwig Ripple, in Pennsylvania in 1807. He was b. on Nov. 20, 1781, and d. on July 18, 1866. They had the following children:

Amanda$^{1.1.4.1g}$, b. in 1808, m. William Mell (1802-1866) on Feb. 10, 1828, and d. in 1888.

Lydia$^{1.1.4.2g}$, m. John Ludwick and ___ Patton.

Elizabeth$^{1.1.4.3g}$, m. John Foos and Daniel Craver.

Leah$^{1.1.4.4g}$, m. Samuel Shaffer, Daniel Lawrence, and Daniel Craver.

Samuel$^{1.1.4.5g}$, m. Eve Gilbert and Mary Ann Rorak.

George$^{1.1.4.6g}$, m. Susan Overlander.

John$^{1.1.4.7g}$, m. Caroline Fowler.

William$^{1.1.4.8g}$, m. Emily Almyra Shaffer.

Jacob Harruff

Jacob$^{1.1.5g}$ d. in Portage County, Ohio, on Apr. 5, 1863, and is buried in the Brunstetter cemetery in Austintown. He m. ___ Eastman. Jacob had the following children:

Jacob$^{1.1.5.1g}$.

Andrew$^{1.1.5.2g}$, m. Sally Morse on July 15, 1832.

Catherine$^{1.1.5.3g}$, m. Levi Little on Jan. 29, 1853.

Amanda$^{1.1.5.4g}$, m. Andrew Foos on July 2, 1848.

William$^{1.1.5.5g}$, m. Catherine Kistler on Aug. 13, 1846.

Mary$^{1.1.5.6g}$, m. Conrad Lodowick on May 8, 1836.

Leah$^{1.1.5.7g}$, m. Daniel Roof in Trumbull County on May 4, 1844.

Samuel$^{1.1.5.8g}$.

Jacob Harruff

Jacob$^{1.1.5.1g}$ m. Catherine in 1826, and Hannah Bauman (1820-1889) in 1846. He d. in Portage County, Ohio, on July 28, 1871, and had the following children:

John$^{1.1.5.1.1g}$.

Andrew$^{1.1.5.1.2g}$, b. about 1828, and m. Catherine Boley in Trumbull County on June 22, 1849.

Susan$^{1.1.5.1.3g}$.

Julius$^{1.1.5.1.4g}$.

William$^{1.1.5.1.5g}$.

Viola$^{1.1.5.1.6g}$.

Henrietta$^{1.1.5.1.7g}$.

Amelia[1.1.5.1.8g].
Rebecca[1.1.5.1.9g], m. John Casey.
Ann Maria[1.1.5.1.10g], m. Solomon Carns.
Belinda[1.1.5.1.11g], m. Edward Garvey.
Homer[1.1.5.12g], b. in 1853, m. Amy Sisco (b.1873) on Oct. 15, 1894, and resided in New Waterford, Ohio.
Howard[1.1.5.1.13g], b. in 1855, and d. in 1937.
Katherine[1.1.5.1.14g], b. in 1857, and m. Frank Ludwick.

William Harruff

William[1.1.6g] d. in Trumbull County, Ohio, on Jan. 9, 1861. He m. Magdalena in Trumbull County, Ohio, in 1825. She was b. on Dec. 23, 1795, and d. in Austintown Township on Mar. 17, 1873. They are buried in Smith Corners cemetery. They had the following children:
William[1.1.6.1g], m. Hannah Hadasser on Sep. 12, 1848.
Polly[1.1.6.2g], m. Jacob Bauman in Trumbull County, Ohio, on Nov. 21, 1844.

Andrew Harruff

Andrew[1.1.7g] m. Eve Hull (1794-May 5, 1866) in Trumbull County, Ohio, on Oct. 10, 1833, and d. in Austintown Township on Aug. 6, 1865. He was a M. E. minister. They are buried in Brunstetter cemetery and had the following children:
Cornelius[1.1.7.1g], b. in 1834, and m. Belinda Leonard (1834-1912) on Apr. 24, 1851. He was a carpenter, auctioneer, and managed the American Hotel. He d. in Canfield, Ohio, in Austintown Township in 1908.
Polly[1.1.7.2g], m. Jacob Bauman, and resided in Austintown.
Rachel[1.1.7.3g], m. Benjamin Clapsaddle, and resided in Bellefontaine, Ohio.
Leah[1.1.7.4g], m. David Bennett, and resided in Bellefontaine, Ohio.
Andrew[1.1.7.5g], b. in 1837, and m. Orpha Flick (1838-1899) in Mahoning County, Ohio, on May 9, 1856. He worked in a flour mill, and was the local jailer. He d. in Canfield in 1902.

Lewis Harruff

Lewis[1.1.8g] m. Mary Albert (1806-Oct. 1880) in Trumbull County, Ohio, on May 11, 1827, and had the following children:
William[1.1.8.1g], b. in 1829, and m. Polly Brunstetter (b.1830) on Nov. 4, 1851.

Catherine$^{1.1.8.2g}$, b. in 1831, and d. young.
Sarah$^{1.1.8.3g}$, b. in 1835, and d. young.
Lewis$^{1.1.8.4g}$, b. in 1833, and d. in Boardman Township in 1915. He m. Rebecca Brunstetter (1836-1909) on Nov. 11, 1859. He was a cabinet maker, wagon maker, and carpenter.
Mary Ann$^{1.1.8.5g}$, b. in 1840, m. John Franklin (1840-1939), and d. in 1880.

Ludwic Harruff

Ludwic$^{1.2g}$ served in the Revolutionary War, d. in Lancaster County, Pennsylvania, on Oct. 10, 1843. He m. Margaretha, and had the following children in Dauphin County, Pennsylvania:

Maria Magdalena$^{1.2.1g}$, baptized on May 11, 1783 at 10 weeks old, and sponsored by Peter and Maria Magdalena Radebach.

Andrew$^{1.2.2g}$, b. on July 21, 1786, baptized on Sep. 17, 1786, and sponsored by his mother.

Jacob$^{1.2.3g}$, b. on Nov. 8, 1788, baptized on Jan. 21, 1799, and sponsored by his mother.

Peter$^{1.2.4g}$, b. about 1790, and m. Barbara Cassel (widow) in Dauphin County, Lower Paxton Township, Ohio, on Dec. 10, 1812.

Barbara$^{1.2.5g}$, b. about 1792, and m. Henrich Seider in Dauphin County, Lower Paxton Township, Pennsylvania.

Rebecca$^{1.2.6g}$, b. on Apr. 9, 1802, and baptized on May 23, 1802.

Andreas Harruff

Andreas$^{1.3g}$ m. Catharina (Elisabeth), and moved to Augusta County, Jennings Gap, Virginia, between 1789 and 1796. They had the following children:

Elisabeth$^{1.3.1g}$, b. on Jan. 2, 1786, baptized on Jan. 22, 1786, and sponsored by Justina Fierin.

Salome$^{1.3.2g}$, b. on Mar. 20, 1788.

Ludwick$^{1.3.3g}$, b. about 1797, and m. Margaret Huffman in Augusta County, Virginia, on Feb. 6, 1818.

Jacob$^{1.3.4g}$, b. about 1805, and m. Peggy Keller in Augusta County, Virginia, on Mar. 12, 1829.

Rebecca$^{1.3.5g}$, b. about 1807, and m. Samuel Keller in Augusta County, Virginia, on July 31, 1828.

Peter Harruff

Peter$^{1.4g}$ m. Margaret about 1783. He was an inmate in Dauphin County, East Hanover Township, Pennsylvania, in 1786, and 1787. In 1790, he resided in Hummelstown in Derry Township. He moved to Augusta County, Jennings Gap, Virginia, between 1794 and 1798. In 1799, he was a Deacon in the Jennings Gap Congregation. They moved to Fairfield County, Bloom Township, Ohio, between 1800, and 1805, and Franklin County, Montgomery Township, Ohio, between 1806 and 1807 (purchased land on Mar. 27, 1807). In 1801, Peter Heroff was listed as insolvent and delinquent in Augusta County, because he had moved to the West Country. Peter owned the first tavern in Franklin County, Montgomery Township. It was in his home, which consisted of four connected log cabins. It was located on the Old Columbus Road, where Ohio University now stands. In 1818, he sold part of the 4000 acres in Franklin County that he has owned for over 20 years to Philip Zinn. Peter d. in Montgomery Township in Dec. 1818, and Margaret d. sometime after Aug. 3, 1819. In the Franklin Chronicle on Aug. 6, 1821, a child of the widow Harruff from the north side of Columbus was reported murdered by a thief on the preceding Tuesday night. Peter and Margaret had the following children:

David$^{1.4.1g}$, b. about 1784.

Catherine$^{1.4.2g}$, b. in East Hanover Township on Sep. 9, 1786, baptized at Swatara Reformed Lutheran Church at Lebanon County, Jonestown on Mar. 10, 1787, and sponsored by Christian Herschberger and wife.

William$^{1.4.3g}$, b. in 1788.

John$^{1.4.4g}$, b. in 1791.

Jacob$^{1.4.5g}$, b. about 1794. He may be the child that was killed by a thief in Aug. 1821.

Mary$^{1.4.6g}$, b. about 1798, and m. Moor Justice in Franklin County, Ohio, on July 29, 1819.

Susan$^{1.4.7g}$, b. about 1800, and m. Francis Gross in Franklin County, Ohio, on Nov. 9, 1820.

Margaret$^{1.4.8g}$, b. on Aug. 3, 1805. On Aug. 3, 1819, Thomas Moore and James Culbertson were appointed as her guardians.

David Harruff

David$^{1.4.1g}$ m. Julia Ann. They moved to Vermillion County, Vermillion Township, Indiana, between 1819 and 1824. David d. in Vermillion Township in 1832. After David's death, Julia m. John Leagle

58   EARLY FAMILIES OF PENNSYLVANIA

in Vermillion County on Nov. 25, 1833. Julia d. in 1834. They had the following children:

Mary$^{1.4.1.1g}$, b. about 1808, and m. John Alexander in Vermillion County on Jan. 1, 1828.

Peter$^{1.4.1.2g}$, b. about 1810, and m. Margaret Hinton in Vermillion County on June 26, 1835.

John$^{1.4.1.3g}$, b. about 1812, and m. Jane Roberts in Vermillion County on Aug. 2, 1836.

Phebe$^{1.4.1.4g}$, b. about 1814, and m. William W. Wellburn in Vermillion County on Jan. 16, 1834.

Margaret Ann$^{1.4.1.5g}$, b. about 1824, and m. William Roberts in Parke County, Indiana, on Aug. 12, 1844.

William$^{1.4.1.6g}$, b. on Apr. 14, 1827, and m. Sarah Jane Oldridge in Vermillion County on Sep. 7, 1852. She was b. on Feb. 8, 1834, and d. in Copan, Oklahoma on Nov. 23, 1924. William d. in Vermillion County, Newport, Indiana, on May 27, 1854.

Catherine Harruff

Catherine$^{1.4.2g}$ m. John Wimsett in Franklin County, Ohio, on Aug. 29, 1808. He was b. in Maryland in 1788, and d. in Vermillion County, Vermillion Township, Indiana, in 1849. She d. in Vermillion Township in 1861. They had the following children (the first five in Ohio):

Joseph$^{1.4.2.1g}$, b. in 1809, and m. Cynthia Powers in Vermillion County, Indiana, on Sep. 28, 1833. He d. in Edgar County, Illinois, in 1882.

Margaret$^{1.4.2.2g}$, b. in 1811.

John$^{1.4.2.3g}$, b. in 1813, and m. Hermina Stokes in Vermillion County, Indiana, on Oct. 16, 1834.

James$^{1.4.2.4g}$, b. in 1815, and m. Hester A. Southard in Vermillion County, Indiana, on Aug. 29, 1838.

David$^{1.4.2.5g}$, b. in 1819, and m. Mary S. Stokes in Vermillion County, Indiana, on Aug. 20, 1839. He d. in Edgar County, Scotland, Illinois, in 1907.

Andrew$^{1.4.2.6g}$, b. in 1823, m. Nancy, and d. in Kansas City, Missouri, in 1901.

Jacob$^{1.4.2.7g}$, b. in 1826, and m. Rachel Ann Wiley in Vermillion County, Indiana, in 1848. He d. in Vermillion County in 1913. Rachel was b. in 1832, and d. in 1878.

William Harruff

William[1.4.3g] m. Elizabeth, widow of Isaac Hess, in Franklin County, Montgomery Township, Ohio, on May 7, 1813. She was b. in Pennsylvania in Feb. 1789, and d. in the home of her son, Samuel, on Nov. 12, 1878. William was a Private Dragoon in the War of 1812 from 1812-13. They moved to Marion County, Ohio, in 1820, and William d. in Richland Township on July 10, 1843. The Whetstone River ran through his land. In 1834, he had 80 acres and 3 cattle. In 1835, he had 80 acres. They are buried in Smith cemetery. William and Elizabeth had the following children:

Christina[1.4.3.1g], b. about 1814 in Franklin County, Clinton Township, Ohio, and m. Levi Watson in Marion County, Ohio, on Feb. 5, 1837.

John[1.4.3.2g], b. on Apr. 24, 1817.

Henry[1.4.3.3g], b. on Feb. 24, 1820.

Samuel[1.4.3.4g], b. on Jan. 3, 1824.

Rebecca Ann[1.4.3.5g], b. on Aug. 15, 1825.

Hannah E.[1.4.3.6g], b. about 1830, and m. John Stose in Marion County, Ohio, on Dec. 25, 1855.

William[1.4.3.7g], b. on Sep. 17, 1834, and d. on June 21, 1850. He is buried in Smith cemetery.

John Harruff

John[1.4.3.2g] m. Rebecca Emory in Marion County, Ohio, on Sep. 1, 1838. She was b. in 1821, and d. in Marion County, Richland Township, Ohio, in 1887. John d. there on May 5, 1898. In 1870, they were residing in Allen County, Ohio. They had the following children in Marion County, Richland Township, Ohio:

William[1.4.3.2.1g], b. in 1839, m. Elizabeth Richardson (b. in Ohio in 1838) in Allen County, Ohio, on Sep. 5, 1866, Sarah E. King in Mercer County, Ohio, on Sep. 2, 1877, and Amanda J. Counts in Allen County on Feb. 18, 1881. William d. in Allen County, Ohio, in 1904, and is buried in Spencerville cemetery.

Jane Ann[1.4.3.2.2g], b. in 1842, and m. Harrison Hanley in Allen County, Ohio, on June 8, 1862.

James Wesley[1.4.3.2.3g], b. on Oct. 3, 1844, m. Sarah Strine in Marion County, Ohio, on Jan. 22, 1867, and d. in Marion County, Ohio, on Sep. 8, 1919. She was b. in Ohio in 1843. They resided in Morrow County, Westfield Township, Ohio, in 1880.

Catherine[1.4.3.2.4g], b. in 1847.

Martin[1.4.3.2.5g], b. on July 15, 1849, and d. on Sep. 11, 1853. He is buried in Smith cemetery.

John[1.4.3.2.6g], b. in 1849, and m. Manerva E. Rupp in Marion County on Nov. 16, 1876.

Samuel[1.4.3.2.7g], b. in 1852.

Mary A.[1.4.3.2.8g], b. in 1859.

Susan F.[1.4.3.2.9g], b. in 1863, and m. John H. Brennemon in Allen County on Apr. 11, 1882.

George[1.4.3.2.10g], b. in 1865.

Henry Harruff

Henry[1.4.3.3g] m. Nettie Alma Williams in Marion County, Ohio, on Sep. 1, 1838, and Christina Bennet on Dec. 29, 1842. Christina was b. in Harrison City, Virginia (now West Virginia), in 1826. Henry d. in Marion County, Richland Township, Ohio, on Aug. 16, 1898. During the Civil War, Henry served from Sep. 13, 1864 to July 10, 1865 in Company K, 174 O.V.I.. He is buried in Salem Evangelical Lutheran cemetery. Henry had the following children:

Mary C.[1.4.3.3.1g], b. in 1846, and m. William Berridge in Marion County on Sep. 12, 1865.

Hannah E.[1.4.3.3.2g], b. in 1847.

Levi[1.4.3.3.3g], b. in 1849, and m. Margaret Hile (b.1851) in Morrow County, Ohio, on Dec. 24, 1872.

Anthony B.[1.4.3.3.4g], b. in Nov. 1855, m. Esther Fiant in Marion County on Jan. 6, 1872, and d. in Marion County in 1922. She was b. in Ohio in Oct. 1858, and d. in 1933. They are buried in Salem cemetery.

Samuel Harruff

Samuel[1.4.3.4g] m. Nancy Neff, widow of ___ Griffith, in Marion County, Richland Township, Ohio, on Feb. 20, 1845. Nancy was b. in Ohio on Nov. 4, 1824 (she may have been a daughter of Abraham Neff). On her daughter, Nancyan's, death certificate her maiden name was said to be Neff (informant, Audie Dull (her son)). Samuel was a farmer in Richland Township until his death on Oct. 26, 1861. He is buried in Smith cemetery. In 1882, Nancy moved to Mercer County, Dublin Township, Ohio, and settled in section ten, where she d. on Nov. 1, 1884. She is buried in Mount Olive cemetery. Nancy and Samuel had the following children (except the first, who was by Nancy's first marriage):

LANCASTER, LEBANON & DAUPHIN COUNTIES 61

James P.$^{1.4.3.4.1g}$, b. on Apr. 30, 1844. He is listed in the family Bible, but is not listed with the family in 1850 and 1860. On his death certificate, James's parents are listed as Samuel and Nancy Harruff. In 1860, he was farming the land of Alice Geyer in Richland Township. James m. Julia Ann Bader in Marion County, Ohio, on Nov. 1, 1863. She was b. in 1845, and d. in Madison Township on July 30, 1919. They moved to Jay County, Madison Township, Indiana, between 1867 and 1873. James d. at Salamonia on Nov. 5, 1913

Solomon$^{1.4.3.4.2g}$, b. on Apr. 28, 1846, and d. on Sep. 8, 1858. He is buried in Smith cemetery.

Julian$^{1.4.3.4.3g}$, b. on Oct. 18, 1847, and m. Frederick Yahn in Marion County, Ohio, on Nov. 23, 1865. He was b. on Feb. 22, 1838, and d. in Mercer County, Dublin Township, Ohio, on May 25, 1912. Julian d. there on June 6, 1894. They are buried in Mount Olive cemetery.

Charles$^{1.4.3.4.4g}$, b. on Feb. 4, 1850, and m. Paulina Fields in Marion County, Ohio, on Jan. 18, 1872. She was b. in Ohio in 1851, and d. in 1894. Charles d. in Marion County, Claridon Township, Ohio, in 1924. They are buried in Thew cemetery.

Harvey H.$^{1.4.3.4.5g}$, b. on Apr. 2, 1852, and m. Susanna Elizabeth, daughter of Daniel Paul and Mary (Strait) Teeter, in Adams County, Indiana, June 24, 1875. She was b. in Darke County, Ohio, in 1853, and d. in Adams County, Decatur, Indiana, on Mar. 23, 1929. Harvey came to Adams County, Indiana, in 1873, and worked as a carpenter, wagonmaker, and later a contractor and builder in Berne. He was a post master in Adams County, Berne, Indiana, for four years, and was elected the Adams County, Recorder in 1894. He took the position in 1895, and served one term. He then engaged in the real estate and insurance business in Berne till 1911, when he moved to Fremont, Michigan on a temporary basis, so he could attend to the fruit farm he had bought there. He was a member of the I.O.O.F.. He d. in Newaygo County, Fremont, Michigan in 1912.

John$^{1.4.3.4.6g}$, b. on June 22, 1854, and m. Ianthe Martha Jane, daughter of Emanuel and Eliza (Roebuck) Putman, in Mercer County, Ohio, on Aug. 4, 1878. She was b. in Mercer County, Dublin Township, Ohio, in Dec. 1859. John was a carpenter. They moved to Allen County, Lima, Ohio, between 1884, and 1895. They resided there in Aug. 1910.

Albert$^{1.4.3.4.7g}$, b. on Nov. 15, 1856, and m. Susan Mae, daughter of John and Mariah Higgins, in Marion County, Ohio, on Oct. 3, 1878. She was b. in Marion County, Ohio, on Apr. 22, 1859, and d. in

Van Wert County, Ohio, on May 10, 1928. Albert d. in Mercer County, Dublin Township, Ohio, on Jan. 13, 1933.

Louisa$^{1.4.3.4.8g}$, b. on July 31, 1859, m. J. F. Underwood, and d. in Marion County, Claridon Township, Ohio, on Nov. 3, 1881.

Nancyan$^{1.4.3.4.9g}$, b. on Dec. 24, 1861, and m. Clayborn Hancock, son of John and Susan (Roebuck) Dull, in Mercer County on Feb. 2, 1886. Clayborn farmed 40 acres on the Louis Godfrey Reserve, adjacent to his father's land. Clayborn was a farmer, carpenter, and drainage contractor, until he had a stroke, and was afflicted with partial paralysis in 1914. This ailment forced his retirement, and the family moved to Rockford in 1919. Clayborn was an active member of the I.O.O.F and Local Order of Red Men. Annie worked as a housekeeper after her husband's death on Dec. 18, 1927. She resided in Rockford, living with her grandson Leo, and his wife, Dorothy, until her death on Oct. 11, 1936. Clayborn was b. in Mercer County, Dublin Township, Ohio, on Nov. 23, 1862. They are buried in Riverside cemetery.

Rebecca Ann Harruff

Rebecca Ann$^{1.4.3.5g}$ m. Levi J. Cramer in Marion County, Ohio, on Feb. 18, 1847. Rebecca d. in Marshall County, Center Township, Indiana, on Oct. 6, 1900. They had the following children (the first three in Marion County, Ohio, and the rest in Marshall County, Indiana):

Catherine$^{1.4.3.5.1g}$, b. in 1848.

William Harruff$^{1.4.3.5.2g}$, b. in 1850.

Luther James$^{1.4.3.5.3g}$, b. in 1853.

Emaretta$^{1.4.3.5.4g}$, b. in 1855, and m. George Harvey Joyce.

Cyrus C.$^{1.4.3.5.5g}$, b. in 1860.

Samuel$^{1.4.3.5.6g}$, b. in 1861, and d. in Marshall County, Center Township in 1931.

Martin A.$^{1.4.3.5.7g}$, b. in 1863, and m. Nellie Holloway in Marshall County on Oct. 14, 1890.

John R.$^{1.4.3.5.8g}$, b. in 1867, and m. Hattie Hess in Marshall County on Sep. 30, 1893, and Amanda Ross in Marshall County on June 5, 1898.

John Harruff

John$^{1.4.4g}$ served in the War of 1812 from Franklin County, resided in Vermillion County, Vermillion Township, Indiana, from

1825-1829, and later moved to Allen County, Ohio. He m. Barbara (b. 1794), and had the following children:

Caroline$^{1.4.4.1g}$, b. about 1817, and m. Peter Roerbaugh in Allen County on Aug. 12, 1839.

Lydia$^{1.4.4.2g}$, b. about 1819, and m. Michael Keifer in Allen County on Sep. 17, 1840.

Charlotta$^{1.4.4.3g}$, b. about 1821, and m. John Walsch in Allen County on Oct. 3, 1842.

Leah$^{1.4.4.4g}$, b. in 1823, m. Joseph Linder in Allen County on July 5, 1842, and d. in 1898.

Lewis$^{1.4.4.5g}$, b. about 1825, and m. Polly Osewalt in Allen County on Dec. 9, 1847.

Sarah$^{1.4.4.6g}$, b. about 1826, and m. Samuel Waggoner in Allen County, on May 25, 1847.

Margaret Harruff

Margaret$^{1.4.8g}$ m. James Condren in Franklin County, Ohio, on Nov. 9, 1820. He was b. in Pennsylvania in 1800. They resided in Auglaize County, Moulton Township, Ohio, in 1860. They had the following son:

John$^{1.4.8.1g}$, b. in Franklin County, Columbus, Ohio, in 1826.

Nicholas Harruff

Nicholas$^{1.5g}$ had the following daughter in Dauphin County, Pennsylvania:

Elisabeth$^{1.5.1g}$, baptized on Aug. 8, 1784, and sponsored by Dary and wife.

Johan Henrich Harruff

Johan$^{1.6g}$ resided in Fairfield County, Bloom Township, Ohio, in 1806, Union County, Mill Creek Township, Ohio, in 1820 (he was also there in 1824), Butler County, Madison Township, Ohio, in 1830, and d. in Shelby County, Washington Township, Ohio, on Jan. 5, 1848. He m. Mary S. She was b. on Sep. 5, 1763, and d. in Miami County, Monroe Township, Ohio, on Nov. 5, 1838. Johan had the following children:

David$^{1.6.1g}$, b. on Jan. 9, 1799, and d. in Auglaize County, Pusheta Township, Ohio, on Sep. 19, 1878. He m. Rosina Julius in Miami County, Ohio, in 1838, and Sarah Ann Mowery in Miami County, on Mar. 17, 1840.

William$^{1.6.2g}$, b. about 1806, and resided in Butler County, Madison Township, Ohio, in 1830.

Peter$^{1.6.3g}$, b. in 1809, and resided in Shelby County, Washington Township, Ohio, in 1850.

George$^{1.6.4g}$, b. about 1813, and m. Elizabeth Gray in Preble County, Ohio, on Mar. 23, 1834.

Elizabeth$^{1.6.5g}$, b. about 1815, and m. Isaac Newton in Preble County, Ohio, on Dec. 31, 1837.

Barbary$^{1.6.6g}$, b. about 1817, and m. John Allen in Butler County, Ohio, on May 25, 1837.

Lewis$^{1.6.7g}$, b. on Feb. 13, 1822, and d. in Auglaize County, Pusheta Township, Ohio, on Mar. 20, 1863. He m. Mary McClintock, who d. in Auglaize County in 1855, and is buried in Harruff cemetery, and Sarah H. Bixler in Auglaize County on Sep. 2, 1855.

Sarah Ann$^{1.6.8g}$, b. about 1822, and m. Joseph Baughman in Miami County on May 28, 1843.

Adam$^{1.6.9g}$, b. about 1824, and m. Lucy Baker in Clark County, Ohio, on Feb. 18, 1847.

Peter Harruff

Peter$^{1.6.3g}$ m. Elizabeth (b. in Pennsylvania in 1811), and had the following children:

Isaac$^{1.6.3.1g}$, b. about 1833, d. on Mar. 20, 1839, and is buried in Loy cemetery.

John H.$^{1.6.3.1g}$, b. in 1835, and m. Sallie C. Mizener in Shelby County, Ohio, on Mar. 14, 1865.

Mary$^{1.6.3.2g}$, b. in 1837.

Susan$^{1.6.3.3g}$, b. in 1840.

David$^{1.6.3.4g}$, b. in 1842.

William S.$^{1.6.3.5g}$, b. in 1844.

Elizabeth$^{1.6.3.6g}$, b. in 1846.

Jacob A.$^{1.6.3.7g}$, b. in 1849, and m. Catharine Hammaker in Shelby County on Apr. 7, 1864.

****

Johan Haushalter

Johan^{1h} was b. in Baden, Germany. He left Germany, but d. en route to America. His family arrived on the ship *Friendship* on Sep. 3, 1739. He had the following children (possibly his widow was the

Elizabeth Hausholder that m. Jonathan Weir in Berks County on Dec. 29, 1741):
    Johan Adam$^{1.1h}$, b. in 1719.
    Margaretha$^{1.2h}$, b. about 1719, and m. Johannes Weidman in Cocalico on July 6, 1741.
    Elizabetha$^{1.3h}$, b. about 1721, and m. Joseph Obold in Cocalico on Mar. 29, 1742.
    Anna Barbara$^{1.4h}$, b. about 1723, and m. Johan Georg Wittman in Warwick on Jan. 1, 1744.
    Johann Georg$^{1.5h}$, b. in 1725.
    Heinrich$^{1.6h}$, b. about 1727, and was in Warwick in 1754.

Johan Adam Haushalter

Johan Adam$^{1.1h}$ m. Maria Elisabetha Weidman in Warwick on Oct. 17, 1743, and d. in Washington County, Hagerstown, Maryland. His will was written on July 22, 1791, and probated on Jan. 2, 1798. He was naturalized in Berks County in 1761. He arrived on the ship *Friendship* on Sep. 3, 1739. Maria Elisabetha d. before 1791. Adam and Maria Elisabetha had the following children:
    Johan Adam$^{1.1.1h}$, b. in Lancaster County on Nov. 1, 1744.
    Adam$^{1.1.2h}$, b. on Oct. 10, 1746, and d. before 1791.
    Maria Barbara$^{1.1.3h}$, b. on Mar. 16, 1749.
    Andreas$^{1.1.4h}$, b. about 1751.
    Matthias$^{1.1.5h}$, b. about 1753.
    Elisabetha$^{1.1.6h}$, b. in Lancaster County, Gummery on Jan. 19, 1754.
    Eva$^{1.1.7h}$, b. about 1756, and d. before 1791.
    Christian$^{1.1.8h}$, b. in Berks County about 1759, and d. before 1791.
    Maria Margaretha$^{1.1.9h}$, b. in Berks County on Dec. 15, 1761.
    Catharina$^{1.1.10h}$, b. in Berks County on July 19, 1764.
    Anna Maria$^{1.1.11h}$, b. in Berks County on Dec. 27, 1765.

Johan Adam Haushalter

Johan$^{1.1.1h}$ m. Maria Margaretha, and had the following children baptized at the Reformed Congregation in Washington County, Hagerstown, Maryland:
    Georg$^{1.1.1.1h}$, baptized on Sep. 15, 1771.
    Georg Peter$^{1.1.1.2h}$, baptized on June 13, 1773.

Matthias Haushalter

Matthias[1.1.5h] m. Eva had the following son (they resided in Berkeley County, Virginia, in 1782):

Johannes[1.1.5.1h], baptized at Hain's Church in Berks County, Heidelberg Township on Mar. 31, 1776, and sponsored by Frantz and Catharina Crick.

Catharina[1.1.5.2h], baptized in Washington County, Maryland, at the Reformed Congregation of Hagerstown on Apr. 9, 1780.

Johan Georg Haushalter

Johan Georg[1.5h] m. Margaretha Balmer in Warwick on Nov. 18, 1746, and d. in Washington County, Maryland, in 1794. He served in the Revolutionary War, and had the following children in Lancaster County:

Heinrich[1.5.1h], b. about 1747, and m. Mary Jonas in Baltimore County, Baltimore, Maryland, on Feb. 16, 1769. This has not been confirmed.

Georg Adam[1.5.2h], b. on Oct. 22, 1749.

Jacob[1.5.3h], b. about 1751. This has not been confirmed.

Simon[1.5.4h], b. about 1752 (1745). This has not been confirmed. He may be the Georg Simon Haushalter that immigrated to Philadelphia in 1765.

Georg Michael[1.5.5h], b. on Feb. 20, 1753.

Catharina Margaretha[1.5.6h], b. on July 13, 1755.

Johannes[1.5.7h], b. on July 13, 1756.

Elisabetha[1.5.8h], b. about 1758.

Christine[1.5.9h], b. about 1759, and m. Georg Schwingel in Washington County, Maryland, on Apr. 23, 1778. This has not been proven.

Jacob Haushalter

Jacob[1.5.3h] m. Catharina (?a Jacob m. Eliza White in Baltimore on Nov. 8, 1770), and had the following children baptized at the Reformed Lutheran Congregation at Washington County, Hagerstown, Maryland:

Catharina Margaretha[1.5.3.1h], baptized on Dec. 25, 1771.

Simon Haushalter

Simon[1.5.4h] m. Elisabetha, and d. about 1781. He served in the Revolutionary War, and had the following children baptized in the Reformed Congregation in Washington County, Hagerstown, Maryland:

Elizabeth[1.5.4.1h], baptized on Nov. 18.26, 1774.
Susanna[1.5.4.2h], baptized on Nov. 15, 1776.
Catharina[1.5.4.3h], baptized on Feb. 7, 1779.
Georg[1.5.4.4h], baptized on Feb. 10, 1782.

Georg Michael Haushalter

Georg Michael[1.5.5h] m. Susanna Hager in Washington County, Maryland, in 1778, and d. about 1822. He served in the Revolutionary War, and had the following children baptized in Washington County, Maryland:

Daniel[1.5.5.1h], baptized in Washington County, Williamsport on Feb. 8, 1795.

Heinrich Haushalter

Heinrich[1.6h] is presumed to be the father of the following children, but it has not been confirmed:
Heinrich[1.6.1h], b. about 1754.
Jacob[1.6.2h], b. about 1757.

Heinrich Haushalter

Heinrich[1.6.1h] m. Anna Maria. He d. in York County, Hopewell Township, Pennsylvania. His will was written on Mar. 9, 1809, and probated on Mar. 18, 1809. They had the following children in York County:

Nancy[1.6.1.1h], b. on Feb. 9, 1776, baptized at Blymir's (St. John's) Union Church on Apr. 28, 1776, and sponsored by her parents.

Anna Maria[1.6.1.2h], b. on June 15, 1778, baptized at Blymir's on Oct. 25, 1778, and sponsored by her parents.

Johannes[1.6.1.3h], b. on Dec. 22, 1780, baptized at Blymir's on May 20, 1781, and sponsored by Casper and Barbara Klemmer.

Abraham[1.6.1.4h], b. on Sep. 15, 1782, baptized at Blymir's, and sponsored by Casper and Barbara Klemmer.

Henrich[1.6.1.5h], b. about 1784.
Jacob[1.6.1.6h], b. about 1786.
Elisabeth[1.6.1.7h], b. on Apr. 6, 1788, baptized at Blymir's on Nov. 8, 1788, and sponsored by Christian and Elizabeth Bleymeyer.

Jacob Haushalter

Jacob[1.6.2h] m. Elisabeth, and had the following children in York County:

Elisabeth$^{1.6.2.1h}$, b. on Oct. 23, 1778, baptized at Blymir's on June 6, 1779, and sponsored by her parents.
Temperance$^{1.6.2.2h}$, b. on Nov. 3, 1780, baptized at Blymir's on May 20, 1781, and sponsored by her parents.
Heinrich$^{1.6.2.3h}$, b. on June 5, 1788, baptized at Blymir's on June 5, 1789, and sponsored by Conrad and Dorothy Miller.

****

Hess

____ Hess^{1i}, possibly from Bucks County, Pennsylvania, and had the following children:
Abraham$^{1.1i}$, b. in 1765, and d. in Delaware County, Berkshire Township, Ohio, on Apr. 23, 1839. He is buried in Sunbury cemetery.
George$^{1.2i}$, b. on Mar. 28, 1771. He spoke imperfect English, was said to be from Bucks County, Pennsylvania. He served in the War of 1812. He d. in Delaware County, Porter Township, Ohio, on Apr. 28, 1838. He had no children, and left parts of his estate to Isaac's daughters. He came to Delaware County, Kingston, Ohio, in 1807 with John Phillips. George m. Mary. She was b. in 1778, and d. on Apr. 19, 1856. They are buried in Stark cemetery.
Isaac$^{1.3i}$.

Isaac Hess

Isaac$^{1.3i}$ m. Elizabeth ____. Isaac d. in Franklin County, Ohio, sometime between 1810 and 1813. Isaac's will/estate, probated in 1816, names his brothers George and Abraham. On May 2, 1816, William Harruff and Francis Smith were appointed guardians of Isaac's daughters, Catherine and Polly. After Isaac's death, Elizabeth m. William Harruff. Isaac and Elizabeth had the following children:
Mary$^{1.3.1i}$, b. in Virginia (?) on July 14, 1807.
Catherine$^{1.3.2i}$, b. in Virginia (?) in 1808.

Mary Hess

Mary$^{1.3.1i}$ m. Ansel, son of Nathaniel and Althea (Field) Mattoon, in Franklin County, Ohio, on July 14, 1823. Ansel was b. in Vermont on May 24, 1794. Mary d. in Franklin County, Worthington, Ohio, on June 23, 1844. After Mary's death, Ansel m. Almira Mattoon on Apr. 17, 1845. Ansel and Mary had the following children:
Isaac$^{1.3.1.1i}$, b. in (Maryland?) in 1819.
Harriet$^{1.3.1.2i}$, b. in Ohio in 1824.

Rosalie$^{1.3.1.3i}$, b. in Ohio in 1842.
Mary$^{1.3.1.4i}$, b. in Ohio in 1844.

Catherine Hess

Catherine$^{1.3.2i}$ m. James H. Martin in Marion County, Ohio, on May 30, 1826. They had the following children in Marion County, Richland Township, Ohio:
May$^{1.3.2.1i}$, b. in 1827.
Jane$^{1.3.2.2i}$, b. in 1830.
Susan$^{1.3.2.3i}$, b. in 1832.
Isaac$^{1.3.2.4i}$, b. in 1833.
Elizabeth$^{1.3.2.5i}$, b. in 1835.
George$^{1.3.2.6i}$, b. in 1836.
Rachel$^{1.3.2.7i}$, b. in 1838.
Wells$^{1.3.2.8i}$, b. in 1839.
Kessiah$^{1.3.2.9i}$, b. in 1847.
James$^{1.3.2.10i}$, b. in 1848.

****

Lorentz Houtz

Lorentz^{1j} was b. in Hassloch in 1652, and had the following son there:
Johann Wendel$^{1.1j}$, b. in 1669.

Johann Wendel Houtz

Johann Wendel$^{1.1j}$ m. Anna Catharina, and d. at Hassloch on Feb. 5, 1726 (1723). She d. on Mar. 16, 1716. They had the following children at Hassloch, Bayern Pflaz, Germany:
Juliana Sophia$^{1.1.1j}$, b. about 1697, and m. Johann Nikolaus Fuesser.
Anna Catharina$^{1.1.2j}$, b. in 1699, and m. Johan Wilhelm Leichthaminer on Feb. 2, 1725.
Johann Jacob$^{1.1.3j}$, b. on Jan. 22, 1702, and d. in 1702.
Johann Jacob$^{1.1.4j}$, b. on Feb. 9, 1703.
Catharina Margaretha$^{1.1.5j}$, b. on Apr. 9, 1704, and m. Moses Voelkle on Feb. 20, 1726.
Johann Ulrich$^{1.1.6j}$, b. on Sep. 1, 1706.
Johann Philip$^{1.1.7j}$, b. on Oct. 28, 1708, and baptized on Nov. 26, 1708.

Johann Henrich Christopher[1.1.8j], b. on Feb. 15, 1711.
Philip Lorentz[1.1.9j], b. on Sep. 10, 1715.

Johann Philip Houtz

Johann Philip[1.1.7j] m. Anna Margaretha, daughter of Sebastian and Agnes (Flockirth) Royer, in 1733, and d. in Lebanon County, Bethel Township, Pennsylvania, in 1766. She was b. in Hassloch on June 1, 1713, and d. in Bethel Township in Dec. 1798. They had the following children in Pennsylvania:

Magdalena[1.1.7.1j], b. about 1736, and m. Johan Jacob Werns on Mar. 22, 1757.

Johann Wendel[1.1.7.2j], b. on May 30, 1739, m. Anna Catharina Elisabeth Riegel (Reiger) on May 20, 1760, and d. in Shenandoah County, Edinburgh, Virginia, in 1797.

Philip Lorentz[1.1.7.3j], b. in 1740, m. Anna Maria Mueller on Mar. 7, 1764, and Anna Catharina Daub. He d. in Cumberland County, Pennsylvania, on Dec. 6, 1796.

Elisabeth[1.1.7.4j], b. in 1742, and m. Johannes Weber on Mar. 22, 1759.

Heinrich[1.1.7.5j], b. on Oct. 10, 1745, m. Maria Barbara Dups on Sep. 12, 1769, and d. in Lebanon County, Hamlin, Pennsylvania, on Sep. 30, 1796.

Georg[1.1.7.6j], b. in 1748, m. Maria Elisabeth Conrad, and d. in Feb. 1782 (July 6, 1782/83).

Juliana[1.1.7.7j], b. about 1750, m. Jacob Laubsher on May 2, 1770, and d. in 1784 (?1842).

Johan Christopher[1.1.7.8j], b. on Jan. 29, 1753, m. Susannah Ellis, and d. in Greene County, Tennessee about 1842/43.

Anna Maria[1.1.7.9j], b. in 1759, m. Christopher Kueble, and d. in 1802.

Philip Lorentz Houtz

Philip Lorentz[1.1.9j] m. Eva Anna, daughter of Christian and Catharina Elisabeth (Batdorf) Walb.. She was b. in Schoharie, New York in 1720. He immigrated to America on the ship *Friendship* on Sep. 20, 1738, and d. in Berks (?Lebanon) County, Bethel Township, Pennsylvania, on Oct. 22, 1788. They had the following children:

Johann Christian[1.1.9.1j], b. on Aug. 16, 1741, m. Barbara Emmerr, and d. on Jan. 1, 1826.

Maria Elisabetha[1.1.9.2j], b. on Jan. 25, 1744, m. Samuel Royer, and d. on Sep. 17, 1817.

Anna Catharina$^{1.1.9.3j}$, b. on Aug. 6, 1745, and m. John Gunckel.

Maria Barbara$^{1.1.9.4j}$, b. in 1749, and m. Martinus Batdorf on Dec. 31, 1769.

Jacob$^{1.1.9.5j}$, b. about 1753, m. Anna Maria Gunckel in 1782, and d. in Perry County, Somerset, Ohio, in 1836.

Baltzer$^{1.1.9.6j}$, b. on July 28 (3), 1757, m. Elisabeth Minnich, and d. on Feb. 4, 1836.

Johann Wendel$^{1.1.9.7j}$, b. on May 30, 1760, m. Catarina Eitzlerin Ditzler on Apr. 18, 1785, and d. on Nov. 3, 1845.

Johan$^{1.1.9.8j}$, b. on Dec. 26, 1762, m. Catharina Elisabeth Winter and Catharina (Dubbs) Snavely, and d. on Mar. 10, 1829.

Anna Maria$^{1.1.9.9j}$, b. in 1763, and d. on May 15, 1795.

****

Unknown Kern

Unknown^{1k} had the following children (presumed to be brothers):

Johan Nicholas$^{1.1k}$, b. about 1720.

Georg Michael$^{1.2k}$, b. about 1729.

Johan Nicholas Kern

Johan Nicholas$^{1.1k}$ m. Maria Apollonia. They arrived at Philadelphia on the ship *Edinburgh* on Sep. 16, 1751. Nicholas d. in York County, York Township, Pennsylvania, before 1779, and Maria Apollonia d. after 1779. Nicholas and Maria Appolonia had the following children:

Jacob$^{1.1k}$, b. in Germany about 1740.

Nicholas$^{1.2k}$, b. in Germany about 1742.

Adam$^{1.3k}$, b. in Germany about 1744.

Henry$^{1.4k}$, b. in Germany about 1746.

Maria Magdalena$^{1.5k}$, b. on Oct. 11, 1751, and baptized at Christ's Lutheran Church on Oct. 20, 1751. She may have been the daughter that m. ____ Nevill, and resided in York County, Pennsylvania.

Carl$^{1.6k}$, b. in York County, York Township, Pennsylvania, on Mar. 23, 1753, and baptized at Christ's Lutheran Church of York on Apr. 1, 1753.

John$^{1.7k}$, b. in York Township on Sep. 15, 1754, and baptized at Christ's Lutheran Church of York on Sep. 21, 1754.

72   EARLY FAMILIES OF PENNSYLVANIA

John$^{1.8k}$, b. in York Township on Aug. 14, 1756, and baptized at Christ's Lutheran Church of York on Sep. 2, 1756.

Anna Maria$^{1.9k}$, b. in York Township on Aug. 14, 1756, baptized at Christ's Lutheran Church of York on Sep. 2, 1756, m. John Wright, and resided in Frederick County, Virginia.

Jacob Kern

Jacob$^{1.1k}$ m. Catherine Funk in York County, York, Pennsylvania, on Nov. 28, 1762. He d. in York Township on May 20, 1799. They baptized the following children in Christ's Lutheran Church of York:

John$^{1.1.1k}$, b. on June 11, 1767, and baptized on July 12, 1767.

Jacob$^{1.1.2k}$, b. on Apr. 7, 1770, and baptized on May 20, 1770.

Joseph$^{1.1.3k}$, b. on Aug. 30, 1772, m. Margaret Stinebach in 1799, and d. in Greensburgh, Pennsylvania, in 1846. He was baptized on Oct. 18, 1772.

George$^{1.1.4k}$, b. on Oct. 11, 1775, and baptized on Nov. 26, 1775. He may have d. before 1799.

Michael$^{1.1.5k}$, b. on Dec. 17, 1778, and baptized on Feb. 7, 1779. He may have d. before 1799.

John Kern

John$^{1.1.1k}$ m. Catherine, and had the following children baptized at Christ's Lutheran Church of York:

Jacob$^{1.1.1.1k}$, b. on Apr. 8, 1795, and baptized on May 6, 1795.

Elizabeth$^{1.1.1.1.2k}$, b. before 1799.

Jacob Kern

Jacob$^{1.1.2k}$ had the following daughter:

Catherine$^{1.1.2.1k}$, b. before 1799.

Nicholas Kern

Nicholas$^{1.2k}$ m. 1st Catherine, daughter of Stephen and Elisabeth (Brumbach) Hotsinpiller, in Frederick County, Virginia, about 1764. He them m. 2nd an unknown woman about 1782 (probably the unknown Carn that m. Jean Lewis in Rockingham County in 1782). He m. 3rd Mary Elisabeth Dailey, widow of Christian Painter, in Rockingham County, Virginia, on June 10, 1805. Catherine was b. in Frederick County, Virginia, about 1742, and d. in Rockingham County, Virginia, before Apr. 1776. Nicholas purchased 335 acres in Augusta County, Virginia, from Michael and Barbara Hover on Aug. 3, 1772.

This land was patented to Rudolph Mack on Aug. 30, 1763, and was located on the North Fork of the Shenandoah, on the head of Fort Run, and the corner of Frederick Woolfort. This land transaction was rendered void, because Hover was not naturalized at the time of purchase. Johan/Adam Painter/Bender d. on Sep. 1, 1773/Nov. 16, 1773, and Nicholas was named an administrator to the estate, and made the guardian of Adam and Catharine's daughters, Barbara, and Margaret. Nicholas was the teste for Mathias Rodes will in Augusta County on May 14, 1774. Nicholas was a Lt. in the Revolutionary War in the 7th Class, 7th Virginia Regiment of the Continental Line from Rockingham County on May 25, 1778. Nicholas resided in Rockingham County, Virginia, in 1787, and 1804. On Feb. 10, 1813, Nicholas deeded land to Abraham and Alexander, sons of Christian Painter. Nicholas had the following children:

Nicholas$^{1.2.1k}$, b. on Feb. 26, 1765, and m. Nancy Lanah Vanorsdal in Rockingham County, Virginia, on May 7, 1795. He d. in Hocking County, McArthur, Ohio, on Mar. 13, 1844. He resided in Greenbriar County, Virginia, in 1801, and was listed as a surviving heir of Catherine Kern. He was taxed as Nicholas Carins in Greenbriar County, Hanna District in 1800.

Elizabeth$^{1.2.3k}$, b. about 1767 (68). She was a surviving heir of Catherine in 1801.

Catherine$^{1.2.4k}$, b. about 1769, and m. Henry, son of John and Catherine (Miller) Baer, in Rockingham County, Virginia, in 1788 (bondsman, Nicholas Kern). She was not listed as a surviving heir of Catherine Kern in 1801, so she either d. before that date, or is a daughter or widow of Henry Kern.

Frederick$^{1.2.5k}$, b. about 1770, and resided in Gallia County, Green Township, Ohio, in 1799. He was a surviving heir of Catherine residing in Greenbriar County in 1801. He is probably the Frederick Carins taxed in Greenbriar County, Hanna District in 1800.

Magdalena$^{1.2.6k}$, b. on Apr. 5, 1771.

Jacob$^{1.2.7k}$, b. about 1772, and m. Mary Lew in Greenbriar County, Virginia, on June 19, 1799 (placed with Nicholas). He was a surviving heir of Catherine in 1801.

John$^{1.2.8k}$, b. about 1774, and m. Eliza Pope in Greenbriar County, Virginia, on July 9, 1805 (placed with Nicholas). He was a surviving heir of Catherine in 1801. He is the John Carins taxed in Greenbriar County, Hanna District in 1800 there were also two Henry Carins (one may be a reprint) in Greenbriar County, Hanna District in 1800.

Mary$^{1.2.9k}$, b. about 1776, and m. Jacob, son of John and Catherine (Miller) Baer, in Rockingham County on Mar. 19, 1798 (bondsman Mathias Moyer) (placed with Nicholas). She was a surviving heir of Catherine residing in Greenbriar County in 1801.

Susan$^{1.2.10k}$, b. about 1783, and m. Mathias Miller in Rockingham County in 1804 (bondsman Abraham Painter, and consent of Nicholas Kern). She was not listed as one of Catherine's heirs in 1801.

Magdalena Kern

Magdalena$^{1.2.6k}$ m. Abraham, son of Christian and Mary Elisabeth (Dailey) Painter, in Rockingham County, Virginia, on Feb. 24, 1799 (bondsman Louis Swern and the father of the bride), and d. in Middletown, Indiana, on Jan. 27, 1856 (placed with Nicholas). She was a surviving heir of Catherine in Greenbriar County in 1801. Abraham was b. in Rockingham County, Virginia, on Dec. 9, 1774, and d. in Middletown, Indiana (?Highland County, Ohio), on Dec. 9, 1840. They had the following children:

Mary$^{1.2.6.1k}$, b. about 1800, and d. of consumption at a young age.

Elizabeth$^{1.2.6.2k}$, b. about 1802, and d. of consumption at a young age.

Rachel$^{1.2.6.3k}$, b. about 1804, and m. Christian Blazer.

John$^{1.2.6.4k}$, b. on Nov. 17, 1806, baptized at Rader's Lutheran Church on Apr. 26, 1807, sponsored by John Kern, and d. of consumption at a young age.

Henry Kern

Henry$^{1.3k}$ d. in Rockingham County, Virginia, sometime before June 25, 1787 (his will was probated in Shenandoah County, Virginia, in 1781, and he was believed to have been killed during the Revolutionary War). He resided in Frederick County, Virginia, prior to Oct. 3, 1766, when he was referred to as a resident of that place, when he purchased a half of an acre in the town of Stephensburg, and 2 additional lots consisting of 5 acres (land of Lawrence Stephens) for the rent of one pepper corn (Nov. 4, 1766/Nov. 6, 1766 release for £20). Henry and Michael Kern were litigants in a law suit in Frederick County, Virginia, in 1770. Henry was a witness to the lease between James Willson and William Gilkison, concerning 220 acres bordering Stephen Hotspiler (Opequon Creek ca. 1767). Henry was sued for debt in Shenandoah County by Isaac Hite on June 25, 1772, and on Apr. 28,

1773; Bernard Reedy on Apr. 29, 1773; Samuel Beale on June 22, 1773, and William Savage assignee for Adam Holker on May 24, 1774. A Henry Carn was taxed in Timberville District in 1788 (this may refer to the widow of Henry Carn). Henry m. Catherine, and had the following children (possibly the Heinrich and Catharina Kern that had Maria Magdalena baptized in Frederick County, Frederick Evangelical Lutheran Church, Maryland, on Oct. 1, 1770/71):

$Mary^{1.3.1k}$, b. about 1767 (possibly the Maria Magdalena baptized to Heinrich and Catharina Kern in Frederick County, Frederick Evangelical Lutheran Church, Maryland, on Oct. 1, 1770/71), and m. Adam Pup in Rockingham County in 1787 (bondsman, Nicholas Kern (Mary is an orphan of Henry Kern, and daughter of Catherine Kern)).

$Frederick^{1.3.2k}$, b. in Frederick County, Stephensburg, Virginia, on Jan. 1, 1776, m. Susannah, daughter of Christian and Margaret (Groover) Syler, on Mar. 22, 1807, and d. in Gallia County, Ohio, on Apr. 6, 1867. She was b. on Oct. 13, 1787, and d. on Nov. 6, 1874. He was the only minor orphan of Henry in 1787. On June 25, 1787, he was bound to Michael Grove in Rockingham County.

Adam Kern

$Adam^{1.4k}$ m. Maria Esther, daughter of Samuel and Catharina (Francois) Moser, in York County, York Township, Pennsylvania, on July 17, 1766, Ruth Snyder in Frederick County, Virginia, on Apr. 18, 1788, and Christina Andrews, widow of ___ Enders in Frederick County, Virginia, on Oct. 25, 1791. Maria Esther was b. in Bischwiller, Bas-Rhin, France, on Sep. 18, 1746, and d. in Frederick County, Kernstown, Virginia, in 1788. Adam moved to Frederick County Virginia, about 1765, and purchased three and a half acres on the south side of Hogg's Run, and on the west side of a smith's shop (on Opequon Creek) from Robert Wilson for three and a half shillings on Sep. 30, 1765. After this purchase, he returned to Pennsylvania to marry Maria Esther. He and his wife returned to Virginia on Oct. 1, 1766. By Nov. 1, 1773, Michael Kern (presumed brother of Adam) had moved to Dunmore (now Shenandoah) County, Virginia, and on that date sold his 33 acres and 4 poles on Hog's Run, to Adam Kern for five shillings. Also, on Nov. 1, 1773, Michael and Catherine Kern, sold Adam Kern for five shillings the 20 acre tract and 16 acre tract they received from William Cochran (also on that date three additional tracts for £130?). On Mar. 3, 1784, Adam and Esther deeded the 10,400 square feet that Adam currently resided on to Henry Eley, and on June 1,

1784, they deeded land on the east side of the great road from Winchester to Stephensburg to Henry Huver. On May 14, 1787 (June 5, 1787) Adam deeded part of the tract he purchased from Robert Wilson to Isaac Brown. Adam was a blacksmith, and was residing in Kernstown in Sep. 1798. He is presumed to have d. between 1799-1801. The town of Kernstown was established on Adam's land in 1799 through an act of the Virginia Assembly. Prior to this act, the town was called Karnsville, and was a major stopping place for travelers in the valley. They had the following children in Frederick County, Opequon Creek, Virginia:

John$^{1.4.1k}$, b. in 1767, and was an executer for a will in Frederick County on Oct. 26, 1784. Tradition states that John d. young, and his widow, and son moved to Kentucky.

Nicholas$^{1.4.2k}$, b. on May 8, 1768.

Adam$^{1.4.3k}$, b. on Oct. 25, 1773.

Samuel$^{1.4.4k}$, b. on Nov. 14, 1775, m. Susanna, daughter of Christian Grabill, on Apr. 9, 1801, and d. in Shenandoah County, Virginia, on July 6, 1857. She was b. on Dec. 6, 1782, and d. on Nov. 21, 1856.

Henry$^{1.4.5k}$, b. on Nov. 14, 1775.

Rebecca$^{1.4.6k}$, b. about 1777, and d. about 1797.

Jacob$^{1.4.7k}$, b. on July 4, 1779, m. Sarah, daughter of Darby and Anna (Semmes) Ryan, in Frederick County on Dec. 16, 1801, and d. in Shelby County, Van Buren Township, Indiana, on Jan. 19, 1843. After Sarah's death, he m. Delphia Ann Stanley.

Nicholas Kern

Nicholas$^{1.4.2k}$ m. Ann Groves in Frederick County on Sep. 23, 1788, and Mary Carroll in Apr. 1802. He ran a blacksmith shop on the west side of Valley Pike. He d. in Frederick County, Kernstown, Virginia, on Oct. 16, 1843, and had the following children:

John$^{1.4.2.1k}$, b. on Dec. 22, 1788, m. ____ Haynes, and was killed by a horse in Ohio in 1837.

Mary$^{1.4.2.2k}$, b. on Oct. 17, 1789, m. Elisha Smallwood, and d. on Sep. 3, 1839.

Margaret$^{1.4.2.3k}$, b. on Apr. 9, 1790, m. William Strother, and d. on Mar. 17, 1828.

Samuel$^{1.4.2.4k}$, b. on Jan. 2, 1792, m. Mary M. Balthis and Nancy ____, and d. in Indiana on June 13, 1870.

Henry$^{1.4.2.5k}$, b. on Nov. 10, 1793, and d. unmarried in Indiana.

LANCASTER, LEBANON & DAUPHIN COUNTIES

Elizabeth$^{1.4.2.6k}$, b. on Dec. 29, 1796, m. John Beemer, and d. on May 23, 1836.

Anna E.$^{1.4.2.7k}$, b. on July 26, 1800, and d. in Apr. 1883. She m. John F. Peters. and resided in Moorefield, West Virginia.

Adam Kern

Adam$^{1.4.3k}$ m. Ella Bennett on Apr. 2, 1796, and Margaret Rittenouer in Frederick County on May 18, 1807. He d. in Frederick County, Kernstown, Virginia, on Oct. 23, 1855, and had the following son:

John Thompson$^{1.4.3.1k}$, b. on Jan. 26, 1797, and d. in Richmond, Virginia, in 1864. He was a member of Jefferson Davis's administration. He m. Rebecca T. Mason. She d. in Hampshire County, West Virginia, on Jan. 13, 1874.

Matilda$^{1.4.3.2k}$, b. on Dec. 25, 1798, and m. Andrew Hineman.

Sarah$^{1.4.3.3k}$, b. on Dec. 29, 1800, and m. Edward Hines.

James$^{1.4.3.4k}$, b. on Apr. 1, 1805, and m. Ann.

Joseph$^{1.4.3.5k}$, b. on Apr. 1, 1805, m. Elizabeth, widow of ____ Hendricks, on Feb. 15, 1829, and moved to Fairfield County, Ohio, where he d.. He was a farmer, and Methodist minister, and is buried in Kernstown.

Eliza$^{1.4.3.6k}$, b. on Feb. 29, 1808, and m. Mager Steele.

Zacheriah$^{1.4.3.7k}$, b. on Aug. 10, 1809, and m. Sarah Ann Hamilton.

Nimrod$^{1.4.3.8k}$, b. on May 10, 1811, and m. Elizabeth Bently on Feb. 12, 1840.

Ephrium$^{1.4.3.9k}$, b. on Mar. 14, 1813, and m. Mary Elizabeth Hamilton.

Maranda$^{1.4.3.10k}$, b. on Feb. 15, 1815, m. William Weaver, and resided in Stephens City, Virginia.

William Henry$^{1.4.3.11k}$, b. on Jan. 24, 1817.

Philoma$^{1.4.3.12k}$, b. on Apr. 9, 1819, and m. John W. Steele of Ohio.

Alcinda Jane$^{1.4.3.13k}$, b. on Nov. 1, 1825, m. Adam Dean, and resided in Kernstown.

Caroline$^{1.4.3.14k}$, b. on Aug. 15, 1823, and m. James Schryock.

Margaret Catherine$^{1.4.3.15k}$, b. on Mar. 19, 1827, and m. John R. Eblin.

Henry Kern

Henry[1.4.5k] m. Rachel, daughter of Benjamin and Catherine (Rudolph) Kackley (Elijah and Catherine Richards (Benjamin d., and his widow rem. Henry Richards)), in Frederick County on Sep. 12 (17), 1801, and d. after being thrown from a horse in Shenandoah County, Virginia, on Aug. 28, 1828. She was b. on Feb. 1, 1783, and d. on Sep. 2, 1874. They had the following children in Shenandoah County:

Catherine[1.4.5.1k], b. on Mar. 29, 1802, m. John, son of Mathias Smootz, on Dec. 29, 1821, and d. in Shenandoah County in the 1860s.

Sarah Ann[1.4.5.2k], b. on Aug. 28, 1804, m. Daniel Neff in Shenandoah County on June 15, 1826, and Abraham Miller on Feb. 13, 1833. Sarah and Abraham moved to Ohio.

Rachel[1.4.5.3k], b. on Dec. 25, 1806, m. Reuben Hoover on Nov. 11, 1838, and resided in Shenandoah County.

Lucy[1.4.5.4k], b. on Feb. 27, 1809, m. Frederick A. Shrum on Nov. 17, 1830, and moved to Indiana.

Jacob[1.4.5.5k], b. on Mar. 21, 1811, and m. Peggy Ann Rosenberger in Shenandoah County on Jan. 23, 1833.

John Nicholas[1.4.5.6k], b. on May 31, 1813, and d. in Indiana, unmarried, in 1894. He may be buried in Kernstown.

Henry[1.4.5.7k], b. on Apr. 23, 1816.

Samuel[1.4.5.8k], b. on Feb. 14, 1820, and m. Clarissa Pirkey.

Henry Kern

Henry[1.4.5.7k] m. Catherine Bowman on Feb. 15, 1843. She was b. on July 26, 1826. They had the following children in Shenandoah County, Virginia:

Mary Catherine[1.4.5.7.1k], b. on Nov. 23, 1843.
Isaac[1.4.5.7.2k], b. on Aug. 4, 1845, and d. on Feb. 20, 1909.
Almedia Jane[1.4.5.7.3k], b. on Feb. 26, 1847.
Calvin[1.4.5.7.4k], b. on Apr. 12, 1849.
Milton[1.4.5.7.5k], b. on Nov. 4, 1852.
Rachel Ann[1.4.5.7.6k], b. on Jan. 24, 1851.
James Henry[1.4.5.7.7k], b. on July 12, 1854.
Leah Ellen[1.4.5.7.8k], b. on July 10, 1856.
William Ashby[1.4.5.7.9k], b. on Dec. 12, 1863.
Albert Lee[1.4.5.7.10k], b. on Apr. 27, 1867.
George Washington[1.4.5.7.11k], b. on June 29, 1868.

Georg Michael Kern

Georg Michael[1,2k] m. Anna Charitas (Engen) about 1751. Her name appears as Charitas or Caritas on the baptismal records of York and Lancaster County, Pennsylvania, and as Catherine on deed records, the Virginia baptism, deed records, and communicant register for Trinity Lutheran Church. Georg Michael arrived at Philadelphia on the ship *Duke of Wirtenberg* on Aug. 16, 1751, and settled in Lancaster County, Lancaster, Pennsylvania. Georg Michael Kern was a communicant at Trinity Lutheran Church in Lancaster on Easter, 1752, and Anna Catharina Kernin appeared as a communicant at the same church on the second Sunday after Trinity in 1752. In 1766, he purchased 33 acres on the southern side of Hog's Run in Frederick County, Virginia, from Stephen Pritchard (2 acres being excepted where the meeting house now stands). On Mar. 4, 1767, Michael leased land in Frederick County, Winchester from William Cochran. He purchased 2 lots near Winchester, Frederick County, Virginia, on Mar. 5, 1767, and purchased the land of Lawrence Stevens on German Street in Frederick County, Stephensburg, Virginia, in 1766 (?). After purchasing this land, Michael moved back to Pennsylvania, briefly in 1769, where he had his daughter, Anna Catharina baptized. By Nov. 1, 1773, Michael had returned to Virginia, and settled in Dunmore (now Shenandoah) County, Virginia, and on that date sold his 33 acres and 4 poles on Hog's Run, to Adam Kern for 5 shillings. During the time he spent in York, he may have been residing with the family of his presumed brother, Nicholas. Also, on Nov. 1, 1773, Michael and Catherine Kern, sold the 20 acre tract and 16 acre tract they received from William Cochran (also on that date 3 additional tracts for £130?) to their presumed nephew, Adam Kern, for 5 shillings. In 1777, Michael Kern was listed as a resident of Augusta County, South River. On Mar. 18, 1777, Michael Kern purchased 139 acres from John and Susanna Yancey, that had been patented to William Thompson on Aug. 20, 1748, and 6 acres that had been patented to Samuel Hinds on Feb. 14, 1761. This land was located in Augusta County, Virginia (note that Rockingham was created from Augusta in 1778). In Rockingham County, Virginia, on May 22, 1780, Michael Cairn had his deposition taken in a debt law suit between Rush and Craig, because Michael was about to leave these parts. Michael and Catherine (Caty) Carn/Kearn deeded land to Thomas Turk (delivered to John Byers in 1780) in Augusta County, Virginia, on Mar. 18, 1780. On May 30, 1782, Michael Carns purchased a bell from someone's estate. On May 30, 1782, he was allowed a Revolutionary War claim in Rockingham County. He served in the 7th Class, 7th Virginia Continental Line. He is thought to have d. in Rockingham County, Virginia, between 1781 and 1787, but his deposition seems to indicate that he moved away. Michael received an indenture of lease and release form Henry and Eve Mier in Shenandoah County in 1773, and was a surety along with John Fitsmire for Eve Mier, executrix for the estate of Henry Mier, deceased, on Nov. 23, 1773. On May 24, 1774, Michael believed that he was in danger of suffering from this roll, and petitioned Eve Mier for relief by counter security. Michael sued Henry Fry for debt on June 23, 1773, and was sued for debt by Samuel Beale on Apr. 29, 1773, and Lawrence Hoff on June 23, 1773. They had the following children (the only ones given were Adam, Michael, and Abraham, and this is taken from the record that stated he m. Catherine Engen)):

Adam$^{1.2.1k}$, possibly b. about 1751. Presumed to be the Adam that m. Elisabeth about 1768, and resided in Rockingham County, Virginia.

Michael$^{1.2.2k}$, b. about 1753 (perhaps he m. Catherine, and had Charles) (unproven).

Abraham$^{1.2.3k}$, b. about 1755 (unproven).

Maria Margaretha$^{1.2.4k}$, b. on Mar. 29, 1757, baptized at Trinity Lutheran Church in Lancaster County, Lancaster, Pennsylvania, on May 30, 1757, and sponsored by Martin and Margaretha Hoffman.

Margaret Elisabet$^{1.2.5k}$, b. on Apr. 8, 1760, baptized at Trinity Lutheran Church in Lancaster County, Lancaster, Pennsylvania, on May 11, 1760, and sponsored by Peter and Margaret Schindel. She is probably the Elizabeth, b. in 1759, that m. John Robertson in Frederick County, Virginia, in 1775/76, and d. in Montgomery County, Virginia, sometime after 1840. John was b. on Aug. 12, 1749, and d. in Botetourt County, Virginia, on Nov. 23, 1820. They had a daughter, b. in 1804. John enlisted in the Fourth Virginia Regiment, of the Frederick County, Militia in 1781. In 1786, they moved to Montgomery County, Virginia. John was pensioned in 1818, and Elizabeth received her husband's pension in 1840. In 1840, Nicholas Karn of Frederick County, Virginia, nephew of Elizabeth, made an affidavit that he was present at Elizabeth and John's wedding (this would have been Nicholas, son of Adam and Esther (Moser) Kern). This relationship to Nicholas may be explained if Michael took care of Nicholas's children after his death.

LANCASTER, LEBANON & DAUPHIN COUNTIES 81

Anna Barbara[1.2.6k], b. on July 18, 1762, baptized at Trinity Lutheran Church in Lancaster County, Lancaster, Pennsylvania, on Aug. 15, 1762, and sponsored by Michael and Anna Barbara Schindel.

Johann Peter[1.2.7k], b. on Oct. 3, 1765, baptized at Trinity Lutheran Church in Lancaster County, Lancaster, Pennsylvania, on Oct. 20, 1765, and sponsored by Michael and Barbara Schindel. He was taxed in Rockingham County, Virginia, in 1787 (listed as under 21 years old). He purchased land from Adam and Elisabeth Carn (Kern) in Rockingham County, Virginia, on July 28, 1788. Peter was taxed 1788 with one tithable and two horses, and in Keezeltown District in 1792. A Peter Kerns was listed as Insolvent and Delinquent in Augusta County, Virginia, in 1802, because he was removed from the area.

Nicholas[1.2.8k], b. about 1767 (unproven).

Anna Catharina[1.2.9k], b. in York County, Pennsylvania, on Mar. 29, 1769, baptized at Christ's Lutheran Church of York on July 23, 1769. Questionable, as Michael was residing in Virginia at this time, but Adam that m. Maria Esther Moser went back and forth to Pennsylvania.

Charles[1.2.10k], b. on Apr. 1, 1773, and baptized in Shenandoah County, Virginia, on June 13, 1773 (to Michael and Catherine Kern (Same Wayland source as Adam's child)).

Adam Kern

Adam[1.2.1k] m. Elisabeth about 1772. In Shenandoah County, in July 1779, Adam sued George and Solomon Witzell for threatening to take his life, and destroy his property (the complaint was ordered dismissed). Adam and Elisabeth sold land to Adam's brother, Peter Carn, in Rockingham County, Virginia, on July 28, 1788. Adam had a discontinued law suit from the Virginia Commonwealth in Rockingham County on Mar. 28, 1791. Elisabeth was said to have d. in Shelby County, Orange Township, Ohio, at 113 years of age. She is possibly the Elizabeth Kern whose estate was settled in Miami County, Ohio, in 1850 (placing her birth about 1737), but other Kerns of Miami County are from Rowan County, North Carolina). Possibly, Elisabeth is the Elisabeth Carness that m. Ludwig Levarrance in Rockingham County in 1793. Adam and Elisabeth had the following children:

Ann Rosina[1.2.1.1k], b. on Jan. 23, 1773, baptized in Shenandoah County, Virginia, on May 12, 1773 (Wayland to Adam and Elisabeth Kern), and m. Ludwig Boyer (bondsman John Rush, and daughter of Adam Kern (German)).

?Elisabeth Carness$^{1.2.1.2k}$, b. about 1775, and m. Ludwig Levarrance in Rockingham County in 1793 (bond, Mathias Myers (Moyer)) (unproven perhaps this is Adam's widow).

?John$^{1.2.1.3k}$, b. about 1778 (John, son of Nicholas, was in Greenbriar County in 1801) (unproven). Possibly the John Carn that was taxed in Rockingham County, Harrisonburg/Mole Hill/West District with no property in 1792. A Johan Kern was confirmed at Rader's on Oct. 28, 1803, at age 21 (1782), and a Susanna was confirmed on the same day at age 19 (1784).

?George Karns$^{1.2.1.4k}$, b. about 1779, and m. Barbara Pence in Rockingham County on Jan. 13, 1803 (unproven). He was a member of the Kieseltown Congregation in 1799 (Kerns).

John Kern

John$^{1.2.1.3k}$ m. Barbara Weber in Rockingham County on May 8, 1805, and Anna Barbara, daughter of Henry Eates, in 1813. Anna Barbara was b. on June 20, 1779, and d. in Rockingham County on June 30, 1849 (aged 70 years and 10 days). She is buried at Rader's Lutheran Church cemetery. John had the following children baptized at Rader's:

Jacob$^{1.2.1.3.1k}$, b. on Feb. 13, 1806, baptized on May 25, 1806, and sponsored by his parents.

Catharina$^{1.2.1.3.2k}$, b. on Apr. 11, 1807, baptized on Aug. 23, 1807, and sponsored by her parents.

Elizabeth$^{1.2.1.3.3k}$, b. on Oct. 23, 1808, baptized on May 28, 1809, and sponsored by her mother.

Maria$^{1.2.1.3.4k}$, b. on Dec. 12, 1812, baptized on Apr. 16, 1813, and sponsored by Magdalena Bender.

Nicholas Kern

Nicholas$^{1.2.8k}$ m. Elizabeth about 1789 (the presence of Michael Kern in Rockingham County, Virginia, indicates that this Nicholas Kern remained there, while Nicholas, son of Nicholas was in Greenbriar County in 1801). Nicholas Kaern was a communicant at Rader's Lutheran Church in Mar. 1807. Nicholas and Elizabeth had the following sons in Rockingham County, Virginia:

Michael$^{1.2.8.1.k}$, b. on Apr. 28, 1790, baptized at Rader's Lutheran Church on Aug. 22, 1790, and sponsored by his parents.

Son$^{1.2.8.2k}$, b. on Oct. 24, 1792, baptized at Rader's on May 15, 1793, and sponsored by his parents.

Adam$^{1.2.8.3k}$, b. on May 25, 1795, baptized at Rader's on Aug. 16, 1795, and sponsored by his parents (mother's name not listed).

Michael Kern

Michael$^{1.2.8.1k}$ m. Elizabeth Miller in Rockingham County in 1814, and had the following children baptized at Rader's Lutheran Church in Rockingham County:

Rebecca$^{1.2.8.1.1k}$, b. on Jan. 1, 1815, baptized on June 6, 1815, and sponsored by her parents.

Susanna$^{1.2.8.1.2k}$, b. on Aug. 21, 1816, baptized on June 30, 1817, and sponsored by her parents.

John$^{1.2.8.1.3k}$, b. on Oct. 10, 1818, baptized on June 5, 1819, and sponsored by his parents.

Maria$^{1.2.8.1.4k}$, b. on June 29, 1820, baptized on Nov. 16, 1820, and sponsored by her parents.

****

Other Kern Families

John Kern

John$^{1k(a)}$ resided in Frederick County, Virginia. On Sep. 27/Oct. 20, 1765, Jno. Kern of Frederick County leased .5 acres lying in Mecklenburgh for five shillings, and the rent of one pepper corn on Lady Day next. On Sep. 28, 1765/Oct. 2, 1765, a Jno. Kern leased an additional .5 acre lot from John Hogdon for £40 (lease and release of same transaction?). He leased land to Thomas and Elizabeth Shepherd in Frederick County, Virginia, on June 29, 1767.

****

Jacob Kern

Jacob$^{1k(b)}$ m. Sarah, and resided in Frederick County, Virginia. On Aug. 19, 1778, he is referred to in a deed, as having land adjacent to Conrad Heironimus, and in May 1780 on the road from Winchester to Great Cape Capon. They resided on Little Timber Ridge, Frederick County, Virginia, near the Hampshire County Line. On Sep. 28, 1793, he purchased 225 acres from the heirs of John Noble, and this land was transferred to his children (Nathan, George, Mary, Jacob, and John) from Aug. 5, 1811 to Nov. 1811. Jacob d. between Aug. and Nov.

1811, and his wife signed the final deed. Jacob and Sarah had the following children:

John[1.1k(b)], b. about 1760, m. Elizabeth, daughter of Frederick and Catherine Light in Frederick County on Jan. 30, 1787. He d. in Hampshire County, Virginia, near Capon Bridge about 1846. On Sep. 8, 1811, he received a portion of his father's land on Little Timber Ridge. His will was filed at Romney in 1843.

Jacob[1.2k(b)], b. about 1762, m. Rachel, daughter of Elisha and Martha (Ewing) Cowgill, in Frederick County, Virginia, on Feb. 15, 1791, and d. in Hampshire County, Virginia, in 1826. He purchased 22 acres in Hampshire County on Little Timber Ridge on June 6, 1795.

Elizabeth[1.3k(b)], b. about 1765, and m. George Marricle in Frederick County on July 3, 1786.

George[1.4k(b)], b. about 1772, m. Elizabeth, daughter of Jerimiah Reid, and d. in Frederick County, Ridgecrest, Virginia, in 1854.

Mary[1.5k(b)], b. about 1775, and m. Asa Rosenberger on Aug. 26, 1794.

Nathan[1.6k(b)], b. about 1776, m. Rachel Reid, and Sarah Whitacre. He was alive in 1850.

Joseph[1.7k(b)], b. about 1778, and was residing in Hampshire County in 1840.

****

Abraham Kern

Abraham[1k(c)] m. Maria Catharina, and immigrated to Pennsylvania on the ship *Britannia* on Sep. 11, 1731. Abraham, son of Hans/Johannes Kern of Kurburg, Nassauischen Graffschafft, and Elisabetha Gruber, was b. in Hochfurst, baptized at Hirschland, Northern Alsace, on July 16, 1708, and m. Maria Catharina, daughter of Conrad Muller (schoolmaster at Lehmbach), at Sultzbach/Langensoultzbach on Feb. 18, 1731. Abraham's parents were m. at Diedendorf on Sep. 24, 1706. Abraham's grandparents were Georg Kern and Ulrich Gruber (of Betterchingen). Abraham's mother, Elisabeth (b. in 1676), immigrated with them. Maria Catharina was b. in 1709. They settled in Lancaster County, Cocalico Township, Pennsylvania (resided there in 1746), and had the following children:

Johannes[1.1k(c)], b. about 1732 (not proven as a son).

Johan Christophel[1.2k(c)], b. in Feb. 1735, baptized at Muddy Creek on May 26, 1735, and sponsored by Johan Christophel Steinle. He m. Margaret Catharine.

Johan Heinrich[1.3k(c)], b. on Sep. 24, 1737, baptized at Muddy Creek on Dec. 21, 1737, and sponsored by Heinrich and Anna Catharina Haller. He m. Anna Barbara.

Abraham[1.4k(c)], b. about 1739, and m. Anna Maria Barbara Brendel at Trinity Lutheran Church of New Holland, Pennsylvania, on Nov. 26, 1764.

Maria Catharina[1.5k(c)], baptized at Muddy Creek on July 19, 1743, and sponsored by Christophel and Anna Catharina Steinel.

Anna Catharina[1.6k(c)], b. on Apr. 14, 1746, baptized at Muddy Creek on May 19, 1746, and sponsored by Andreas and Margaretha Gansert.

Johan Peter[1.7k(c)], b. on Aug. 1, 1749, baptized on Aug. 1, 1749, and sponsored by Peter Tritt and wife.

****

Johan Thomas Kern

Johan Thomas[1k(d)] was the son of Peter Kern. He was b. in Freisbach, Germany, on Sep. 19, 1700, and m. Anna Maria Margaretha, daughter of Michel Jopp of Ottersheim, Germany, at Freisbach, on Feb. 17, 1733. They came to America on the ship *Samuel* on Aug. 30, 1737, and settled in Lancaster County, Pennsylvania. They had the following children:

Anna Elisabetha[1.1k(d)], b. on Nov. 20, 1733.

Johan Christoph[1.2k(d)], b. on Jan. 25, 1736.

Johan Michael[1.3k(d)], baptized at the First Reformed Congregation at Lancaster, Lancaster County, Pennsylvania, on May 12, 1739.

****

Unknown (James) Kern

Unknown[1k(e)] m. an unknown woman, and d. before 1750. This was probably the James Curn/Kern that appears on the early rentals of Augusta County, Virginia, in 1749/50. His widow m. Matthew Shaup/Mathias Schaub/Schaup. Mathias's will was written in Augusta County, Virginia, on Nov. 3, 1750, and proved there on Nov. 28, 1750.

He names his eldest sons in law, Michael Carn, and George Carn (both to receive the full estate that their father left them). One third of Matthew's estate was to be divided between eight children, and one third was to be divided between his own six children. Matthew named his two eldest sons, John and Adam Shaup (a Michael and George Carn appear as purchasers of Matthew's estate on Feb. 20, 1750/51 (recorded on May 18, 1762)). Unknown Carn/Kern had the following children:

Michael$^{1.1k(e)}$, b. in 1727, or before. Michael Carn was listed as not found on the delinquents list of Augusta County, Virginia, in 1755. He was a juror in Augusta County, Virginia, on May 24, 1765, and listed as a witness from Bedford (80 miles away) on the same date. He resided in Bedford County, Bedford, Virginia.

George$^{1.2k(e)}$, b. in 1729 or before. He d. in Bedford County, Virginia, in 1767.

****

Michael Kern

Michael$^{1k(f)}$ was said to be a pioneer settler of Morgan District by 1772, and Kern's Fort was built on the lands he owned. He was said to have served in the Revolutionary War, and d. in 1778. He is buried near the site of Kerns Fort. There are several Kerns in Monongalia County, but further research needs to be done to determine their parentage. Michael had the following children:

Michael$^{1.1k(f)}$, b. about 1750.

Michael Kern

Michael$^{1.1k(f)}$ received a land grant of 215 acres at the mouth of Decker's Creek in Monongalia County, Virginia, in 1784, and a Michael Kearn received a land grant for 710 acres in Monongalia County in 1795. In Monongalia County, Trickett District, Virginia, in 1800, a Michael Kerns Sr. is taxed with two tithable males, four slaves over 16, and six horses, and a Michael Kerns Jr. with one tithable male, and two horses Michael Kern of Monongalia County, (in 1782/85, there is no mention of a Michael Kern, but there is a Michael Kain).

Michael$^{1.1.1k(f)}$, b. about 1774.

Susannah$^{1.1.2k(f)}$, b. about 1788, and m. Reuben Chalfant in Monongalia County on Nov. 2, 1809.

****

Maurer

These Maurers have not been confirmed as siblings, but it is quite possible that they were (it is believed that at least Michael and Georg were). They are placed here to add some clarity to the Maurer families in the region.

Johan Phillip^{1m}, b. about 1719.
Johann Michael^{2m}, b. about 1721.
Georg^{3m}, b. about 1725.
Peter^{4m}, b. about 1736.
Henrich^{5m}, m. Anna Elisabetha, and they were sponsors for the baptism of Anna Elisabetha, daughter of Jacob and Maria E. Kuhborts, at Trinity Lutheran Church in 1751. He d. in Lancaster County in 1767.
Johann^{6m}, confirmed at Trinity Lutheran Church in 1748.
Thomas^{7m}, confirmed at Trinity Lutheran Church in 1748.

Johan Phillip Maurer

Johan Phillip^{1m} m. Catarina, daughter of Leonhardt and Margareth Ramler, in Berks County, Tulpehocken Township, Pennsylvania, on May 27, 1740. He received a 500 acre land warrant in Lebanon County, Heidelberg Township on June 14, 1765. In 1754, he was in East Hanover/Lebanon Township, and in 1770, was in Heidelberg Township. On Nov. 16, 1755, he was one of the people in East Hanover Township when Indians crossed the Susquehanna and attacked settlers. They had the following children:

Catarina Margaretha$^{1 \cdot 1m}$, b. on May 30, 1744.
Johan Phillip$^{1 \cdot 2m}$, b. on Nov. 15, 1746.
Johan Jacob$^{1 \cdot 3m}$, b. on June 9, 1748.
Eva Margaretha$^{1 \cdot 4m}$, b. on Oct. 30, 1749.
Johan Georg$^{1 \cdot 5m}$, b. on Apr. 23, 1751.
Maria Elisabetha$^{1 \cdot 6m}$, b. on July 25, 1754.
Georg Michael$^{1 \cdot 7m}$, b. on Jan. 13, 1756.

Johan Phillip Maurer

Johan Philip$^{1 \cdot 2m}$ m. Anna C.. His will was written on Feb. 10, 1778, and probated on May 23, 1786. the executers were his wife Anna C. and Wendle Bartholomew. They had the following children:

Simon$^{1 \cdot 2 \cdot 1m}$; Eva$^{1 \cdot 2 \cdot 2m}$; Margaret$^{1 \cdot 2 \cdot 3m}$; Catharine$^{1 \cdot 2 \cdot 4m}$; Anna$^{1 \cdot 2 \cdot 5m}$, m. Christopher Brown; George$^{1 \cdot 2 \cdot 6m}$.

Johann Michael Maurer

Johann Michael[2m] m. Maria Christina, daughter of Johann Nickel and Maria Barbara (Anschuetz) Schwingel, in Trinity Lutheran Church of Lancaster, Lancaster County, Pennsylvania, on June 14, 1743, and had the following children:

Hans Georg[2·1m], b. on Apr. 1, 1744, baptized at Trinity Lutheran Church on Apr. 9, 1744, and sponsored by Paul and Rosine Reuter.

Anna Caterina[2·2m], b. about 1745, and m. Johan Georg Schock[1·1h].

Rosina Barbara[2·3m], b. on Jan. 29, 1745/46.

Johan Nicholas[2·4m], b. about 1748.

Anna Margaretha[2·5m], b. about 1750, and m. Johan Christoph Frank in Lebanon County, Lebanon, Pennsylvania, on Aug. 30, 1774.

Hans Georg Maurer

Hans Georg[2·1m] m. Maria Magdalena, daughter of Peter and Salome (Frey) Heylmann, in Lebanon County, Lebanon, Pennsylvania, on Apr. 8, 1766. She was b. in Lebanon/North Annville Township on May 1, 1746, and baptized by Johan Casper Stoever on June 24, 1746. They moved to Washington County, Hagerstown, Maryland, where the baptized the following children at St. John's Lutheran Church (the Evangelical Lutheran Church at Elizabethtown (Hagerstown)):

Johan Henrich[2·1·1m], b. on Apr. 3, 1774, and baptized on Apr. 24, 1774.

Margarethe[2·1·2m], b. on Apr. 3, 1774, and baptized on Apr. 24, 1774.

Rosina Barbara Maurer

Rosina Barbara[2·3m] m. Anastasius, son of Peter and Salome (Frey) Heilmann, in Lebanon County, Lebanon on Apr. 8, 1766 by Johan Casper Stover (he was from Lebanon, and she from Heidelberg). Rosina d. in Lebanon County on Apr. 11, 1799. Anastasius was b. in Lebanon/North Annville Township on Mar. 3, 1742, baptized by Johan Casper Stoever on Apr. 15, 1742, and d. in Lebanon County on Mar. 18, 1815. They had the following children:

Frederic[2·3·1m], b. on Dec. 5, 1766, baptized at Hill Lutheran on Dec. 25, 1766, and sponsored by Johan Nicholas Maurer and Elisabeth Heilmann.

LANCASTER, LEBANON & DAUPHIN COUNTIES

Anna Catharina$^{2.3.2m}$, b. on Dec. 3, 1768, baptized at Hill Lutheran on Dec. 3, 1768, and sponsored by Peter and Salome Heilmann.

Johan Adam$^{2.3.3m}$, b. on Sep. 29, 1771, baptized on Oct. 12, 1771, and sponsored by Anton Stoever and wife. He m. Eleonora Imboden on Jan. 31, 1808, and was killed by falling under a wagon on Feb. 22, 1809.

Maria Christina$^{2.3.4m}$, b. on Sep. 14, 1773, baptized at Hill Lutheran on Oct. 21, 1773, and sponsored by John Heylmann and wife.

Rosina Barbara$^{2.3.5m}$, b. on Apr. 4, 1776, baptized at Hill Lutheran on Apr. 18, 1776, and sponsored by John Heilmann and wife.

Johan$^{2.3.6m}$, b. on Oct. 17, 1778, baptized at Hill Lutheran on Oct. 20, 1778, and sponsored by John Heilmann and wife.

Johan Georg$^{2.3.7m}$, b. on June 16, 1780, baptized at Hill Lutheran on Sep. 3, 1780, and sponsored by Johan Georg and Maria Heilmann.

Johan Nicholas Maurer

Johan Nicholas$^{2.4m}$ m. Maria Catarina, and was taxed in Lebanon Township in 1769. They had the following daughter in Lebanon:

Rosina Barbara$^{2.4.1m}$, b. on Nov. 22, 1769, baptized at Hill Lutheran on Dec. 2, 1769, and sponsored by Anastasius and Rosina Heilman.

Georg Maurer

Georg^{3m} m. Anna Maria. He may be the George Mauerer, who was killed and scalped in Lebanon County on Aug. 11, 1757, and the George Mowerer whose will was probated in Lancaster County in 1759. They baptized the following daughter in Trinity Lutheran Church of Lancaster:

Anna Maria$^{3.1m}$, b. on Oct. 25, 1748, baptized on Oct. 30, 1748, and sponsored by Benjamin and Barbara Spieker.

Peter Maurer

Peter^{4m} m. Catarina Elisabeth Kniesz in Lebanon Bethel on Apr. 20, 1756. He d. in Bethel Township between Aug. 4, 1780 and Sep. 10, 1781, and had the following children:

Magdalena$^{4.1m}$; Anna$^{4.2m}$; Barbara$^{4.3m}$; Elizabeth$^{4.4m}$; John$^{4.5m}$; Ernestina$^{4.6m}$; Henry$^{4.7m}$.

****

Hans Jacob Miller

Hans Jacob[1o] was b. to Hans and ____ (Schneider) Miller, in 1628, and m. Vrenilli Gubleman. He immigrated to America on the ship *Mary Hope* from London on June 29, 1710, and arrived at Philadelphia in Oct. 1710. He had the following children:

Rudliffe[1.1o], b. in 1658.

Hans Jacob[1.2o], b. on Mar. 20, 1663 (SWI?).

Rudliffe Miller

Rudliffe[1.1o] m. Barbara, and d. in Lancaster County, Conestoga Township, Pennsylvania, in 1732. Rudliffe's wife d. sometime after that date. In 1719, Rudliffe was listed as an English settler in Conestoga Township. In 1720, he is listed as Rudith Miller (and son); in 1721, on the English assessments as Rudy; in 1722, as Ralph (and son); in 1724, Rudall (and son); and in 1725/26, as Rudy (and son). His will was written on Nov. 27, 1731, and probated on Feb. 1, 1732. Perhaps Barbara is the Bru Miller, whose estate was filed at Lancaster in 1740. Rudliffe and Barbara had the following children:

Henry[1.1.1o], b. about 1796, and was taxed in Conestoga in 1719, 1721, 1722, 1724, 1725, 1726.

Jacob[1.1.2o], b. about 1798 (possibly the Jacob whose estate was filed in Lancaster County in 1737).

Anna Margaretha[1.1.3o], b. about 1700, and m. Michael Sprinckel. He was taxed in Conestoga Township in 1724, and 1726. They moved to York County, Manchester Township, Pennsylvania.

Hans Jacob Miller

Hans Jacob[1.2o] m. Magdalena on Apr. 2, 1693. In 1710, he had 1,000 acres surveyed in the Pequea Valley (+6% for roads). He was taxed in Lancaster County, Conestoga Township in 1718; as Jacob and son in 1719; and Jacob Elder in 1725. He was naturalized in 1717. He d. on Apr. 20, 1739, and is buried in Tchantz Graveyard. His estate was filed in Lancaster County in 1740. They had the following children:

Jacob[1.2.1o], b. about 1694.

Hance[1.2.2o], b. about 1796, and taxed in Conestoga in 1718, 1719.

Martin[1.2.3o], b. about 1798, and was taxed in Conestoga in 1719, 1725, 1726. He was naturalized in 1717, and his estate was filed in Lancaster County in 1743.

Michael[1.2.4o], b. about 1700.

Jacob Miller

Jacob$^{1.2.1o}$ was taxed in 1719 as freeman with his father; Jacob Jr. in 1720, 1725, 1726, 1724. He was naturalized in 1717. On Nov. 19, 1754, Jacob deeded 100 acres (part of a 1,000 acre patent to Jacob Miller on June 30, 1711) to his son, Martin in Strasburg Township. This land was adjacent to Jacob Miller Jr., Amost Strettell, and Jacob Miller. He m. Catharina, and had the following children:

Jacob$^{1.2.1.1o}$.

Martin$^{1.2.1.2o}$ was b. in Switzerland about 1720, m. Margareth Neff, and d. in Strasburg Township between Jan. 7, and Mar. 15, 1773 (will dates). On Dec. 1, 1744, Jacob and Catherine Miller deeded 100 acres in Strasburg Township to Martin that was part of the 150 acres that had been granted to them on Apr. 29/30, 1731.

Michael Miller

Michael$^{1.2.4o}$ m. Barbara. He may be the Michael Miller that resided in York County on Oct. 16, 1727. His will was written on Mar. 23, 1737, and probated on Aug. 26, 1739. He was taxed in Conestoga in 1718, 1719, 1720, 1721, 1725, 1724, 1726. In May 1718, he had 1,200 acres on the North West side of the Conestoga River. His will was probated in Lancaster County in 1739. He had the following children:

Jacob$^{1.2.4.1o}$.

****

Samuel Moser

Samuel^{1q} was b. in 1689, and d. on Feb. 22, 1755. He m. Catharina Weiss in Bischwiller, Bas-Rhin, France, on May 14, 1714. She was b. in 1693. They has the following children in Birschwiller:

Samuel$^{1.1q}$, b. on Mar. 31, 1715.

Hans Michael$^{1.2q}$, b. on July 11, 1717.

Johan Peter$^{1.3q}$, born on July 16, 1724.

Anna Maria$^{1.4q}$, b. on Sep. 21, 1729.

Samuel Moser

Samuel$^{1.1q}$ m. Catharina Francois in Langensoultzbach, Bas-Rhin, France, on Nov. 23, 1739. They arrived at Philadelphia in 1749, on the ship *Lydia*. He was taxed in York in 1762. Samuel may have been the Samuel who wrote his will on Feb. 2, 1796, probated in York Borough on June 2, 1796, and executed by Henry Tyson and

John Herbach. The will referred to a wife Salome, son Samuel, and other children. Samuel and Catharina had the following children:

Maria Esther$^{1.1.1q}$, b. in Bischwiller, France, on Sep. 18, 1746, and m. Adam Kern.

Samuel$^{1.1.2q}$, baptized in York County, Pennsylvania, by Reverend Jacob Lischy on Mar. 3, 1750/1, and sponsored by Christian and Anna Maria Leonhardt.

Maria Elisabeth$^{1.1.3q}$, baptized in York County by Reverend Jacob Lischy on May 11, 1755, and sponsored by Christian and Anna Maria Leonhardt.

Samuel Moser

Samuel$^{1.1.2q}$ m. Eva Margaret, daughter of Michael and Margaret Geisselman, sometime before 1780, and Anna Maria before 1787. He may be the Samuel who wrote his will on Aug. 1, 1811, probated in York Borough on May 20, 1816, and executed by Adam and George Moser. The will refers to a wife, Barbara, and children Adam, George, and Catharine. Samuel had the following children in York County, Pennsylvania:

Catharine$^{1.1.2.1q}$, b. on Aug. 9, 1780, and baptized at Christ Lutheran Church on Aug. 27, 1780.

Adam$^{1.1.2.1q}$, b. on Jan. 27, 1783, and baptized at Christ's Lutheran Church of York on Feb. 24, 1783.

Mary Magdalene$^{1.1.q}$, b. on Jan. 9, 1787, baptized at Blymir's Union on Aug. 26, 1787, and sponsored by Mary Magdalene Miller.

John Conrad$^{1.1.2.3q}$, b. on June 31, 1789, and baptized at Christ's Lutheran on Aug. 15, 1789.

Hans Michael Moser

Hans Michael$^{1.2q}$ m. Eva Maria, daughter of Melchior Elsasser, at Billigheim, Germany, on Jan. 16, 1741. She was b. in Billigheim on Sep. 11, 1717, and d. in Columbiana County, Ohio, on June 27, 1807 (moved there with son Samuel in 1801). They arrived at Philadelphia in 1749 on the ship *Lydia* and settled in York County, Manchester Township, Pennsylvania. Michael was taxed there in 1762, and d. there in 1789. They had the following children:

Hans Michael$^{1.2.1q}$, b. in 1742.

Peter$^{1.2.2q}$, b. in 1744, m. Margaret Wortman (possibly the John Peter Moser that m. Margaret Wollmer at the First Reformed Congregation at Lancaster, Pennsylvania, on May 21, 1765), and d. in 1808 (buried in Petersburg, Ohio). In 1801, they moved to Jefferson

County, Ohio (now Mahoning County). During the Revolutionary War, he served as a Private in Captain Wright's Company in 1776, and Captain Smythe's Company Lancaster County, Militia. She was b. in 1743, and d. in 1821.

Samuel$^{1.2.3q}$, b. on Feb. 16, 1746.
Abraham$^{1.2.4q}$, b. about 1748, and d. in 1822.
Johannes$^{1.2.5q}$, b. about 1750, and d. in 1826.
Johan Jacob$^{1.2.6q}$, b. on Aug. 29, 1756 (he moved to Ohio).
Daniel$^{1.2.7q}$, b. on Apr. 4, 1759, m. Catherine, and d. in Petersburg, Ohio, in 1817. He was a Private in Captain Strahler's Company, 6th Battalion Northampton County, Militia in the Revolutionary War. He was taxed as single in York Township in 1779. Daniel and his wife were sponsors at the baptism of Daniel Moser at BLY in 1792.

Hans Michael Moser

Hans Michael$^{1.2.1q}$ m. Maria Anna Shaffer, and d. in 1811. They had the following children:

Johan Michael$^{1.2.1.1q}$, b. on Apr. 29, 1773, baptized at Blymir's Union on Aug. 4, 1776, and sponsored by Conrad and Maria Agathe Giesy.

Catherine$^{1.2.1.2q}$, b. on Aug. 21, 1778, baptized at the First Reformed Church of York on Aug. 28, 1778, and sponsored by Catharine Lindis.

Juliana$^{1.2.1.3q}$, b. on Feb. 9, 1795, baptized at the First Reformed Church on June 14, 1795, and sponsored by Georg and Barbara Lotman.

Samuel Moser

Samuel$^{1.2.3q}$, m. Elizabeth, and d. in Tuscarwas County, Bolivar, Ohio, in 1808 (1810/12). They had the following children in York:

Samuel$^{1.2.3.1q}$, b. on July 14, 1767, baptized at Christ's Lutheran Church on Oct. 23, 1767, and sponsored by Michael and Eva Maria Moser.

Abraham Moser

Abraham$^{1.2.4q}$ m. Barbara, and had the following children in York County, Pennsylvania:

Maria Elizabeth$^{1.2.4.1q}$, b. on Oct. 25, 1776, baptized at Christ's Evangelical Church of York on Jan. 13, 1777.

Abraham[1.2.4.2q], b. on Apr. 27, 1794, baptized at the First Reformed Church of York on Aug. 31, 1794, and sponsored by Michael and Maria Moser.
Elizabeth[1.2.4.3q], b. on Aug. 25, 1796, baptized at the First Reformed Church on Nov. 2, 1796, and sponsored by Elizabeth Moser.
Elizabeth[1.2.4.4q], b. on Sep. 13, 1798, baptized at Blymir's Union Church on Jan. 27, 1799, and sponsored by George Minnich and wife.

Johannes Moser

Johannes[1.2.5q] m. Catherine, daughter of John Lindy, and had the following children in York County, Pennsylvania:
Johannes[1.2.5.1q], b. on Aug. 25, 1789, baptized at Blymir's Union on Sep. 30, 1789, and sponsored by John and Anna Maria McDowell
Daniel[1.2.5.2q], b. on Mar. 12, 1792, baptized at Blymir's Union Church on Apr. 9, 1792, and sponsored by Daniel and Catherine Moser.
Elisabeth[1.2.5.3q], b. on July 16, 1800, and baptized at The First Reformed Church of York on Dec. 19, 1800.

Johan Jacob Moser

Johan Jacob[1.2.7q] m. Catharine, and had the following children at York:
Peter[1.2.7.1q], b. on May 17, 1797, and baptized at Christ's Lutheran Church on Sep. 3, 1797.
Henry[1.2.7.2q], b. on Jan. 23, 1800, and baptized on Nov. 3, 1800.

****

Johan Leonhard Mueller

Johan Leonhard[1r] m. Catharina, and Maria Sophia (possibly Maria Sophia Catharina). Leonard had the following children in Lancaster County, Earl Township:
Johan Jacob[1.1r], b. on Jan. 12, 1733, baptized in Apr. 1733, and sponsored by Johan Jacob Weiss and Susanna Wolff.
Susanna[1.2r], b. on July 16, 1734, baptized at Muddy Creek on Aug. 4, 1734, and sponsored by Johan Jacob Weiss and Susanna Wolff.
Maria Magdalena[1.3r], b. on Oct. 9, 1735, baptized on Oct. 30, 1735, and sponsored by Maria Magdalena Wagner.

Sophia[1.4r], b. on May 6, 1737, baptized at Muddy Creek on May 30, 1737, and sponsored by Jacob Weiss Jr. and Sophia.

Anna Elisabetha[1.5r], b. in Dec. 1739, baptized at Muddy Creek on Dec. 16, 1739, and sponsored by Jacob and Sophia Weiss.

Anna Barbara[1.6r], b. on Dec. 27, 1740, baptized at Muddy Creek on Jan. 3, 1741, and sponsored by Jacob and Sophia Weiss.

Anna Catharina[1.7r], b. on Jan. 2, 1742, baptized on Jan. 4, 1742, and sponsored by Sophia Weiss.

Eleonore[1.8r], b. about 1744.

Maria Dorothea[1.9r], b. on Oct. 16, 1745, baptized at Trinity Evangelical Lutheran Church of New Holland on Nov. 3, 1745, and sponsored by Johannes Eyd and wife.

Sophia Catharina[1.10r], b. on July 1, 1748, baptized at Trinity Evangelical Lutheran Church of New Holland on July 31, 1748, and sponsored by Benjamin Lessly and Catharina Werndtin (her mother is listed as Sophia).

Anna Maria Sophia[1.11r], b. about 1751, and m. Johan Peter Grimm.

Anna Christina[1.12r], b. on Sep. 19, 1753, baptized on Oct. 14, 1753, and sponsored by Johan Jacob Werns and Christina, daughter of John Dieffendorffer. She m. Johan Heinrich Grimm.

Eleonore Mueller

Eleonore[1.8r] m. Johan Michael, son of Christian Schnoeder, on Nov. 25, 1766, and had the following children:

Maria Sophia[1.8.1r], b. on July 30, 1767, baptized at Seltenreich on Sep. 27, 1767, and sponsored by Leonard and Maria Sophia Mueller.

Johan Christian[1.8.2r], b. on Nov. 30, 1768, baptized at Seltenreich on Jan. 8, 1769, and sponsored by John Stein and Sophia Mueller.

Johan Michael[1.8.3r], b. on July 27, 1771, baptized at Seltenreich on Sep. 1, 1771, and sponsored by Philip and Dorothea Schnoeder.

Eleonore[1.8.4r], b. on Nov. 9, 1773, baptized at Seltenreich on Apr. 10, 1774, and sponsored by Leonard and Sophia Mueller.

****

Ulrich Neff

Ulrich[1s], had the following son in Hausen am Albis, Canton Zurich, Switzerland:

Felix$^{1.1s}$, b. on Oct. 4, 1587.

Felix Neff

Felix$^{1.1s}$ m. Anna Ringger in Hausen am Albis about 1607. She d. of the plague in Affoltern am Albis on Nov. 16, 1628, and Felix d. there after 1643. Felix was a constable in 1634. They had the following children in Heisch (near Hausen):

Jogli "Jacob"$^{1.1.1s}$, b. about 1613.

Jorg$^{1.1.2s}$, baptized on May 14, 1615, and sponsored by Jorg Wirtz and Elsie Aberli.

Henrich$^{1.1.3s}$, baptized on Mar. 2, 1617, and sponsored by Henrich Grob and Elsbeth Huber.

Baschi "Sebastian"$^{1.1.4s}$, baptized on Sep. 5 (6), 1619 (20), and sponsored by Baschi Hage and Madale Grob.

Hans Rudolf$^{1.1.5s}$, baptized at Heisch, Canton Zurich on Apr. 14, 1622, and sponsored by Rudi Russer and Margaret Sessler.

Anna$^{1.1.6s}$, baptized on Mar. 7, 1624, and sponsored by Hans Santmann and Anna Bar.

Trineli "Catharine"$^{1.1.7s}$, baptized on Oct. 30, 1625, and sponsored by Hans Funk and Catherin Binder.

Verena$^{1.1.8s}$, baptized on July 7, 1627, and sponsored by Mathis Kunzli and Verona Suter.

Hans Rudolf Neff

Hans Rudolf$^{1.1.5s}$ m. Ragula, daughter of Kasper and Anna (Lussi) Zimmerman in Affoltern am Albis on Nov. 5, 1648. She was baptized at Affoltern am Albis on Dec. 13, 1629, sponsored by Adam Steinbruckel and Regula Schwytzer, and d. at Baden Heidelberg, Michelfeld, Germany, on Sep. 3, 1679. In 1624, Rudolf moved with his parents to Affoltern. In 1661, he moved to Germany, and settled in Bockshof, and in 1665, moved to Michelfeld. While in Michelfeld, Rudolf was a farmer for the Junker (Reinhardt of Gemmingen).

Kasper, son of Heinrich and Elsbet (Winterlin/Winterli) Zyberman/Zimmerman (m. at Affoltern on Aug. 6, 1580) was baptized at Alffoltern am Albis on Jan. 21, 1588 (sponsored by Kaspar Schneebeli and Margaretha Usteri), m. Anna, daughter of Thomas Lussi (d.1643), at Alffoltern am Albis on Nov. 20, 1627, and d. there on Dec. 2, 1681. Kasper was a bailiff, innkeeper, and butcher.

Hans Rudolf Neff d. from the plague in Baden, Heidelberg, Michelfeld on Oct. 19, 1677. Hans Rudolf and Raugla baptized the following children at Alffoltern am Albis (unless otherwise noted):

Ulrich$^{1.1.5.1s}$, baptized on Oct. 7, 1649, and sponsored by Ulrich Ringger and Barbol Huni. He m. Catharina, daughter of Michael and Anna Maria Endress on Nov. 2, 1669.

Barbel$^{1.1.5.2s}$, baptized on May 8, 1651, and sponsored by Hans Fugli and Barbara Stoltz.

Heinrich$^{1.1.5.3s}$, baptized on Jan. 30, 1653, and sponsored by Heinrich Weiss and Freni Vollenweid.

Margaretha$^{1.1.5.4s}$, baptized at Benken on June 11, 1654, and sponsored by Rudolf Bram and Margaretha Strasser.

Jacob$^{1.1.5.5s}$, baptized at Benken on Nov. 18, 1655, and sponsored by Hans Jacob Haupt and Margaretha Strasser.

Verena$^{1.1.5.6s}$, baptized on Mar. 4, 1657, and sponsored by Hans Schneebeli and Verena Dubs.

Hans Jacob$^{1.1.5.7s}$, baptized on Jan. 30, 1658/59, and sponsored by Hans Jacob Stoltz and Margaretha Gunthard.

Hans Rudolf$^{1.1.5.8s}$, baptized at Reichen, Germany, on June 9, 1661, sponsored by Hans Jacob Huprecht and Barbara Huber, and d. on Apr. 4, 1662.

Hans Rudolf$^{1.1.5.9s}$, baptized at Reichen on Mat 3, 1663, and sponsored by Jacob Huprecht and Barbara Huber.

Catharina$^{1.1.5.10s}$, baptized at Michelfeld on Oct. 19, 1666, and sponsored by Catharina Muller.

Catharina$^{1.1.5.11s}$, baptized at Michelfeld on July 5, 1668, sponsored by Catharina Endress, and d. on July 7, 1668.

Anna$^{1.1.5.12s}$, baptized at Michelfeld on July 18, 1669, sponsored by Anna, wife of Hanns Rudisiler, and d. on Aug. 14, 1669.

Cleophe$^{1.1.5.13s}$, baptized at Michelfeld on Oct. 9, 1671, and sponsored by Cleophe.

Anna$^{1.1.5.14s}$, baptized at Michelfeld on Jan. 10, 1673, and sponsored by Anna, wife of Hans Rudisiler.

Hans Jacob Neff

Hans Jacob$^{1.1.5.7s}$ m. Anna Barbara, daughter of Mathusalem/Matthias and Margaretha (Lang) Donner, at Michelfeld on Feb. 5, 1683/84. She was b. in Michelfeld on Sunday Cantate, baptized on May 12, 1658, sponsored by Anna Elisabeth, wife of Georg Herbert, and Barbara, wife of Bernard Rattermann, and d. in Michelfeld on Dec. 21, 1700.

Mathusalem/Matthias Donner, son of Mathusalem and Anna (Handt) Donner was b. in Luckau near Niederlaussnitz, Germany, about 1606, m. Margaretha, daughter of Jacob and Magdalena (Meitz)

Lang, in Biberach, Swabia, Germany, in 1632, and d. at Michelfeld on Sep. 11, 1669. Matthias Donner was a tailor, soldier, and Lords Court Farmer (gamekeeper). Margaretha Lang was b. in Biberach in 1607, and d. at Michelfeld on Apr. 15, 1692. Jacob Lang was a baker.

Hans Jacob Neff was killed in a shooting accident at Michelfeld on June 30, 1718. Hans Jacob and Anna Barbara Neff had the following children in Michelfeld:

Anna Catharina$^{1.1.5.7.1s}$, b. on Mar. 30, 1685, baptized on Mar. 31, 1685, and was sponsored by Anna Catharina, wife of Weirich Seltzer Becker. She m. Hans Rudolph.

Reuss/Reiss in Michelfeld on Mar. 29, 1712. They immigrated to Pennsylvania on May 11, 1738.

Johan Michael$^{1.1.5.7.2s}$, b. on Feb. 21, 1686/87, baptized on Feb. 23, 1687, and sponsored by Michael Georg Schoeffer.

Hans Jacob$^{1.1.5.7.3s}$, b. on Feb. 7, 1690, baptized on Feb. 9, 1690, and sponsored by Hans Jacob Renkhert.

Maria Catharina$^{1.1.5.7.4s}$, m. Heinrich Seltzer in Michelfeld on Feb. 9, 1709, and immigrated to Pennsylvania on May 16, 1730.

Johann Michael Neff

Johann Michael$^{1.1.5.7.2s}$ m. Anna Dorothea, daughter of Hans Jacob and Catherina Saur, at Michelfeld on Nov. 11, 1710. She was b. at Michelfeld on Sep. 26, 1690, and sponsored by Dorothea, housewife of Felix Mauer, at her baptism.

Hans Jacob, son of Joachim and Appel Saur, was b. at Michelfeld in 1646, m. Catherina, daughter of Melchior (Mayer of Eschelbach) and Anna Becker, and d. on Mar. 17, 1728/29. Hans Jacob was a court official in Michelfeld. Catherina d. in Michelfeld on Nov. 27, 1725.

Joachim, son of Jacob and Appolonia (Schwifer) Saur, was b. at Michelfeld about 1599, m. Appel, daughter of Philip and Anna (?Saur) Baur, at Michelfeld in 1642, and d. around midnight at Michelfeld on Sep. 9/10, 1656. Joachim was a Cooper, and served in the Dutch War (30 years War?). Appel was b. in 1613, and was alive in 1680.

Michael Neff was a farmer, and d. in Lancaster County, Heidelberg Township, Pennsylvania, sometime after Apr. 1756. He arrived in Philadelphia on the ship *James Goodwill* on Sep. 11, 1728, and was naturalized on Apr. 11, 1743. He purchased 250 acres in Lancaster County, Heidelberg Township, on Nov. 28, 1734, and 427 acres in Heidelberg Township in 1744 (patented in 1749). He was on the church council, and a Deacon of Christ's Lutheran Church of

Tulpehocken from 1745 until his death. Michael distributed his 482 acres between his sons on Apr. 13, 1756. Michael and Anna Dorothea had the following children:

Johann Michael$^{1.1.5.7.2.1s}$, b. at Michelfeld on July 23, 1712, baptized on July 24, 1712, and sponsored by Georg Michael Brecht.

Johann Jacob$^{1.1.5.7.2.2s}$, b. at Michelfeld on Feb. 13, 1714/15, baptized on Feb. 15, 1715, and sponsored by Johann Jacob Heberle.

Anna Catharina$^{1.1.5.7.2.3s}$, b. in Michelfeld on Nov. 22, 1716, baptized on Nov. 23, 1716, and sponsored by Anna Catharina, wife of Jacob Heberle.

Georg Abraham$^{1.1.5.7.2.4s}$, b. at Michelfeld on Oct. 2, 1719, baptized on Oct. 11, 1719, and sponsored by Georg Abraham Dietz.

Maria Catharina$^{1.1.5.7.2.5s}$, b. in Michelfeld on Jan. 25, 1722/23, baptized on Jan. 27, 1723, sponsored by Anna Catharina Scherber, and d. in Michelfeld in 1725.

Hans Leonhard$^{1.1.5.7.2.6s}$, b. in Michelfeld on Mar. 8, 1724/25, baptized on Mar. 12, 1725, and sponsored by Leonhard Gebhard.

Anna Maria$^{1.1.5.7.2.7s}$, b. on the Atlantic Ocean about 1727, and m. John Schaeffer of Schafferstown.

Johann Georg$^{1.1.5.7.2.8s}$, b. in Berks County, Tulpehocken Township, Pennsylvania, on Dec. 1, 1729, baptized on May 3, 1730, and sponsored by Johann Georg Schwab.

Johann Michael Neff

Johann Michael$^{1.1.5.7.2.1s}$ m. Anna Maria, daughter of Ludwig and Anna Margaretha Miller, and d. in Dauphin County, Heidelberg Township, Pennsylvania, about 1799. He was naturalized on Apr. 13, 1743. They had the following children:

Michael$^{1.1.5.7.2.1.1s}$, b. in 1736, m. Anna Christina, and resided in Franklin County, Letterkenny Township, Pennsylvania.

Jacob$^{1.1.5.7.2.1.2s}$, b. in 1739, and resided in Franklin County, Pennsylvania, in 1800.

Leonard$^{1.1.5.7.2.1.3s}$, b. about 1742, and resided in Franklin County, Pennsylvania, in 1800.

Johann Georg$^{1.1.5.7.2.1.4s}$, b. on Feb. 3, 1744, m. Maria Elisabeth, daughter of Georg Buhlmann, on May 28, 1771, and d. about 1812.

Johannes$^{1.1.5.7.2.1.5s}$, b. in 1746, and resided in Franklin County, Letterkenny Township in 1800.

Maria Catharina$^{1.1.5.7.2.1.6s}$, b. on Jan. 5, 1749, and baptized on Apr. 16, 1749. She m. Christian Kohr (b. 1747).

Johann Peter[1.1.5.7.2.1.7s], b. in Mar. 1751, and baptized on May 5, 1751.

Anna Maria[1.1.5.7.2.1.8s], b. on May 18, 1752, and m. John Baker.

Abraham[1.1.5.7.2.1.9s], b. on Aug. 26, 1753, and m. Anna Susanna Phillippi on June 18, 1776.

Johann Jacob Neff

Johann Jacob[1.1.5.7.2.2h] m. Eva Christina, daughter of Johann Caspar Stover, in Lancaster County, Warwick Township, Pennsylvania, on May 11, 1742, and d. in Dauphin County, Heidelberg Township, Pennsylvania, in 1770 (will probated in Lancaster County on Jan. 4, 1790). They had the following children:

Johann Jacob[1.1.5.7.2.2.1h], b. on Jan. 3, 1743, and m. Anna Maria Eichelberger in July 1771.

Johannes[1.1.5.7.2.2.2h], b. on Jan. 11, 1744, m. Maria, and d. in Heidelberg Township in 1812.

Michael[1.1.5.7.2.2.3h], b. on May 22, 1745, and m. Anna Maria.

Catharina Margaretha[1.1.5.7.2.2.4h], b. on Aug. 19, 1747, m. Christopher Eichelberger about 1768, and d. about 1776.

Abraham[1.1.5.7.2.2.5h], b. about 1748, and d. in Swatara Township in 1803.

Johann Georg[1.1.5.7.2.2.6h], b. in 1750.

Eva Christina[1.1.5.7.2.2.7h], b. on May 5, 1752, and m. Georg Albright.

Maria Elisabeth[1.1.5.7.2.2.8h], b. on Apr. 15, 1754, and m. Frederick Wolfersperger.

Maria Barbara[1.1.5.7.2.2.9h], b. on Sep. 8, 1755, and m. Christopher Eichelberger on Apr. 21, 1777.

Eva Elisabeth[1.1.5.7.2.2.10h], b. on May 7, 1758, and m. Georg Weiman.

Johann Peter[1.1.5.7.2.2.12h], b. on Apr. 3, 1764, and may have m. Susannah Blaser on June 27, 1783.

Anna Catharina Neff

Anna Catharina[1.1.5.7.2.3s] m. Michael Stump in Berks County, Tulpehocken Township, Pennsylvania, on Sep. 10, 1739, and d. in Hardy County, Virginia, in 1794. Her will was written on Dec. 4, 1783, and probated in 1793. His will was written on July 2, 1767, and probated on Mar. 8, 1768. They moved to Hampshire (now Hardy)

County, Moorfield, Virginia, with Leonhard Neff sometime before Apr. 1748. They had the following children:

Michael$^{1.1.5.7.2.3.1s}$, b. about 1742, m. Sarah, daughter of Thomas and Mary (Baker) Hughs, in 1763, and d. in June 1799. She d. on June 15, 1821.

Georg$^{1.1.5.7.2.3.2s}$, b. on Apr. 8, 1744, m. Elizabeth Massey, and d. in 1805.

Catharina$^{1.1.5.7.2.3.3s}$, b. about 1746, m. Jacob Brake, and d. in 1816.

Leonhard$^{1.1.5.7.2.3.4s}$, b. on Nov. 21, 1749, m. Catharina Elisabeth See, and d. in 1829.

Elisabeth$^{1.1.5.7.2.3.5s}$, b. on July 13, 1752, m. David (Elias) Welton, and was alive in 1815. Elias d. in 1815.

Maria Magdalena$^{1.1.5.7.2.3.6s}$, b. on Dec. 17, 1754, and m. Solomon Welton in 1772, and ___ Yoakham before 1783.

Georg Abraham Neff

Georg Abraham$^{1.1.5.7.2.4s}$ m. Anna Christina Loesh in Berks County, Tulpehocken Township, Pennsylvania, on June 8, 1742, and d. in Dauphin County, Pennsylvania, in 1803. They had the following children:

Sophia$^{1.1.5.7.2.4.1s}$, b. about 1743, and m. ___ Hogmire.

Johann Jacob$^{1.1.5.7.2.4.2s}$, baptized on Sep. 16, 1744, m. Barbara Kapp, and d. in Somerset County, Pennsylvania, in 1809.

Christina$^{1.1.5.7.2.4.3s}$, baptized on May 22, 1746, and m. ___ Graffin.

Maria Catharina$^{1.1.5.7.2.4.4s}$, baptized on July 16, 1747, and m. Michael Kapp.

Maria Magdalena$^{1.1.5.7.2.4.5s}$, b. on Nov. 25, 1748, baptized on Dec. 25, 1748, and m. ___ Smith.

Johann Georg$^{1.1.5.7.2.4.6s}$, b. on Feb. 24, 1751, and baptized on Mar. 3, 1751. He d. before 1756.

Anna Maria$^{1.1.5.7.2.4.7s}$, b. on May 18, 1752, and m. ___ Tussing/Tuping.

Abraham$^{1.1.5.7.2.4.8s}$, b. on July 15, 1753, and baptized on Aug. 12, 1753. In 1790, he resided in Franklin County, Pennsylvania, and in 1800, resided in Somerset County, Pennsylvania. He d. in Fairfield County, Ohio, about 1824.

Johann Georg$^{1.1.5.7.2.4.9s}$, b. on Jan. 14, 1756, and baptized on Feb. 15, 1756. He m. Elisabeth.

Johann Leonhard$^{1.1.5.7.2.4.10s}$, b. on Apr. 10, 1757, baptized on May 8, 1757. He d. in Greene County, Ohio, in 1809.

Michael$^{1.1.5.7.2.4.11s}$, b. on July 1, 1759, and baptized on Aug. 19, 1759. He was not mentioned in the will.

Anna Margaretha$^{1.1.5.7.2.4.12s}$, b. on Aug. 28, 1761, baptized in 1761, and d. on Aug. 6, 1792. She m. Adam Reis Jr. on Aug. 22, 1784.

Johann Heinrich$^{1.1.5.7.2.4.13s}$, b. on July 4, 1764, baptized on July 29, 1764, and m. Anna Maria in 1784.

Hans Leonhard Neff

Hans Leonhard$^{1.1.5.7.2.6s}$ m. Elisabetha Magdalena, daughter of Leonhardt and Anna Catharina Faeg/Feg, in Berks County, Tulpehocken Township, Pennsylvania, in 1745. Elisabetha Magdalena was b. in Tulpehocken Township about 1724, and d. in Hardy County, Virginia, in Jan. 1817 (her son George was the executer of her will).

Leonhardt, son of Johannes and Anna Margaretha Schneider, aka Faeg, was b. in Idar-Oberstein, Nastau-Sig, Germany, about 1695, m. Anna Catharina, daughter of Conrad and Anna Schutz in Schoharie County, Neu-Stuttgardt, New York, on Nov. 1, 1715, and d. in Berks County, Tulpehocken Township, Pennsylvania, in Sep. 1743. His will was written on May 23, 1743, and probated on Sep. 2, 1743. Anna Catharina Schutz was b. in Langenselbold/Niedergrundau, Hesse, Germany, on Apr. 29, 1696.

Johannes Schneider, aka Faeg, son of Johannes Schneider of Vollmersbach, Germany, m. Anna Margaretha, daughter of Martin and Anna Margaretha Becker, in Idar-Oberstein on Apr. 12, 1689, and resided in Neu Stuttgardt, New York, in 1716. Anna Margaretha Becker was b. in Idar-Oberstein on Oct. 28, 1672, and resided in Berks County, Tulpehocken Township, Pennsylvania, in Apr. 1745. Johannes Schneider, aka Faeg, was listed on Captain Johan Encrist's ship in Holland in 1709, and was in New York on July 4, 1710. He was a soldier/volunteer from Queensbury on an expedition to Canada in 1711. He was naturalized on Oct. 11, 1715, and was at Neu-Stuttgardt in 1716.

Conrad, son of Hermann Schutz of Altenburschia, Hesse, Germany, m. Anna, daughter of Clas and Margaretha Eichelborner, in Langenselbold, Hesse, Germany, on May 19, 1687, and d. in Berks County, Tulpehocken Township, Pennsylvania, sometime after May 1723. Conrad was a linen weaver at Lieblos in 1705. Anna Eichelborner was baptized at Langenselbold on Aug. 15, 1661 (sponsored by Anna wife of Peter Kirschner), and d. in Neu-Heessberg, New York before 1715. Conrad resided at Neu-Heessberg in 1716/17, and by May 13, 1723, was residing in Berks County, Tulpehocken.

Hans Leonhard Neff moved to Hampshire County, Moorfield, Virginia, sometime before 1748 (he and Michael Stump had land surveyed there on Apr. 2, 1748), and d. there in May 1778. His will was written on Mar. 16, 1778, and probated on May 12, 1778. Hans Leonhard and Elisabetha Magdalena Neff had the following children:

Leonhard$^{1.1.5.7.2.6.1s}$, b. about 1748, and d. before Mar. 1778.
Michael$^{1.1.5.7.2.6.2s}$, b. about 1751.
Henry$^{1.1.5.7.2.6.3s}$, b. about 1753.
Daughter$^{1.1.5.7.2.6.4s}$, b. about 1757.
Daughter$^{1.1.5.7.2.6.5s}$, b. about 1760.
George$^{1.1.5.7.2.6.6s}$, b. about 1763.
Jacob$^{1.1.5.7.2.6.7s}$, b. about 1766.

Leonhard Neff

Leonhard$^{1.1.5.7.2.6.1s}$ d. before Mar. 1778, and had the following children:
John$^{1.1.5.7.2.6.1.1s}$.

Michael Neff

Michael$^{1.1.5.7.2.6.2s}$ m. Mary, daughter of Jacob and Ann/Nancy Reed, and d. in Hardy County, Virginia, in Nov. 1826. She d. about 1829. He received the land his father purchased from Thom/Thorn from his father's will. The 1782 and 1784 tax list of Hampshire County, Virginia, shows his household having 8 people. On Mar. 30, 1779, he purchased 396 acres on the South Branch from Solomon and Elizabeth Reed. Michael and Mary had the following children:

Daughter$^{1.1.5.7.2.6.2.1s}$, b. about 1778, and m. George Stump.
Isaac$^{1.1.5.7.2.6.2.2s}$, b. in 1780.
Daughter$^{1.1.5.7.2.6.2.3s}$, b. about 1782, and m. Felix Seymour.
Jacob$^{1.1.5.7.2.6.2.4s}$, b. in 1784, m. Catherine Clark and Margaret, and resided in Pickaway County, Darby Township, Ohio, in 1850.
Abraham$^{1.1.5.7.2.6.2.5s}$, b. on Jan. 22, 1788.
??Michael$^{1.1.5.7.2.6.2.6s}$, b. about 1792, and m. Rebecca Yoacum in Hardy County on Nov. 10, 1813 (not proven to be a son).
Daughter$^{1.1.5.7.2.6.2.7s}$, probably the Sarah, that m. John Stump in Hardy County on June 4, 1814 (not proven to be a daughter).

??Ann$^{1.1.5.7.2.6.2.8s}$, b. about 1800, and m. William Miller in Hardy County on Apr. 25, 1821 (not proven to be a daughter).

Isaac Neff

Isaac$^{1.1.5.7.2.6.2.2s}$ m. Jane, son of Charles and Esther Wilson, in Hardy County, Virginia, on May 19, 1806. She was b. in Hardy County, Virginia, in 1783. They resided in Madison County, Pleasant Township, Ohio, in 1830. In about 1833, they moved to Marion County, Salt Rock Township, Ohio, where he had 185 acres. Between 1836 and Jan. 1837, he moved to Indiana. He purchased 160 acres in Delaware Township on Aug. 1, 1840 (purchased from John Russell of Marion County, Ohio). They resided in Delaware County, Delaware Township, Indiana, in Sep. 1850. Isaac and Jane had the following children:

Daughter$^{1.1.5.7.2.6.2.2.1s}$, b. in Hardy County, Virginia, about 1807.

Charles$^{1.1.5.7.2.6.2.2.2s}$, b. in Hardy County in 1810.

Isaac$^{1.1.5.7.2.6.2.2.3s}$, b. in Hardy County in 1812.

Mary Ann$^{1.1.5.7.2.6.2.2.4s}$, b. in Hardy County about 1814, and m. Christopher Wilson in Delaware County, Indiana, on Jan. 22, 1837.

Daughter$^{1.1.5.7.2.6.2.2.5s}$, b. in Hardy County about 1816.

Amelia$^{1.1.5.7.2.6.2.2.6s}$, b. in Hardy County in 1818.

Catherine J.$^{1.1.5.7.2.6.2.2.7s}$, b. in Hardy County in 1820.

Son$^{1.1.5.7.2.6.2.2.8s}$, b. in Hardy County in 1822.

Adelia$^{1.1.5.7.2.6.2.2.9s}$, b. in Hardy County on Aug. 6, 1823, m. Henry Bright in Delaware County, Indiana, on Mar. 26, 1850, and d. in Buchanan County, Otterville, Iowa, on Aug. 23, 1898.

John M.$^{1.1.5.7.2.6.2.2.10s}$, b. in Hardy County in 1826.

Van Seymour$^{1.1.5.7.2.6.2.2.11s}$, b. in Hardy County in 1829.

Charles Neff

Charles$^{1.1.5.7.2.6.2.2.2s}$ m. Abigail Greene (b. in New Jersey in 1819) in Marion County, Ohio, on Sep. 1, 1834, and resided in Franklin County, Clinton Township, Iowa, in 1860. They resided in Delaware County, Indiana, in 1850. They had the following children:

John G.$^{1.1.5.7.2.6.2.2.2.1s}$, b. in 1842.

Isaac Neff

Isaac$^{1.1.5.7.2.6.2.2.3s}$ m. Sarah Cochran in Delaware County, Indiana, on Aug. 8, 1841, and resided in Delaware Township in 1860. They had the following children:

Archibald S. H.$^{1.1.5.7.2.6.2.2.3.1s}$, b. in 1844, m. Isabella Moore on Dec. 29, 1867, and Viola M. Travel on June 16, 1900, and d. in Delaware County, Eaton, on Aug. 14, 1911.

George W.$^{1.1.5.7.2.6.2.2.3.2s}$, b. in 1846.

Marietta$^{1.1.5.7.2.6.2.2.3.3s}$, b. in 1848.

Delila J.$^{1.1.5.7.2.6.2.2.3.4s}$, b. in Dec. 1849.

Amelia Neff

Amelia$^{1.1.5.7.2.6.2.2.6s}$ m. Charles Flamerfelt (b. in New Jersey in 1811) in Marion County, Ohio, on Sep. 19, 1836, and had the following children:

John W.$^{1.1.5.7.2.6.2.2.6.1s}$, b. in Ohio in 1838.

Genetta$^{1.1.5.7.2.6.2.2.6.2s}$, b. in Indiana in 1845.

Rachel$^{1.1.5.7.2.6.2.2.6.3s}$, b. in 1848.

Catherine J. Neff

Catherine J.$^{1.1.5.7.2.6.2.2.7s}$ m. William Russell in Delaware County, Indiana, on July 1, 1841, and had the following children there:

Sarah E.$^{1.1.5.7.2.6.2.2.7.1s}$, b. in 1842.

Stephen S.$^{1.1.5.7.2.6.2.2.7.2s}$, b. in 1844.

Mariah C.$^{1.1.5.7.2.6.2.2.7.3s}$, b. in 1848.

John M. Neff

John M.$^{1.1.5.7.2.6.2.2.10s}$ m. Eveline Fishburn in Delaware County, Indiana, on Sep. 25, 1851, and d. in Delaware County, Eaton, Indiana, on June 18, 1892. Eveline d. in Eaton on Nov. 23, 1912, aged 78. They had the following children in Delaware Township:

David M.$^{1.1.5.7.2.6.2.2.10.1h}$, b. in 1855.

Viola$^{1.1.5.7.2.6.2.2.10.2h}$, b. in 1858.

Van Seymour Neff

Van Seymour$^{1.1.5.7.2.6.2.2.11s}$ m. Alice Ross in Delaware County, Indiana, on May 28, 1852. They had the following children in Delaware Township:

John H.$^{1.1.5.7.2.6.2.2.11.1s}$, b. in 1855 in Indiana.

William J.$^{1.1.5.7.2.6.2.2.11.2s}$, b. about 1857 in Iowa.

Mary Jane$^{1.1.5.7.2.6.2.2.11.3s}$, b. in 1859 in Indiana.

Abraham Neff

Abraham$^{1.1.5.7.2.6.2.5s}$ m. _____ _____ (probably Rachel, daughter of Charles and Esther Wilson) about 1808/9, and Margaret Osborne in Madison County, Ohio, on Apr. 1, 1831. Abraham's first wife d. in Madison County, Pleasant Township, Ohio, sometime before 1830. Margaret was b. on Mar. 2, 1794, and d. in Marion County, Salt Rock Township, Ohio, on Feb 22, 1849. Abraham moved to Madison County, Ohio, between 1820 and 1821, and moved to Marion County, Ohio, in 1830. On Jan. 8, 1831, Marion County officials asked him to appraise a black gelding found by Moses Sailor. Abraham d. in Salt Rock Township on Apr. 30, 1846. Abraham and Margaret are buried in Neff cemetery. Abraham had the following children (Nancy is listed here because her marriage was in Marion County, Ohio, after Abraham's brother, Isaac, moved to Indiana, and Rebecca is placed here because she was b. in the same year as Isaac's son, Isaac, but they do not appear in Abraham's will):

Elizabeth Davis$^{1.1.5.7.2.6.2.5.1s}$, b. in Hardy County about 1809.

Esther Ann$^{1.1.5.7.2.6.2.5.2s}$, b. in Hardy County in 1811.

Rebecca$^{1.1.5.7.2.6.2.5.3s}$, b. in Hardy County in 1812. She was not listed in the will, and has not been proven as a daughter of Abraham.

Charles W.$^{1.1.5.7.2.6.2.5.4s}$, b. in Hardy County about 1814, and m. Hannah Mariah McCrea in Marion County, Ohio, on Apr. 10, 1836.

John G.$^{1.1.5.7.2.6.2.5.5s}$, b. in Hardy County in 1816.

Jacob R.$^{1.1.5.7.2.6.2.5.6s}$, b. in Hardy County on Aug. 1, 1818.

Corbin I.$^{1.1.5.7.2.6.2.5.7s}$, b. in Madison County, Pleasant Township, Ohio, in 1822.

Nancy$^{1.1.5.7.2.6.2.5.8s}$, b. in Madison County, Pleasant Township, Ohio, on Nov. 4, 1824, and m. _____ Griffith and Samuel Harruff. She was not in the will, and has not been proven as a daughter of Abraham.

Elizabeth Davis Neff

Elizabeth Davis$^{1.1.5.7.2.6.2.5.1s}$ m. John M. Greene in Madison County on Feb. 2, 1830, and d. before July 1846. They had the following children:

Rachel Eliza Ann$^{1.1.5.7.2.6.2.5.1.1s}$, b. about 1831, and mentioned in Abraham Neff's will.

Esther Ann Neff

Esther Ann$^{1.1.5.7.2.6.2.5.2s}$ m. Harvey Tanner in Madison County on Aug. 19, 1830. She resided in Pickaway County, Darby Township, Ohio, in 1850, and 1860. Harvey was b. in Ohio in 1806. They had the following children:

Courtney$^{1.1.5.7.2.6.2.5.2.1s}$, b. in 1835, and m. Hester McDowell in Pickaway County on Apr. 24, 1872. He was a merchant in Darby Township in 1860.

Mary J.$^{1.1.5.7.2.6.2.5.2.2s}$, b. in 1841.

Rebecca Neff

Rebecca$^{1.1.5.7.2.6.2.5.3s}$ m. Archibald S. Hanna in Marion County, Ohio, on Nov. 16, 1837, and d. after 1860 in St. Joseph County, Warren Township, Indiana. She moved to Indiana in 1843. Archibald was b. in Pennsylvania in 1802. Archibald and Rebecca had the following children:

Minerva$^{1.1.5.7.2.6.2.5.3.1s}$, b. in 1840.
Esther$^{1.1.5.7.2.6.2.5.3.2s}$, b. in 1842.
Joseph$^{1.1.5.7.2.6.2.5.3.3s}$, b. in Indiana in 1844.
Daniel$^{1.1.5.7.2.6.2.5.3.4s}$, b. in Indiana in 1845.
Archibald$^{1.1.5.7.2.6.2.5.3.5s}$, b. in 1848, and m. Emiline Mikesell in St. Joseph County on Oct. 31, 1872. Possibly this was a second marriage of his father.

James D.$^{1.1.5.7.2.6.2.5.3.6s}$, b. in 1849, and m. Alwilda Lindley in St. Joseph County on Nov. 13, 1873.

Emma$^{1.1.5.7.2.6.2.5.3.7s}$, m. Wilbur H. Barker in St. Joseph County on Nov. 10, 1874.

John G. Neff

John G.$^{1.1.5.7.2.6.2.5.5s}$ m. Catherine Faroute in Marion County, Ohio, on July 14, 1844. He resided in Marion County, Salt Rock Township, Ohio, in 1850, and in Allen County, German Township in 1870 and 1880. He moved to Marion County, Ohio, in 1832, and Allen County, Lima, Ohio, in 1862. They had the following children:

Corbin C.$^{1.1.5.7.2.6.2.5.5.1s}$, b. on Dec. 22, 1844, and d. on Jan. 24, 1845. He is buried in Neff cemetery.

Henry C.$^{1.1.5.7.2.6.2.5.5.2s}$, b. on June 20, 1846, m. M. Jennie, daughter of Michael Mauk, in Allen County on Oct. 13, 1870. He had children Bert, Blanche, Corbin, Bessie, and Katie (d. age 2). He was the foreman of the Lima Paper Mills.

Princess O.$^{1.1.5.7.2.6.2.5.5.3s}$, b. in 1848. She resided in Marion, Ohio.

Alice L.$^{1.1.5.7.2.6.2.5.5.4s}$, b. in May 1850, m. Henry C. Bolton in Allen County on Nov. 30, 1871, and d. on Mar. 26, 1884. They had a son, Frank.

Esther A.$^{1.1.5.7.2.6.2.5.5.5s}$, b. in 1854, and m. Robert, son of David and Elizabeth (Evans) Davis, on Dec. 14, 1875. He was b. in Butler County, Paddy's Run, Ohio, on Nov. 10, 1852. He was a general merchant in Monroe Township, and was the Mayor of West Cairo. They had Elsie May and Donald.

Howard L.$^{1.1.5.7.2.6.2.5.5.6s}$, b. in 1856.

Harvey T.$^{1.1.5.7.2.6.2.5.5.7s}$, b. in 1863.

Jacob R. Neff

Jacob R.$^{1.1.5.7.2.6.2.5.6s}$ m. Isabella Dalzell in Marion County on Mar. 31, 1841, and d. in Marion County, Salt Rock Township, Ohio, on Aug. 28, 1893. She was b. in Ireland on Apr. 8, 1815, and d. on Aug. 19, 1909. They are buried in Grand Prairie cemetery in Grand Prairie Township. They had the following children in Marion County, Salt Rock Township:

Rachel$^{1.1.5.7.2.6.2.5.6.1s}$, b. on Dec. 30, 1842, and d. on May 4, 1852. She is buried in Neff cemetery.

Eliza$^{1.1.5.7.2.6.2.5.6.2s}$, b. in 1844.

Jane Ann$^{1.1.5.7.2.6.2.5.6.3s}$, b. in 1847.

Abraham$^{1.1.5.7.2.6.2.5.6.4s}$, b. on Dec. 2, 1848, and d. on May 5, 1852. He is buried in Neff cemetery.

Mary$^{1.1.5.7.2.6.2.5.6.5s}$, b. in 1853.

Emma$^{1.1.5.7.2.6.2.5.6.6s}$, b. in 1855.

Willie D.$^{1.1.5.7.2.6.2.5.6.7s}$, b. on Oct. 21, 1857, and d. on Dec. 15, 1891. He is buried in Grand Prairie cemetery.

Jacob$^{1.1.5.7.2.6.2.5.6.8s}$, b. in Feb. 1860.

Corbin I. Neff

Corbin I.$^{1.1.5.7.2.6.2.5.7s}$ m. Harriet E. Faroute (b. in Ohio/New York in 1827) in Marion County, Ohio, on Oct. 20, 1842. They resided in Marion County, Grande Prairie Township, Ohio, in 1850, and Allen County, Lima, Ohio, in 1870. He was a Physician, and in Apr. 1861, agreed to furnish free medical services for families of Civil War volunteers during their absence. On June 2, 1863, he was the surgeon of the enrollment board. He was a trustee in 1860, and Mason in the Lima Lodge in 1874 and 1875. They had the following children:

Infant$^{1.1.5.7.2.6.2.5.7.1s}$, d. on July 12, 1846, and is buried in Neff cemetery.
Frances M.$^{1.1.5.7.2.6.2.5.7.2s}$, b. in 1848.
Howard$^{1.1.5.7.2.6.2.5.7.3s}$, b. on Sep. 19, 1852, and d. on Mar. 17, 1853. He is buried in Neff cemetery.

Henry Neff

Henry$^{1.1.5.7.2.6.3s}$ d. in Hardy County, Virginia, in Apr. 1801. He had 6 people in his household according to the 1782 tax list, and 7 in 1784. He had the following children:
Leonard$^{1.1.5.7.2.6.3.1s}$, b. about 1779, m. Lydia, and resided in Ross County, Ohio, in 1830. He was taxed in Hardy County in 1800.
Daughter$^{1.1.5.7.2.6.3.2s}$, b. about 1781, and m. Jacob Nicholas.
Cornelius$^{1.1.5.7.2.6.3.3s}$, b. about 1784, and m. Catherine Cook in Ross County, Ohio, on Apr. 3, 1805. He resided in Madison County, Ohio, in 1830.
Hannah$^{1.1.5.7.2.6.3.4s}$, b. about 1786.
Lydia$^{1.1.5.7.2.6.3.5s}$, b. about 1787, and m. Thomas McCollister in Ross County, Ohio, on Sep. 21, 1809.
Susanna$^{1.1.5.7.2.6.3.6s}$, b. about 1789, and m. Henry Cutright in Ross County on Oct. 18, 1810.
Jonathan$^{1.1.5.7.2.6.3.7s}$, b. about 1791, and m. Peggy Woods in Ross County on Aug. 15, 1811.
George$^{1.1.5.7.2.6.3.8s}$, b. about 1793, and m. Peggy Harper in Ross County on Dec. 22, 1814.
Samuel$^{1.1.5.7.2.6.3.9s}$, b. about 1795.
Madaline$^{1.1.5.7.2.6.3.10s}$, b. about 1797.
Michael$^{1.1.5.7.2.6.3.11s}$, b. about 1799.

George Neff

George$^{1.1.5.7.2.6.6s}$ resided in Hardy County, Virginia, in 1820 and moved to Pickaway County, Ohio, before 1827. He had 6 people in his household according to the 1782 tax list, and 5 people in 1784. He was taxed in Darby Township from 1827 to 1830. He d. in Pickaway County, Darby Township in Nov. 1840, and his will was probated in Hardy County, Virginia. He had the following children:
George$^{1.1.5.7.2.6.6.1s}$, b. in 1786, m. Elizabeth, and possibly Elizabeth Alkire in Madison County, Ohio, on Oct. 4, 1829. He resided in Pickaway County, Darby Township, Ohio, in 1850.
Elizabeth$^{1.1.5.7.2.6.6.2s}$, b. about 1787, m. ____ Wilson, and d. before 1838.

Absalom[1.1.5.7.2.6.6.3s], b. in 1797, m. Jane, and resided in Pickaway County, Darby Township, Ohio, in 1830 and 1850. He was taxed in Darby Township from 1827 to 1830. He was not mentioned in the will.

Elijah[1.1.5.7.2.6.6.4s], b. in 1799, and m. Mary Ann, daughter of Jacob and Amelia Neff, in Hardy County on June 17, 1830, and granddaughter of Jacob and Margaret Neff.

Peter[1.1.5.7.2.6.6.5s], b. in 1803, m. Lydia, and d. in 1877. She was b. in 1805.

Enoch[1.1.5.7.2.6.6.6s], b. in 1808, and m. Rebecca C. Jefferson in Hardy County on Nov. 27, 1828.

Jacob Neff

Jacob[1.1.5.7.2.6.7s] d. in Hardy County, Virginia, in Feb. 1849. He had 4 people in his household according to the 1784 tax list. He m. Margaret. She was b. in 1762, and was alive in 1850. They had the following children in Hardy County:

Jacob[1.1.5.7.2.6.7.1s], b. in 1783, and d. in Hardy County in May 1865. He m. Amelia. She was b. in 1792, and d. on Mar. 10, 1860.

Abraham[1.1.5.7.2.6.7.2s], b. in 1784, m. Elizabeth Shook, and d. in 1859. She was b. in 1791, and d. before 1860.

Susanna[1.1.5.7.2.6.7.3s], b. about 1786, and m. Edward Hopper in Hardy County on July 31, 1805.

John[1.1.5.7.2.6.7.4s], b. in 1788, and m. Mary, daughter of Charles and Esther Wilson, in Hardy County on June 3, 1813, and resided in Pickaway County, Darby Township, Ohio, in 1850.

Elizabeth[1.1.5.7.2.6.7.5s], b. about 1790, and d. in 1866.

Leonard[1.1.5.7.2.6.7.6s], b. about 1793, and d. before 1839.

Isaac[1.1.5.7.2.6.7.7s], b. about 1796, m. Phebe, and d. in Franklin County, Ohio, before Nov. 1853. He resided in Franklin County in 1830.

Anna[1.1.5.7.2.6.7.8s], b. in 1800, and m. George S. Craigen in Hardy County on Sep. 9, 1816.

Margaret[1.1.5.7.2.6.7.9s], b. in 1803, and was alive in 1860.

Washington H.[1.1.5.7.2.6.7.10s], b. in 1806, and was alive in 1860.

Mary Ann[1.1.5.7.2.6.7.11s], b. about 1808, and m. Elijah, son of George Neff.

Johann Georg Neff

Johann Georg[1.1.5.7.2.8s] m. Maria Elisabeth, daughter of Martin Stupp, and d. in Lancaster County, Heidelberg Township, Pennsylvania, in Mar. 1773. His will was written on Aug. 16, 1772, and probated in Mar. 1775. After Georg's death, she m. Adam Deininger (before 1781). They had the following children:

Johann Georg[1.1.5.7.2.8.1s], b. on Nov. 30, 1754, m. Maria Catharina Moss, and d. in Aug. 1812.

Michael[1.1.5.7.2.8.2s], b. on May 15, 1756, m. Christina Kapp, and d. in Wythe County, Virginia, on Jan. 15, 1825. She was b. in 1756, and d. on Mar. 13, 1830.

Johann Jacob[1.1.5.7.2.8.3s], b. on Oct. 4, 1758, m. Elisabeth, and resided in Somerset County, Pennsylvania.

Christina Elisabeth[1.1.5.7.2.8.4s], b. on Apr. 22, 1759, and m. Peter Kapp.

Catharina[1.1.5.7.2.8.5s], b. in 1761, and m. John Burns.

Leonhard[1.1.5.7.2.8.6s], b. on May 22, 1763, m. Margaretha, daughter of Johannes Salomonmuller in Somerset County, Pennsylvania, about 1785, and Elisabeth Bowing. He d. in Jessamine County, Kentucky in Oct. 1844.

Maria Eva[1.1.5.7.2.8.7s], b. on Mar. 16, 1765, and m. Henry Wiseman.

Elisabeth[1.1.5.7.2.8.8s], b. in 1767.

Peter[1.1.5.7.2.8.9s], b. on June 6, 1770, m. Mary Granfern on Mar. 4, 1794, and d. in Jessamine County, Kentucky on Sep. 22, 1860. She was b. in Pennsylvania in May 1775, and d. in Kentucky on June 24, 1859.

****

Jacob Schock/Schaak

Jacob[1] was taxed in Lebanon County, Lebanon Township on Nov. 8, 1756 (?also in 1755). In 1756, he had 100 acres. He was taxed there in 1757-58 (150 acres). He m. Barbara (possibly she is a second wife). A Jacob Schock immigrated to America on the ship *Robert and Alice* on Sep. 30, 1743; a Hans Jacob Schoch and Jacob (x) Shack immigrated to America on the ship *Shirley* on Sep. 5, 1751; and a Johan Jacob Schock immigrated to America on the ship *Neptune* on Oct. 7, 1755. It is not sure which of these immigrants is the Jacob Schock of Lebanon. He is believed to have been the father of the following children (he and Barbara are the parents of Anna Elisabetha (possibly Anna Elisabetha is a daughter of Jacob Jr. and a previous wife)):

    Johan Nicholas[1.1], b. about 1741.
    Johan Georg[1.2], b. about 1743.
    Jacob[1.3], b. in 1745.
    Georg Adam[1.4], b. about 1747.
    Casper[1.5], b. about 1749, and was a laborer at Lebanon, Pennsylvania, from 1769 to 1772.
    Ann Elisabetha[1.6], b. in Apr. 1765, baptized by Johan Casper Stoever on May 12, 1765, and sponsored by (Nicholas) Schaack and his wife Elisabeth.

Johan Nicholas Schock/Schaack

    Johan Nicholas[1.1] m. Maria Elisabetha before Jan. 13, 1760 (he and his wife are sponsors to a baptism of Georg, son of Jacob and Dorothea Sprecher, at Hill Lutheran Church on this date), and d. in Dauphin (now Lebanon) County, Lebanon Township, Pennsylvania, in 1806. His will was written on Dec. 30, 1805, and probated on Apr. 7, 1806. He was taxed in Lebanon County, Lebanon Township with Jacob Schock/Schaak in 1758, 59 (100 acres), 69, 70, 71, 72, 79, 80 (140 acres), 81, 83, 85, and 87. In 1769, he had 110 cultivated acres and 30 uncultivated. He appears on the 1790 census of Dauphin County, Pennsylvania, with one male above 16, one male below 16, and two females in his household. His will refers to his land, adjacent to Philip Shack, and the tract that Nicholas and Jacob Shack held together (which Jacob's son, Philip, agreed to divide). Maria Elisabetha's will was written in Dauphin County, Lebanon Township on Dec. 19, 1806, and probated on Aug. 21/December 10, 1810. They had the following children:

    Maria[1.1.1], b. about 1764.
    Elisabetha[1.1.2], b. about 1766.
    Michael[1.1.3], baptized at Tabor Lutheran Church in Lebanon, Pennsylvania, on Nov. 24, 1768, and sponsored by Adam and Catharina Elisabetha Schally.
    Catharina Elisabetha[1.1.4], b. on May 16, 1771, baptized at Tabor Lutheran on June 23, 1771, and sponsored by Adam and Catharina Elisabetha Schally.
    Magdalena[1.1.5], b. on Sep. 28, 1775, baptized at Tabor Lutheran on Nov. 5, 1775, and sponsored by Adam and Catharina Elisabetha Schally.

Maria Schaak

Maria$^{1.1.1}$ m. Ludwick Dornman, and had the following children:

Magdalena$^{1.1.1.1}$, b. on May 26, 1787, baptized at Tabor Lutheran on July 1, 1787, and sponsored by Maria Elisabetha Schack.

Susanna$^{1.1.1.2}$, b. on May 9, 1789, baptized at Tabor Lutheran on June 14, 1789, and sponsored by Johan Nicholas Schack and wife.

Elisabetha$^{1.1.1.3}$, b. on May 1, 1792, baptized at Tabor Lutheran on May 27, 1792, and sponsored by Gottfried Eichelberger and wife.

Elizabeth Schaak

Elisabetha$^{1.1.2}$ m. Georg Frantz/Francis, and had the following children:

Elisabeth$^{1.1.2.1}$, b. on Dec. 6, 1799, baptized at Bindnagel Lutheran Church in Lebanon County on May 11, 1800, and sponsored by Johannes Zehring.

Catharina Elisabetha Schaak

Catharina Elisabetha$^{1.1.4}$ m. Lucas Schally. Lucas d. before 1806. They had the following children:

Johannes$^{1.1.4.1}$, b. on May 5, 1796, baptized at Tabor Lutheran on Sep. 4, 1796, and sponsored by Nicholas and Maria Elisabetha Schack.

Magdalena$^{1.1.4.2}$, b. on Jan. 3, 1798, baptized at Tabor Lutheran on June 10, 1798, and sponsored by Magdalena Schallin.

Georg Schock

Georg$^{1.2}$ was b. in the Shana River Valley, Germany, about 1743. He is probably the Johan Georg Schock that m. Anna Catarina$^{1.1.2a}$, daughter of Johann Michael and Maria Christina (Schwingel) Maurer, in Lebanon County, Lebanon, Pennsylvania, on June 25, 1765, by Johan Casper Stover (he was of Lebanon, and she of Heidelberg), and the Johann Georg Schick that m. Eva Maria, daughter of Johannes and Susanna Catharina (Sattelthaler) Schoeneberger, in Frederick County, Middletown Evangelical Lutheran Church on May 23, 1774 (proclaimed on May 8, 12, and 13). Johannes Schoeneberger (soldier) m. Susanna Catharina Sattelthaler in Trinity Lutheran Church, Lancaster County, Lancaster, Pennsylvania, on Sep. 19, 1757, and had the following children: Eva Maria, b. on Sep. 25, 1758, baptized at Trinity Lutheran on Oct. 1, 1758, and sponsored by

Andreas and Eva Maria Klein; Michael, who appears on records of Frederick County, Maryland; and Johann Ernst, b. on Sep. 26, 1764, baptized at Trinity Lutheran on Oct. 21, 1764, and sponsored by Ludwig and Juliana Schiller. Johan Georg Schock was a communicant at Trinity Lutheran Church in Lancaster, Pennsylvania, on Mar. 8, 1767, and Catharina was a communicant there in Apr. 1768. Georg Shock was taxed in Bedford County, Hopewell Township, Pennsylvania, from 1774 to 1776, and 1779 to 1783. In 1779, he had 30 acres, two horses, and two cattle, and in 1783, he had two horses. In 1784, and from 1788 to 1791, he was taxed in Bedford (now Somerset) County, Quemahoning Township. In 1784, he was listed with three whites; in 1787, he had a warrantee of 200 acres; in 1788 he had two horses and two cattle; in 1789, he had 100 acres, two horses, and two cattle; in 1790, he had 300 acres, two horses, and three cattle; and in 1791, he had two horses and four cattle. In these records, his name appears as Schock, Shock, Shook, Sheck, Shick, Shake, Shuck, and Sheek, Shuk, and Shooke. In 1789, he is listed in the Quemahoning Township Militia. In 1792, the part of Quemahoning Township that he was residing in became Stoney Creek Township, where he d. sometime after Feb. 1802. He was taxed there from 1792 to 1798. In 1792 and 1796, he is listed as a weaver. In 1797, he had 200 acres, two horses, and four cattle. In 1798, he had a 15' x 25' house and a 25' x 25' barn adjacent to Michael Peterman. He appears on the 1800 census of Stoney Creek Township, and was sued there by Gudleip Nitts in May 1801. In Feb. 1802, a jury was called in the suit. On June 7, 1806, he was certified 206 acres located on the east side of Stoney Creek in Stoney Creek Township, adjacent to Michael Peterson and John Wells, land said to belong to Dr. Smith, and Stoney Creek. Pursuant to a warrant dated May 31, 1787, for 200 acres. That is the last reference found regarding Georg. He had the following children:

George$^{1.2.1t}$, b. about 1766.

Eve$^{1.2.2t}$, b. in 1775, and m. Phillip, son of Johan Nicholas and Catharina Shultz.

Anna Maria$^{1.2.3t}$, b. about 1777.

Catharina$^{1.2.4t}$, b. on Feb. 26, 1778 (to Georg and Eva Scheck), baptized by Baltzer Meyer in Westmoreland County, Hempfield Township, Harrold Zion Lutheran Church on Sep. 13, 1778, and sponsored by Johan Balthasar and Catharina Durr.

Elizabeth$^{1.2.5t}$, b. about 1779. She sponsored her nephew, George Weimer, at his baptism in 1798.

George Shock

George[1.2.1t] m. Elizabeth, daughter of Johann Nicholas and Catharina Shultz, about 1795 in Bedford County, Brother's Valley Township, Pennsylvania. George was a linen weaver. He is presumed to be the George taxed in Quemahoning Township with 2 horses and 2 cattle in 1790, and in 1793. In 1798, he was taxed in Somerset County, Londonderry Township, Pennsylvania, on Savage Mountain, and appeared there in the 1800 census. In 1800, he had a 18' x 20' house and a 18' x 25' barn. In Sep. 1802, he may have been in Elk Lick Township, where he was a tenant in possession, sued for ejectment by Michael Simpson. In May 1805, Michael Simpson sued him again for Capias Trespass Quare Clausum Fregit. He appears on the 1810, 1820, and 1830 censuses of Elk Lick Township. According to family tradition, George and Elizabeth were residing in Coshocton County, Mill Creek Township, Ohio, in 1836, and d. there. They had the following children:

Jacob[1.2.1.1t], b. in Stoney Creek Township about 1796.

George[1.2.1.2t], b. in Londonderry Township, in 1798, m. Elizabeth (b. 1786), and resided in Elk Lick Township in 1840, and Milford Township in 1850.

Daughter[1.2.1.3t], b. about 1799.

Peter[1.2.1.4t], b. on Feb. 5, 1800.

Henry[1.2.1.5t], b. in Elk Lick Township about 1803, and resided in Elk Lick Township in 1830.

Daughter[1.2.1.6t], b. about 1805 (note: an Elizabeth was b. on Apr. 12, 1808, and baptized to a George and Elizabeth Schueck in Westmoreland County, Greensburg First Lutheran Church on Oct. 26, 1808).

Joseph[1.2.1.7t], b. about 1807, and resided in Elk Lick Township in 1830.

Adam[1.2.1.8t], b. on Jan. 20, 1809, baptized at Salisbury German Reformed Church on Apr. 30, 1809, and d. in Elk Lick Township before 1820.

Samuel George Washington[1.2.1.9t], b. in 1810.

Daughter[1.2.1.10t], b. about 1812.

Son[1.2.1.11t], b. about 1814.

Son[1.2.1.12t], b. about 1816.

Jacob Shock

Jacob[1.2.1.1t] m. Catherine Miller about 1816, and d. in Elk Lick Township before 1850. She was residing in Allegany County,

Maryland, in 1850. They had the following children in Elk Lick Township:

Elizabeth$^{1.2.1.1.1t}$, b. about 1817, m. Eli Engle in Somerset County, Pennsylvania, on May 5, 1837, and resided in Allegheny County, Maryland, in 1850.

Jeremiah$^{1.2.1.1.2t}$, b. in 1818, and d. in 1834.

John$^{1.2.1.1.3t}$, b. on Nov. 25, 1822.

Samuel$^{1.2.1.1.4t}$, b. on Jan. 21, 1823.

William Urias$^{1.2.1.1.5t}$, b. on Jan. 7, 1826.

Eliza$^{1.2.1.1.6t}$, b. in 1831, m. Elias Lint in Somerset County on July 31, 1851, and resided in Greenville Township in 1850.

Jeffery$^{1.2.1.1.7t}$, b. in 1833, and resided in Greeneville Township in 1850.

Amos$^{1.2.1.1.8t}$, b. in 1835, and resided in Summit Township in 1850.

John Shock

John$^{1.2.1.1.3t}$ m. Susanna, daughter of Peter and Barbara (Garletts) Engle, and resided in Greenville Township in 1850. They had the following children:

Lydia$^{1.2.1.1.3.1t}$, b. in 1842.

Emily$^{1.2.1.1.3.2t}$, b. in 1843.

James$^{1.2.1.1.3.3t}$, b. in 1845.

Margaret$^{1.2.1.1.3.4t}$, b. in 1846.

Mary F.$^{1.2.1.1.3.5t}$, b. on Feb. 17, 1848.

Elia Noah Webster$^{1.2.1.1.3.6t}$, b. on Apr. 28, 1855.

Samuel Shock

Samuel$^{1.2.1.1.4t}$ m. Catherine Barkley (b. 1825) in Somerset County in 1845, and resided in Elk Lick Township in 1850. They had the following children:

Eliza$^{1.2.1.1.4.1t}$, b. in 1847.

Zacheriah$^{1.2.1.1.4.2t}$, b. in 1848.

William Urias Shock

William Urias$^{1.2.1.1.5t}$ m. Mary Ann Patton (b. 1827) in Somerset County on Dec. 25, 1846, and resided in Elk Lick Township in 1850. They had the following children:

Catherine$^{1.2.1.1.5.1t}$, b. on Apr. 20, 1848.

Eli$^{1.2.1.1.5.2t}$, b. in 1850.

Amanda$^{1.2.1.1.5.3t}$, b. on July 7, 1853.

Maggie A.$^{1.2.1.1.5.4t}$, b. on Aug. 5, 1861.
William Urias$^{1.2.1.1.5.5t}$, b. on Jan. 13, 1862, and m. Rachel Jane May on Oct. 7, 1880.

Peter Shock

Peter$^{1.2.1.4t}$ m. Mary Ann, daughter of James and Anna Maria (Jauler) Boyd, in Somerset County, Pennsylvania, on Apr. 22, 1827. About 1829, Peter moved from Elk Lick/Greeneville Township to Addison Township, where he farmed 40 acres of government land. In Apr. 1832, he and Mary Ann sold their land in Greenville Township (probably Mary Ann's inheritance) to their brother-in-law, Solomon Hutzell, and in Nov. 1835, sold the remainder to John Walker. On June 6, 1837, Peter purchased land in Coshocton County, Ohio, but did not make the move to Ohio until 1840. In 1846, he moved to Allen County, Amanda Township, where he farmed 50 acres in section 34. In 1886, he moved to Mercer County, Black Creek Township, Ohio, and purchased 80 acres. While they resided in Black Creek Township, Peter and Mary lived with their son, Levi, and in 1892, moved in with their daughter, Sarah. Peter and Mary were members of the Dunkard Church until 1855, when they converted to the United Brethren Church. In their old age, both lost their sight. Peter d. in Mercer County, Black Creek Township, Ohio, on Nov. 13, 1895, and Mary Ann on Oct. 1, 1895. They are buried in Fountain Chapel cemetery. They had the following children:

Levi$^{1.2.1.4.1t}$, b. on May 9, 1828, and m. Mary Jane Carr in Allen County, Ohio, on Feb. 8, 1851 and Mary Albert in Coshocton County, Ohio, on Mar. 30, 1869. Mary Carr was b. in Ohio in 1831, and d. in Mercer County, Black Creek Township, Ohio, on Dec. 31, 1868. Mary Albert was b. in Coshocton County, Ohio, on Nov. 27, 1822, and d. in Black Creek Township on July 30, 1905. Levi d. in Mercer County, Rockford, Ohio, on July 3, 1912.

Elizabeth$^{1.2.1.4.2t}$, b. on Dec. 25, 1829, m. David Eaton Baxter in Allen County, Ohio, on Jan. 30, 1851, and d. in Allen County on Nov. 5, 1921. He was b. in Ross County, Ohio, on Apr. 28, 1828, and d. on July 4, 1927.

Huldah Ann$^{1.2.1.4.3t}$, b. on Sep. 1, 1832, m. Reuben R. Carr in Allen County, Ohio, on Dec. 4, 1852, and d. in Lucas County, Toledo, Ohio, on July 2, 1909. He was b. in Ohio on May 2, 1832, and d. in Mercer County, Black Creek Township, Ohio, on June 16, 1909.

Carlisle$^{1.2.1.4.4t}$, b. on Jan. 1, 1835, m. Amos Crites in Allen County, Ohio, on Aug. 17, 1854, and d. in Allen County on May 18,

1918. He was b. in Fairfield County, Ohio, on Nov. 18, 1832, and d. in Buckland, Ohio, on Mar. 4, 1919.

Catherine$^{1.2.1.4.5t}$, b. on May 21, 1837, m. Joseph Daniel Allen in Allen County, Ohio, on Dec. 31, 1859, and d. in Allen County, Allentown, Ohio, on July 4, 1927. He was b. on Dec. 6, 1838, and d. in Allen County on Oct. 29, 1918.

George$^{1.2.1.4.6t}$, b. on Oct. 14, 1839, m. Nancy, daughter of Lewis and Elizabeth (Shope) Herring, in Allen County, Ohio, on Oct. 7, 1862, and d. in Mercer County, Black Creek Township, Ohio, on Nov. 28, 1892. George farmed 20 acres in section 34 in Allen County, Amanda Township, Ohio, until 1886, when he moved to Mercer County, Black Creek Township, Ohio, where he took up 20 acres in section 24. George did from a heart attack suffered while clearing this land. Nancy d. in Paulding County, Payne, Ohio, about 1894, while residing with her sons, that were clearing trees. George is buried in Fountain Chapel cemetery, and Nancy's grave has not been located.

Sarah$^{1.2.1.4.7t}$, b. on Mar. 16, 1842, m. Hiram Baxter in Allen County, Ohio, on Dec. 10, 1863 and William C. Wagoner in Allen County on July 29, 1866. She d. in Mercer County, Rockford, Ohio, on Mar. 19, 1913. William was b. in Allen County, Ohio, on Apr. 26, 1845, and d. in Mercer County, Black Creek Township, Ohio, on Aug. 11, 1926.

Mary Ann$^{1.2.1.4.8t}$, b. on Aug. 17, 1845, had a illegitimate son by Louis McBride, and m. William T. Rumple in Allen County, Ohio, on Apr. 11, 1877. Mary Ann d. in Mercer County, Ohio, on June 13, 1922. William was b. in Carroll County, Ohio, n Jan. 18, 1839, and d. in Mercer County on Dec. 6, 1912.

Elvina$^{1.2.1.4.9t}$, b. on Dec. 11, 1847, m. Asa Binkley in Allen County, Ohio, on Dec. 24, 1871, and d. in Van Wert County, Jackson Township, Ohio, on Aug. 10, 1914. He was b. in Allen County, Ohio, on Dec. 8, 1850, and d. in Van Wert County, Jackson Township, Ohio.

William$^{1.2.1.4.10t}$, b. on Aug. 22, 1850, m. Margaret Elizabeth Kiracoff in Allen County, Ohio, on Apr. 25, 1872, and d. in Allen County, Amanda Township, Ohio, on Nov. 26, 1933. She was b. in Augusta County, Virginia, on Apr. 22, 1951, and d. in Van Wert County, Van Wert, Ohio, on Feb. 1, 1919.

Peter$^{1.2.1.4.11t}$, b. on May 12, 1852, m. Malinda, daughter of Samuel and Catherine (Tester) Shope, in Allen County, Ohio, on Dec. 7, 1876, and d. in Isabella County, Blanchard, Michigan on Mar. 5, 1932. She d. in Defiance County, Ney, Ohio, on Oct. 17, 1918.

Samuel George Washington Shock

Samuel George Washington$^{1.2.1.9t}$ m. Sarah, daughter of Johan Adam and Anna Maria (Glatfelter) Fadley, in Somerset County, Bushtown, Pennsylvania, on Apr. 15, 1824, and d. while serving in the Civil War in Alcorn County, Corinth, Mississippi on Mar. 12, 1863. She was b. in Somerset County, Elk Lick Township, Pennsylvania, in 1808, and d. in Indiana on Sep. 15, 1876. They had the following children:

Infant$^{1.2.1.9.1t}$, b. in Somerset County, Elk Lick Township on Jan. 31, 1825, and d. in 1827.

Infant$^{1.2.1.9.2t}$, b. in Elk Lick Township on Jan. 31, 1825, and d. in 1827.

Elizabeth$^{1.2.1.9.3t}$, b. in Elk Lick Township on Feb. 4, 1826, and d. in Aug. 1826.

Catherine$^{1.2.1.9.4t}$, b. in Elk Lick Township on Feb. 4, 1826, and d. in Aug. 1826.

Azariah R.$^{1.2.1.9.5t}$, b. in Elk Lick Township on Jan. 13, 1828.

Minerva Jane$^{1.2.1.9.6t}$, b. in Elk Lick Township on June 5, 1830, and m. Joseph Miller in Allen County, Ohio, on May 6, 1852.

Lucretia$^{1.2.1.9.7t}$, b. in Elk Lick Township on June 5, 1833, and m. Caspar Smith in Allen County, Ohio, on Aug. 5, 1855.

Marietta$^{1.2.1.9.8t}$, b. in Washington County, Marietta, Ohio, on Mar. 26, 1835.

Infant$^{1.2.1.9.9t}$, b. and d. in Coshocton County, Mill Creek Township, Ohio, on Apr. 23, 1836.

Infant$^{1.2.1.9.10t}$, b. and d. in Coshocton County, Mill Creek Township, Ohio, on Apr. 23, 1836.

Elisha$^{1.2.1.9.11t}$, b. in Mill Creek Township on July 25, 1840, and d. in Indiana.

Mary Magdalene$^{1.2.1.9.12t}$, b. in Mill Creek Township on July 22, 1843, m. David W. Frock in Clay County, Indiana, on Apr. 11, 1869, and d. in Indiana.

George$^{1.2.1.9.13t}$, b. in Mill Creek Township in 1846, and resided in Clay County, Harrison Township, Indiana, in 1880. He has not been confirmed as a son.

Amanda$^{1.2.1.9.14t}$, b. in Mill Creek Township on Aug. 6, 1847, and m. Tobias Wallrick in Allen County, Ohio, on Jan. 1, 1872.

Caroline$^{1.2.1.9.15t}$, b. in Mill Creek Township on Aug. 6, 1847, and d. before 1850.

John$^{1.2.1.9.16t}$, b. in Mill Creek Township about 1848, and m. Mary Berger in Clay County, Indiana, on May 9, 1868. He has not been proven as a son.

120   EARLY FAMILIES OF PENNSYLVANIA

Azariah R. Shock

Azariah R.$^{1.2.1.9.5t}$ m. Elizabeth Van Horn in Coshocton County, Ohio, on Nov. 25, 1853 and Nancy Cherryholmes in Clay County, Indiana, on Nov. 2, 1873. Azariah resided in Clay County, Harrison Township, Indiana, in 1880. Nancy was b. in Ohio in 1850. Azariah and Elizabeth had the following children:
 Ettie$^{1.2.1.9.5.1t}$, b. in Ohio in 1862.
 Josophene$^{1.2.1.9.5.2t}$, b. in Ohio in 1864.
 Mercy$^{1.2.1.9.5.3t}$, b. in Ohio in 1866.
 Amanda$^{1.2.1.9.5.4t}$, b. in Indiana in 1868.
 Wakefield$^{1.2.1.9.5.5t}$, b. in Indiana in 1870.

Jacob Shock

Jacob$^{1.3t}$ m. Anna (Maria) Elisabetha, daughter of Daniel and Maria Elisabetha (Stroeher) Angst, in Lebanon County, Lebanon, Pennsylvania, on May 14, 1765 (by Johan Casper Stover) (he was from Lebanon and she from Hanover). Daniel, son of Daniel and Maria (Junker) Angst, was b. in Enkirch, in the Moselle Valley on Apr. 26, 1723, m. Maria Elisabeth, daughter of Johan Nicholas and Eva Maria Stroeher, in Germany on July 3, 1744, and d. in Lebanon County, Annville Township on Nov. 22, 1803. He was taxed in Lebanon Township in 1769, 1770, 1771, 1772, 1779, 1780 (150 acres), 1781, 1783, 1785, and 1787. In 1769, he has 100 cultivated acres, and 45 uncultivated acres. He appears on the 1790 census of Dauphin County, Pennsylvania, with two males over 16, and one male under 16. He d. before 1800. He owned a tract with Nicholas Schaack. Jacob had the following children (also may have been the father of Carll and Andreas Schaack, who were signers of the petition to form Dauphin County about 1785 (along with Philip, Jacob and Hanickel Schaack)):
 Jacob$^{1.3.1t}$, b. about 1766.
 Johannes$^{1.3.2t}$, b. about 1768.
 Philip$^{1.3.3t}$, b. about 1770.
 Johan Georg$^{1.3.4t}$, b. on May 12, 1773, baptized at Tabor Lutheran Church in Lebanon, Pennsylvania, on July 4, 1773, and sponsored by Johan Georg and Susanna Roeslin.

Jacob Schaak

Jacob$^{1.3.1t}$ was taxed as an inmate in 1787, and appeared on the 1790 census of Dauphin County, Pennsylvania, with two males and two females. In 1800, he was in Lebanon Township. He had the following children:

Johann Michael$^{1.3.1.1t}$, b. on Feb. 21, 1787, baptized at Tabor Lutheran on Apr. 29, 1787, and sponsored by Johan Nicholas Schaack and wife.

Henrich$^{1.3.1.2t}$, b. on Aug. 31, 1790, baptized at Tabor Lutheran in Lebanon on Oct. 3, 1790, and sponsored by Henrich Schantzen and wife.

Johannes$^{1.3.1.3t}$, b. on Apr. 14, 1792, baptized at Tabor Lutheran on May 13, 1792, and sponsored by Peter Stecher and wife.

Johannes Schaak

Johannes$^{1.3.2t}$ m. Anna Maria Stein. He resided in HB Township in 1800. They had the following children:

Frantz$^{1.3.2.1t}$, b. on Mar. 14, 1788, and baptized at Hill Lutheran Church in Lebanon County, Pennsylvania, on Apr. 15, 1788.

Johannes$^{1.3.2.2t}$, b. on July 5, 1793, baptized at Tabor Lutheran on Aug. 4, 1793, and sponsored by Jacob Schaack.

Anna Maria$^{1.3.2.3t}$, b. on Nov. 19, 1794, baptized at Tabor Lutheran on Feb. 8, 1795, and sponsored by Jacob Empich and wife.

Jacob$^{1.3.2.4t}$, b. on Oct. 7, 1799, baptized at Tabor Lutheran on Aug. 2, 1800, and sponsored by his parents.

Elisabeth$^{1.3.2.5t}$, baptized at Salem Lutheran Church in Lebanon in Feb. 1802.

Philip Schaak

Philip$^{1.3.3t}$ m. Madelena. He resided in Lebanon Township in 1810, and 1830. They had the following children (all baptized at Salem Lutheran Church in Lebanon, Pennsylvania):

John$^{1.3.3.1t}$, baptized on Apr. 26, 1795.

Johan Philip$^{1.3.3.2t}$, b. on Apr. 16, 1797, baptized at Tabor Lutheran on June 11, 1797, and sponsored by Jacob Schack.

Catherine$^{1.3.3.3t}$, baptized on July 28, 1799.

Jacob$^{1.3.3.4t}$, baptized on May 14, 1801.

Sara$^{1.3.3.5t}$, baptized on May 29, 1803.

Rudolph$^{1.3.3.6t}$, baptized on may 22, 1808.

Georg Adam Schock/Schaak

Georg Adam$^{1.4t}$ m. Maria Barbara. He was taxed as an inmate in Lebanon County, Lebanon Township, Pennsylvania, in 1771. Adam and Maria Barbara had the following children:

Johan Jacob$^{1.4.1t}$, b. on Nov. 7, 1770, baptized at Tabor Lutheran on Nov. 25, 1770, and sponsored by Jacob and Judith Ziegler.

Maria Barbara[1.4.2t], b. on Aug. 5, 1773, baptized at Tabor Lutheran on Aug. 15, 1773, and sponsored by John and Judith Ziegler.
Catharina Elisabetha[1.4.3t], b. on Oct. 17, 1775, baptized at Tabor Lutheran on Nov. 5, 1775, and sponsored by John Ziegler and Elisabeth Schaque/Schaak.

Anna Elisabetha Schock/Schaak

Anna Elisabetha[1.6] was a sponsor to the baptism of Georg Adam Schock's daughter, Catharina Elisabetha in 1775. She m. Michael Leymann, and d. before 1809. On May 15, 1809, her sons (residents of Centre County, Centre Township, Pennsylvania) filed a petition for a bequest from Jacob Schaack's (late of Lebanon Township, deceased) will that was now in possession of Philip Shaak. Michael's will was written in Centre County, Howard Township, Pennsylvania, on Jan. 2, 1843, and probated on May 10, 1843. Michael and Anna Elisabetha had the following children:

Catharina[1.6.1t], b. on Aug. 25, 1790, baptized at Tabor Lutheran on Oct. 3, 1790, and sponsored by Catharina Schaack. She d. before 1843 (probably before 1809).

Johan Jacob[1.6.2t], b. on Mar. 22, 1792, baptized at Tabor Lutheran in Lebanon, Pennsylvania, on Apr. 29, 1792, and sponsored by Johann Jacob Schack.

Michael[1.6.3t], b. about 1794.

****

Jacob Schwingell

Jacob[1u] resided in Remmesweiler in 1537 and 1542. He had the following son:
Mathis[1.1u].

Mathis Schwingel

Mathis[1.1u] was a farmer in Remmesweiler in 1572, and had the following son:
Georg[1.1.1u].

Georg Schwingel

Georg[1.1.1u] was the richest farmer in Remmesweiler in 1625, and had the following son:
Michael[1.1.1.1u], b. about 1627/28.

Michael Schwingel

Michael[1.1.1.1u] m. Anna, daughter of Hans and Marg. N. Heitz, in Ottweiler on Apr. 23, 1650, and d. on June 5, 1694. He was the mayor of Remmesweiler, Oberlinxweiler, and Niederlinxweiler, and church elder. They had the following children (baptized at the Evangelical Lutheran Church in Ottweiler):

Hans Nickel[1.1.1.1.1u], b. on Feb. 21, 1651, m. Anna Katharina Neunkirchen, and d. on Sep. 28, 1674.

Hans Velten[1.1.1.1.2u], b. on Sep. 25, 1653.

Eva Margaretha[1.1.1.1.3u], b. on Mar. 8, 1655, and m. Hans Mikke Hell.

Georg[1.1.1.1.4u], b. about 1657, and m. Barbara, daughter of Simon Konig, in Ottweiler on Oct. 19, 1680.

Hans Jakob[1.1.1.1.5u], b. on June 3, 1660, and m. Anna Leib, daughter of Caspar Schneider on Nov. 16, 1685.

Barbara[1.1.1.1.6u], b. on Mar. 1, 1664, and m. Hans Stefan Schiffler of Niederlinxweiler on Nov. 16, 1685.

Susanne Elisabeth[1.1.1.1.7u], b. on Apr. 22, 1666.

Nikolaus[1.1.1.1.8u], b. on Dec. 12, 1667.

Nikolaus Schwingel

Nikolaus[1.1.1.1.8u] m. Katharina, daughter of Paulus Henrici, in Neunkirchen on July 17, 1691, and d. in Neunkirchen on May 31, 1713. Paulus was and ordnance blacksmith, and in 1711, he and his wife committed their household (a half house) to Nikolaus because he had "helped them both truely and childly in good and bad times during 23 years". On Mar. 9, 1717, the inheritance of Paulus's grandchildren (children of Nikolaus and Katharina) was calculated, indicating he was deceased. Nikolaus was an ordnance blacksmith and church elder in Neunkirchen. After Nikolaus's death, Katharina m. Hanss Velten Kurtz on Nov. 17, 1716. Hanss Velten became mayor of Neunkirchen. Nikolaus and Katharina had the following children in Neunkirchen, Sarrland (baptized at the Neunkirchen Evangelical Lutheran Church):

Anna Barbara[1.1.1.1.8.1u], b. on Nov. 9, 1692, and d. on Jan. 19, 1697.

Hanss Michael[1.1.1.1.8.2u], b. on July 31, 1695, confirmed in 1708, and d. before Apr. 15, 1719.

Hanns Nikolaus/Johan Nickel[1.1.1.1.8.3u], b. on Jan. 26, 1698, and confirmed in 1711.

Johann Georg[1.1.1.1.8.4u], b. on June 19, 1701, and confirmed in 1714.

Johann Jacob$^{1.1.1.1.8.5u}$, b. on Aug. 17, 1704, and d. on Sep. 5, 1704.

Maria Christina$^{1.1.1.1.8.6u}$, b. on Aug. 24, 1705, confirmed in 1719, and m. Hanss Adam Linxweiler.

Susanna Catharina$^{1.1.1.1.8.7u}$, b. on Dec. 16, 1708, confirmed in 1721, and d. in Steinbach bei Ottweiler on May 10, 1764. She m. Johann Casper Mueller and Johan Peter Bleymehl in Doerrenbach on Jan. 2, 1749. Johan Peter was b. on Dec. 24, 1719, and d. in Steinbach on Feb. 21, 1783.

Eva Catharina$^{1.1.1.1.8.8u}$, b. on Feb. 25, 1712, and d. on Jan. 30, 1714.

Johan Nickel Schwingel

Johann Nickel$^{1.1.1.1.8.3u}$ m. Maria Barbara, daughter of Michael Anschuetz, on May 31, 1718 and Anna Margaretha Haas, widow of Ludwig (and possibly a daughter of Leonard Hoy), about 1742. Michael Anschuetz was a citizen, joiner, glass-blower, and the bellows-maker of Gelnhausen. Michael d. there on July 30, 1730. Barbara was b. about 1700, and moved to Neunkirchen with her brothers, Johann Andreas and Johann Jacob, about 1713. Johann Andreas Anschuetz was a master joiner, and glass blower, and m. Luise Katharina, daughter of Georg Bernhard and Eva Katharina (Werner) Meyer, on May 25, 1723. Johann Jacob Anschuetz was b. on Feb. 2, 1685, was a master joiner and glass-blower, and m. Maria Elisabeth, daughter of Johann Michael and Maria Katharina (Lippin) Meyer, on May 16, 1713. Nickel, Barbara, and their four children left Germany on June 21, 1740, and arrived in Philadelphia on the ship *Samuel* on Dec. 3, 1740. It is not certain if Barbara d. en route or soon after arrival. Nickel was a blacksmith, and settled in the Tulpehocken region of Pennsylvania (then Lancaster County, now Lebanon County, Heidelberg Township). He was church councilman and reader of Christ's Lutheran Church in Stouchsburg in 1752. In Aug. 1758, Margaret and Nickel made a grant of 149 acres near Tulpehocken Creek, that had been patented to Margaret in 1741, and transferred the land to their two sons, and her four daughters by her first marriage. Soon after, Nickel moved to Washington County, Maryland, where he d., and his estate was administered by his widow Margaret, and Garrard Stonebreaker on Apr. 3, 1786. He had the following children (the first four in Neunkirchen and the rest in Berks County):

Johann Michael$^{1.1.1.1.8.3u}$, b. on Apr. 9, 1719, and d. soon after his arrival in America.

LANCASTER, LEBANON & DAUPHIN COUNTIES 125

Maria Christina$^{1.1.1.1.8.3.2u}$, b. on Aug. 10, 1721, and m. Johann Michael Maurer.
Georg Martin$^{1.1.1.1.8.3.3u}$, b. on Feb. 2, 1724.
Johann Nicolaus$^{1.1.1.1.8.3.4u}$, b. on Feb. 23, 1730.
Johann Michael$^{1.1.1.1.8.3.5u}$, b. on Aug. 23, 1743, baptized at Berks County, Stouchsburg, Pennsylvania, and sponsored by Michael and Anna Maria Mueller.
Johann Peter$^{1.1.1.1.8.3.6u}$, b. on Apr. 26, 1750, baptized at Stouchsburg on May 10, 1750, and sponsored by Peter Hallstein and John Feg.

Georg Martin Schwingel

Georg Martin$^{1.1.1.1.8.3.3u}$ m. Anna Margaretta, daughter of Martin Thoma, about 1747. George received a land warrant for 150 acres in Lancaster County, Warwick Township, and on Jan. 8, 1752, 50 acres in Lancaster County, Lebanon Township. On Feb. 4, 1761, he purchased 224 acres in Lancaster County, Heidelberg Township. In 1752 and 1758, Nicholas and George Swingle were taxed in Heidelberg Township. Georg was naturalized on Apr. 8, 1761. He was overseer of roads in 1762 and overseer of the poor in Heidelberg Township in 1764. In 1771, Georg was taxed in Heidelberg Township, and was presumed to have taken his family to Frederick County, Maryland, before Feb. 21, 1771, when he recorded a mortgage paid to him in the Conococheague settlement in Maryland. He purchased 614 acres called *Marsh Head, Resurvey on Addition to Marsh Head, Addition to Laferty's Lott, Resurvey on Part of Shippen's Neglect,* and *Addition to Gook Luck* on Mar. 18, 1772. On Mar. 22, 1773, he bought 100 acres called *John's Lott* and *Resurvey on Dickson's Pleasure,* located on Antietam Creek, with intentions of building a mill or mills. During the Revolutionary War, he was a member of the committee to raise money for arms and ammunition for Marsh Hundred in Frederick County, and was a member of that county's Committee of Observation (elected on Sep. 12, 1775). About 1783, He moved to Baltimore, Maryland, and in 1786, he sold part of his 1772 purchase to his sons, George and Nicholas. About 1800, George and his wife moved to Jefferson County, Tennessee. On Mar. 15, 1802, Georg sold the land from his 1773 purchase, and he and his wife were presumed to have d. soon after that date. Georg and Margaretta had the following children:

Nicholas$^{1.1.1.1.8.3.3.1u}$, b. on Oct. 12, 1748, m. Elisabeth, and d. in Washington County, Hagerstown, Maryland, on Mar. 16, 1842. He served in the Revolutionary War from Maryland.

Anna Maria$^{1.1.1.1.8.3.3.2u}$, b. on May 18, 1752, and m. Gerard Stonebreaker.

Leonhard$^{1.1.1.1.8.3.3.3u}$, b. on Feb. 5, 1755, baptized on Mar. 9, 1755, and sponsored by Leonard and Eva Mueller. He served in the Revolutionary War from Pennsylvania and Maryland, and d. in Tennessee sometime after 1838. In late 1777, early 1778, he moved to Frederick County, Maryland, and in all likelihood, operated the grist and saw mill his father established on Antietam Creek. In 1788, he moved to Baltimore County, Maryland. After becoming bankrupt in 1794, he moved to Washington County, Conococheague Hundred, Maryland, to reside on his father-in-law's land. Sometime after Apr. 1804, he moved to Washington County, Tennessee. He m. Eva, daughter of Michael Theiss.

George$^{1.1.1.1.8.3.3.4u}$, b. on Dec. 11, 1757, m. Christina Householder in Washington County, Maryland, on Apr. 23, 1778, Mary Householder in Baltimore County, Maryland, on Apr. 1, 1793, and Mary Phillips, widow of John Savage, in Lewis County, Kentucky on Jan. 2, 1812. George d. on Nov. 15, 1840. He served in the Revolutionary War from Pennsylvania and Maryland. About 1783, he moved to Baltimore, Maryland. George eventually lost all of his property in Maryland, and applied for, and was granted, 300 acres on the north side of the French River in the area of North Carolina that became Jefferson County, Tennessee. In 1802, the county sold George's land for nonpayment of taxes, and George moved to Montgomery County, Kentucky, and soon after, Lewis County, Kentucky. He applied for pension in Lewis County in 1833. In 1838, he was residing in Greenup County, Greenupsburg, Kentucky, and in 1842, resided in Franklin County, Kentucky, where he died.

Michael$^{1.1.1.1.8.3.3.5u}$, b. on Feb. 25, 1759, m. Mary, daughter of Charles Cummings in Washington County, Virginia, on Sep. 6, 1791, and d. in Washington County, Virginia, on Oct. 18, 1827. She was b. in Lancaster County, Virginia, on Dec. 15, 1771, and d. in Washington County, Virginia, on Dec. 6, 1847. Michael served in the Revolutionary War from Maryland. In 1783, he moved to Baltimore County, Maryland, and purchased land with his brother George, and engaged in milling. By 1789, Michael left this partnership to form a new one in the retail goods, wares, and merchandise business with his brother, John in Washington County, Virginia. On Oct. 1, 1791, he moved to the lead mines in Wythe County, Virginia, and about the same time leased lead mines on the French Broad in Tennessee with his brother, John. In Mar. 1792, this venture failed, and in Apr., he, John, and Garret

Fitzgerald purchased land in Jefferson County, Tennessee. Garret dissolved the partnership in Sep. 1792, and Michael returned to Washington County, Virginia, in Nov. 1792. On Oct. 10, 1798, he moved to the Beaver Creek Iron Works in Sullivan County, Bristol, Tennessee, and on Nov. 21, 1799, he moved to the Investry Iron Works. Later, he and John worked as iron moulders at Embreesville, in Unicoi County, Tennessee. On July 1, 1806, Michael sold his 21 acres on Indian Creek to his nephew, George Swingle, and by Apr. 1813, was residing in Washington County, Virginia

John$^{1.1.1.1.8.3.3.6u}$, b. on May 1, 1761. In 1789, he and his brother, Michael had established a partnership in Washington County, Virginia, and over the next 15 years worked with Michael in Virginia and Tennessee (see Michael's entry). In 1810, John resided in Montgomery County, Kentucky, and on Sep. 2, 1816, was residing in Estill County, Ravenna Township, Kentucky. He served in the Revolutionary War as a Private in the 3rd Class, 4th Battalion, Lancaster County, Militia on July 6, 1781. In 1820, he and his son, John, were in Estill County, Kentucky. In 1830, one of them was in Estill County, and the other in Franklin County, Kentucky. In 1840, one was in Franklin County, and the other in Jefferson County, Kentucky.

Maria Barbara$^{1.1.1.1.8.3.3.7u}$, b. on Oct. 23, 1763, baptized in Berks County, Tulpehocken Township, Stouchsburg, Pennsylvania, on Nov. 9, 1763, and sponsored by Maria Barbara, wife of John Schaeffer.

Magdalena$^{1.1.1.1.8.3.3.8u}$, b. about 1765, and m. Jacob Tice in Baltimore, Maryland, on Oct. 23, 1784.

Johann Nicolaus Schwingel

Johann Nicolaus$^{1.1.1.1.8.3.4u}$ m. Maria Barbara, daughter of Michael and Maria Barbara (Feg) Reidt, in Berks County, Tulpehocken Township, Stouchsburg, Pennsylvania, on May 26, 1752, and d. in Washington County, Maryland, before Apr. 9, 1785, when his will was proved. Maria Barbara was b. in Tulpehocken on Mar. 13, 1732, baptized at Reed's Church, and sponsored by Johan Georg Reidt and her mother. She was confirmed at Tulpehocken on June 3, 1750, and d. in Washington County, Maryland, before Sep. 15, 1805, when her will was proven. On Dec. 23, 1752, Nicholas purchased 81 acres in Plumton Manor in Tulpehocken (now Marion) Township. In 1759, he was taxed in Berks County, Tulpehocken Township. On May 29, 1777, he purchased 138 acres on the Conococheague Creek in Washington County, Maryland, known as Dutch Folly, where he operated a mill. In

1778, he took the Oath of Fidelity. They had the following children in Tulpehocken Township (baptized at Stouchsburg):

Margaretha Elisabeth$^{1.1.1.1.8.3.4.1u}$, b. on Mar. 5, 1753, baptized on Mar. 11, 1753, and sponsored by Michael and Margaretha Elisabeth Theiss. She m. Jacob, son of Abraham Weitmann in Stouchsburg on Dec. 28, 1775, and d. in Washington County, Williamsport, Maryland, between 1800 and 1805.

Johan Georg$^{1.1.1.1.8.3.4.2u}$, b. on Apr. 9, 1754, baptized on Apr. 28, 1754, and sponsored by Johan Georg Schwengel and wife. On July 18, 1799, he bought 200 acres on the south side of the Cumberland River in Wilson County, Tennessee. He bought 640 acres on Barton's Creek in Wilson County on Dec. 28, 1807, where he d. in 1842. He m. Catharine, daughter of Jacob Albert in Stouchsburg on June 9, 1778.

Maria Barbara$^{1.1.1.1.8.3.4.3u}$, b. on Mar. 15, 1756, baptized on Apr. 4, 1756, and sponsored by Johann Nicholas and Maria Barbara Reidt. She m. John, son of Johann Frederick and Anna Dorothea (Mueller) Roemer, Michael Weir before 1789 (he left her), and Henry Kindle before 1805. John was b. in York County, Pennsylvania, on Mar. 1, 1753, and baptized by Reverend Meuer on Mar. 5, 1753. He served in the Revolutionary War from York County in 1778, and d. in Washington County, Conococheague, Maryland, between Sep. 20, 1784, and Oct. 3, 1784. Barbara and Henry were alive and residing in Washington County, Maryland, on Sep. 2, 1806.

Anna Maria$^{1.1.1.1.8.3.4.4u}$, b. on Jan. 11, 1761, baptized on Jan. 18, 1761, and sponsored by Frederick Weiser and wife. She m. George, son of Martin and Margaretha Kershner, in Washington County, Maryland, about 1782. George d. in Washington County, Maryland, before Apr. 11, 1801, when letters of administration were grated to Anna Maria.

Catharina$^{1.1.1.1.8.3.4.5u}$, b. in Mar. 1763, baptized on Apr. 26, 1763, and sponsored by Michael and Anna Catharina Reidt. She m. Henry Seister, and d. in Washington County, Williamsport, Maryland, before July 25, 1805. He served in the Revolutionary War.

Benjamin$^{1.1.1.1.8.3.4.6u}$, b. about Nov. 1, 1764, baptized at 3 years of age on Nov. 16, 1767, and sponsored by Benjamin and Margaret Barbara Spyker. He d. in Berkley County, Gerrardstown, Virginia, on Dec. 10, 1848. He m. Anna Eva, daughter of Nicholas and Barbara Smith in Hagerstown Lutheran Church, Washington County, Maryland, on Oct. 6, 1794. She was b. in 1769, and d. on May 22, 1856.

Benjamin lead a group of German families from the Conococheague Settlement in Maryland to Berkley County, Virginia.

Johannes$^{1.1.1.1.8.3.4.7u}$, b. on Aug. 24, 1765, baptized on Sep. 5, 1765, and sponsored by Johan Ramler and wife. He was not mentioned in his parents will.

Elizabeth$^{1.1.1.1.8.3.4.8u}$, b. about 1769, and m. George Gittinger/Kissinger. He was b. on May 6, 1764, and d. in Washington County, Hagerstown, Maryland, on Nov. 9, 1844.

Christina$^{1.1.1.1.8.3.4.9u}$, b. on Jan. 1, 1773, baptized on Jan. 6, 1773, and sponsored by Henrich and Christina Koppenhefer. She was living with her mother in 1800, and was unmarried in 1805.

Johann Phillip$^{1.1.1.1.8.3.4.10u}$, b. on Nov. 24, 1774, baptized on Dec. 12, 1774, and sponsored by Peter and Etel DeHaas. He m. Sarah, daughter of Jacob and Eleanor Friend, and d. in Washington County, Maryland, between Nov. 25 and Dec. 11, 1802.

Johann Michael Schwingel

Johann Michael$^{1.1.1.1.8.3.5u}$ m. Elizabeth, daughter of Johann Henrich, and Maria Margaretha (Reidt) Zeller, and d. in Northumberland (now Snyder) County, Pennsylvania, in 1794. An inventory of his estate was taken on Dec. 26, 1794. He was a blacksmith. Elizabeth was b. on Nov. 28, 1744, and d. in Northumberland County, Pennsylvania, on Oct. 26, 1823. On Apr. 24, 1769, Michael was a blacksmith in Lancaster County, Heidelberg Township, when he purchased 200 acres on Middle Creek in Northumberland County, Penn Township. It is believed that Michael may have worked on his land in Northumberland County during the summer months, and returned to his family in the Tulpehocken settlement in the winter months like other settlers during that time. He was taxed in Penn Township in 1771, and on Nov. 11, 1772, purchased 50 more acres in the Township. On Apr. 23, 1773, he purchased an additional 50 acres, and sold the first two purchases on May 12, 1778. Michael may have returned to the Tulpehocken region during the Revolution to aid his family in the manufacture of arms (he appeared on the effective supply tax list of Lancaster County, Newman's Town in 1779. On Sep. 12, 1792, he purchased 60 acres in the area that became Union County, and finally Snyder County. They had the following children (the first two and the sixth baptized in Berks County, Tulpehocken Township, Stouchsburg, Pennsylvania):

Johannes$^{1.1.1.1.8.3.5.1u}$, b. on Sep. 5, 1766, baptized on Oct. 9, 1766, and sponsored by Henrich Zeller and wife.

Barbara[1.1.1.1.8.3.5.2u], b. on Apr. 12, 1768, baptized on Apr. 17, 1768, and sponsored by Peter Schutz and wife. She m. Mathias Spotz of Selinsgrove, Pennsylvania.

Eva Margaret[1.1.1.1.8.3.5.3u], b. on Jan. 15, 1770, baptized at Millbach Reformed Church, Lebanon County on June 4, 1770, and sponsored by Margaret Elizabeth Haas. She m. Anthony Gift.

Michael[1.1.1.1.8.3.5.4u], b. on Jan. 13, 1773, m. Esther, daughter of George and Elizabeth (Dreiner/Breimer) Hassinger, and d. in Union County, Penn Township on Apr. 6, 1851. She was b. on May 28, 1777, and d. on Mar. 3, 1858.

Benjamin[1.1.1.1.8.3.5.5u], b. in Union County, Harleton, Pennsylvania, on Aug. 9, 1774, baptized at Rau (Ray) Evangelical Church, and sponsored by Melcher and Orphla Stock.

Johann Peter[1.1.1.1.8.3.5.6u], b. on May 18, 1779, baptized on May 23, 1779, and sponsored by Johannes and Catharine Salzgeber.

Kate[1.1.1.1.8.3.5.7u].

Charles Phillip[1.1.1.1.8.3.5.8u], m. Regina, daughter of William and Anna Maria Gentzel/Gentzler, and moved to Pickaway County, Washington Township, Ohio, about 1831. She was b. on July 12, 1786, and d. in Jackson County, Indiana, on Jan. 10, 1875. Charles served as a Drum Major in the War of 1812.

Johann Peter Schwingel

Johann Peter[1.1.1.1.8.3.6u] d. intestate in Berkley County, Virginia, in 1796. An inventory of his estate was made on Jan. 22, 1798. He was a blacksmith, and served as a Captain in the Maryland Militia during the Revolutionary War. He was residing in Berkley County, Virginia, as early as Oct. 9, 1780. He m. Catherine, daughter of Barnett Bashore. On Aug. 24, 1799, Catherine m. John Kindar. Peter and Catherine had the following son:

Michael[1.1.1.1.8.3.6.1u], b. in Berkley County, Virginia, on Apr. 26, 1785, m. Nancy, daughter of Henry Riner in Berkeley County on Dec. 16, 1809, and d. in Clinton County, Green Township, New Antioch, Ohio, on Oct. 16, 1850. She d. in Berkley County, Virginia, in 1822. Michael moved to Ohio about 1826.

****

Bernard Shope/Schopp

Bernard[1v] m. Nancy. He resided in Pennsylvania in 1793; Fairfield County, Clear Creek Township, Ohio, in 1806, and Ross

County, Scioto Township, Ohio, in 1810. He d. in Scioto Township in Apr. 1813. On Apr. 22, 1813, at Chillicothe, Nancy renounced the administration of his estate, in favor of Henry Johnson and John Edmiston, because of her ill health. This Bernard Shope is presumed to be the Bernard Shope/Schopp of Lancaster County, Pennsylvania, that immigrated to America on the ship *Neptune* on Sep. 24, 1753, and m. Petronilla about 1766. On Easter, 1775, Bernard and Petronilla were baptized at the First Reformed Church of Lancaster, and in this record Petronilla is named as Nancy. They resided in Hempfield Township until about 1787, when the removed to Leacock Township. They were residing there in 1800. Bernard and Nancy/Petronilla had the following children (all baptized at the First Reformed Church of Lancaster except the last two):

Salome$^{1.1v}$, b. on Aug. 12, 1767, baptized on Mar. 12, 1768, and sponsored by Henry and Anna Maria Decker.

Maria$^{1.2v}$, b. on Jan. 16, 1769, and baptized at Trinity Lutheran Church on July 26, 1769.

John$^{1.3v}$, baptized on Aug. 15, 1771, and sponsored by Theobald Roth and wife.

Daniel$^{1.4v}$, b. on May 31, 1773, baptized on Oct. 22, 1773, and sponsored by Nicholas and Elizabeth Job. He m. Barbara Bitscher in Hempfield Township on Mar. 13, 1798. He may be the Daniel Shope on the 1806 tax list of Fairfield County, Hocking Township, Ohio. Daniel of Hocking Township purchased 56 acres in R 19, T14, S26 on Aug. 8, 1807.

Elisabeth$^{1.5v}$, b. on June 15, 1775, baptized on May 27, 1780, and sponsored by Theobald Rod and wife.

Anna$^{1.6v}$, b. on Sep. 30, 1777, baptized on May 20, 1780, and sponsored by John Schry and wife.

Bernard$^{1.7v}$, b. on Feb. 15, 1779, baptized on May 27, 1780, and sponsored by Theobald Rod and wife. He may be the Bernard Shop that m. Elizabeth Crall in Dauphin County, Pennsylvania, in 1805.

Jacob$^{1.8v}$, b. on Jan. 23, 1781, baptized on Nov. 26, 1783, and sponsored by Jacob Stoltz and wife.

Samuel$^{1.9v}$, b. on Mar. 6, 1783, baptized on Nov. 26, 1783, and sponsored by Herman Spohr and wife. He may be the Samuel Schup that m. Barbara about 1799, and had Samuel, b. on July 1, 1800, baptized at Lancaster First Reformed Church on Sep. 30, 1800, and sponsored by his parents.

Susanna$^{1.10v}$, b. on Mar. 25, 1784, baptized on Aug. 23, 1787, and sponsored by Herman and Catharine Spohr.

Helena$^{1.11v}$, b. on June 20, 1787, baptized on Aug. 23, 1787, and sponsored by John and Catharine Hauendupler.

Son$^{1.12v}$, b. about 1790.

William$^{1.13v}$, b. in 1793 (a son b. between 1790 and 1800 on 1800 census).

John Shope

John$^{1.3v}$ may be the John Shope that was taxed in Scioto County, Ohio, in 1806, 1810, and d. there in 1850 (Ver. Township). He m. (?Mary), and had the following children:

Elizabeth$^{1.3.1v}$, b. about 1792, and m. David Wolf in Scioto County, Ohio, on Aug. 22, 1814.

William$^{1.3.2v}$, b. about 1794.

Mary$^{1.3.3v}$, b. about 1798, and m. Isaac Van Bibber in Scioto County on Dec. 16, 1819.

David$^{1.3.4v}$, b. before 1810, and resided in Scioto County (Por. Township) in 1830.

William Shope

William$^{1.3.2v}$ m. Margaret Call in Scioto County on May 11, 1815, and may be the William that resided in Lawrence County, Ohio, and had the following children:

Mahala$^{1.3.2.1v}$, b. about 1815, and m. Daniel Halteman in Lawrence County on Aug. 13, 1835.

Mary$^{1.3.2.2v}$, b. about 1818, and m. John Rawlins in Lawrence County on July 11, 1839.

John$^{1.3.2.3v}$, b. about 1820, and m. Elizabeth Halterman in Lawrence County on Apr. 11, 1843.

William$^{1.3.2.4v}$, b. about 1822, and m. Tempy Corly in Lawrence County on Feb. 8, 1844.

Elizabeth$^{1.3.2.5v}$, b. about 1824, and m. William Thompson in Lawrence County on Feb. 16, 1843.

Timothy$^{1.3.2.6v}$, b. about 1832, and m. Minerva Jane Hobble in Lawrence County on Nov. 20, 1853.

William Shope

William$^{1.13v}$ m. Elizabeth, daughter of George Tester, in Fairfield County, Ohio, on Apr. 22, 1816. In 1810, William resided with his father in Ross County, Scioto Township, Ohio. He served as a

Private in the War of 1812 from Fairfield County, Ohio, from Aug. 30, 1813 to Feb. 28, 1814. He resided in Fairfield County, Greenfield Township until 1828, when he moved to Madison Township. He moved to Allen County, German Township, Ohio, in 1832, and d. there about 1857. He is buried in the south west corner of Greenlawn cemetery. In 1833, William had land in Section 9 of German Township. Elizabeth resided with her son, John, in 1880, and collected a pension for her husband's military service from 1879 to 1883. William and Elizabeth had the following children:

Elizabeth$^{1.13.1v}$, b. on Aug. 18, 1816, and m. Lewis Herring.

George$^{1.13.2v}$, b. about 1818, m. Eliza DeVore in Allen County, Ohio, on Nov. 14, 1857, and d. in German Township in 1858. After George's death, Eliza m. his brother, John.

Nancy$^{1.13.3v}$, b. on Oct. 12, 1820, and m. Henry Herring.

Samuel$^{1.13.4v}$, b. on Apr. 6, 1822.

William$^{1.13.5v}$, b. on Jan. 31, 1825, m. Mary Emmons in Allen County, Ohio, on June 1, 1851, and d. in Mercer County, Black Creek Township, Ohio, on May 23, 1890. She was b. on Dec. 16, 1830, and d. before 1880.

Catharina$^{1.13.6v}$, b. about 1827, and m. John Beierstorfer in Allen County on Apr. 18, 1847. Her name is Schopp in the marriage record.

Polly$^{1.13.7v}$, b. in 1829, and m. Samuel Hart in Allen County, Ohio, on Mar. 26, 1848.

Mary Jane$^{1.13.8v}$, b. about 1829, and m. Bazell Neely in Allen County on Dec. 18, 1853.

Malinda$^{1.13.9v}$, b. on Jan. 2, 1831, m. Jonathan Dillsaver in Allen County, Ohio, on Dec. 14, 1851, and d. in German Township on Nov. 23, 1873. He was b. in Fairfield County, Ohio, on Feb. 8, 1828, and d. in Allen County, Marion Township, Ohio.

Jacob Bernard$^{1.13.10v}$, b. in 1833 (34), and appeared on the 1850 census as Bernard. He m. Elizabeth Jane.

Elendar$^{1.13.11v}$, b. about 1835, and m. George Ward in Allen County, Ohio, on Jan. 22, 1856. She does not appear on the 1850 census, but the marriage record says her name is Shope.

Magdalena/Rebecca$^{1.13.12v}$, b. in 1836, and m. C. H. Stuckey in Allen County, Ohio, on Sep. 9, 1856. The marriage record says Magdalena, and the 1850 census says Rebecca.

John$^{1.13.13v}$, b. on Mar. 16, 1839, m. Eliza DeVore, widow of his brother, George, in Allen County, Ohio, on Jan. 27, 1859, and d. in Allen County, American Township, Ohio, on Dec. 15, 1923. She was b.

in Auglaize County, Ohio, on Nov. 16, 1837, and d. in Allen County, German Township on Jan. 29, 1910.

Susan$^{1.13.14v}$, b. in 1841, and m. John Fifer/Pfiefer in Allen County, Ohio, on Sep. 16, 1858.

Samuel Shope

Samuel$^{1.13.4v}$ m. Catherine, daughter of Jacob and Borial (Naggle) Tester, in Allen County, Ohio, in Dec. 1843, and d. in Allen County, German Township, Ohio, on May 3, 1901. She d. in German Township on July 17, 1899. They had the following children:

Jacob$^{1.13.4.1v}$, b. in 1846, and m. Elizabeth A. Miller in Allen County on Nov. 23, 1869 and Tabitha Place in Allen County on Nov. 13, 1873.

Elizabeth$^{1.13.4.2v}$, b. in 1847, and m. Israel Bower in Allen County on July 19, 1866.

Eleanor$^{1.13.4.3v}$, b. in 1849.

Samuel$^{1.13.4.4v}$, b. in 1850.

John$^{1.13.4.5v}$, b. in 1852.

Louisa$^{1.13.4.6v}$, b. in 1853, and m. Christopher Ely in Allen County on Dec. 9, 1876.

Susan$^{1.13.4.7v}$, b. in 1854.

George$^{1.13.4.8v}$, b. in 1855, and d. before 1870.

William$^{1.13.4.9v}$, b. in 1856, and m. Matilda Bowers in Allen County on Mar. 14, 1878, and Sarah M..

Malinda$^{1.13.4.10v}$, b. on July 13, 1858, and m. Peter Shock.

****

Weipert Stein

Weipert^{1w} d. in "Gerichtsverwandten" before 1677, and had the following son:

Johann Leonhardt$^{1.1w}$, b. in 1652.

Johan Leonhardt Stein

Johan Leonhardt was from Bischofsheim, and resided in Berwangen, Adelshofen, Germany. He m. Anna Margaretha, daughter of Paul Eyermann, citizen at Berwangen, at Neckarbischofsheim on Nov. 20, 1677, and d. in Berwanen on Dec. 1, 1717. Anna Magdalena d. in Berwangen on Aug. 10, 1732, and had the following son:

Johann Leonhardt$^{1.1.1w}$, b. in 1690.

Johann Leonhardt Stein

Johann Leonhardt$^{1.1.1w}$ m. Anna, daughter of Andreas Weidknecht, at Adelshofen on Jan. 13, 1711. Andreas d. in Schultheiss, Adelshofen before 1711. Leonhardt immigrated to America on the ship *Princess Augusta* in 1736. Leonhardt and Anna had the following son: Johann Leonhardt$^{1.1.1.1w}$, b. at Berwangen on Apr. 15, 1712.

Johann Leonhardt Stein

Johann Leonhardt$^{1.1.1.1w}$ d. in 1785. His inventory was taken on Jan. 10, 1785. He immigrated to America on the ship *Hope* in 1733 (1743). He was one of the founders of New Holland, Pennsylvania. He m. Anna Maria Lang in the First Reformed Congregation in Lancaster on Dec. 3, 1745, and had the following children baptized at Seltenreich Lutheran Church in Lancaster County, Earl Township (he may be the Johann Leonhardt Stein that had a Johan Jacob on Jan. 11, 1737, baptized at Trinity Lutheran Church in Lancaster County, and sponsored by Johan Jacob Schlauch, Maria Barbara Firnssler, and Maria Margaretha Wartmannin):

Johan Ludwig$^{1.1.1.1.1w}$, baptized on Oct. 26, 1746, and sponsored by Ludwig Kraft and Catharine Lang.

Johan$^{1.1.1.1.2w}$, baptized on May 29, 1748, and sponsored by John Diefendorffer and Margaret Haess.

Margaretha$^{1.1.1.1.3w}$, b. on Feb. 23, 1750, m. David Diffenderfer (1752-1846), and d. on Feb. 2, 1807.

Maria Sophia$^{1.1.1.1.4w}$, b. in 1752, and m. Johan Heinrich Grimm.

Anna Maria$^{1.1.1.1.5w}$, b. on Sep. 19, 1753, baptized on Oct. 14, 1753, and sponsored by Leonard and Anna Maria Stein.

Leonard$^{1.1.1.1.6w}$, b. in Cocalico on July 20, 1754, baptized on Sep. 1, 1754, and sponsored by Leonhardt and Catharina Mueller. He was confirmed on May 11, 1771.

Eva Elisabeth$^{1.1.1.1.7w}$, b. on Jan. 10, 1756, baptized on Dec. 19, 1756, and sponsored by Johannes Dieffendorfer and Eva Elisabetha Lang. She was confirmed on Apr. 11, 1773, and d. on July 20, 1774.

Jacob$^{1.1.1.1.8w}$, baptized on Feb. 25, 1759, and sponsored by Leonard Mueller and wife.

Johan Georg$^{1.1.1.1.9w}$, baptized on Mar. 14, 1762, and sponsored by Johan Leonhard and Sophia Mueller.

Johan Stein

Johan[1.1.1.1.2w] m. Regina (?Gray) in 1769. She was b. on Apr. 1, 1748, and baptized at Muddy Creek on Mar. 24, 1771. In 1770, they settled in Lancaster County, Brecknock Township, and in 1800, settled in Cumberland County, Newton Township, where John d. in 1809. They had the following children:

Anna Maria[1.1.1.1.2.1w], b. on Apr. 3, 1770, baptized at Seltenreich on June 20, 1770, and sponsored by John and Eva Elizabeth Diefendorffer.

Johan[1.1.1.1.2.2w], b. on June 8, 1773, baptized at Seltenreich on July 4, 1773, and sponsored by Leonard and Anna Maria Stein.

Hannah[1.1.1.1.2.3w], b. on Sep. 16, 1775, baptized at Muddy Creek on Oct. 12, 1775, and sponsored by Margaret Stein, single.

Jonas[1.1.1.1.2.4w], b. on Dec. 25, 1777, baptized at Muddy Creek on Apr. 12, 1778, and sponsored by Leonard and Anna Maria Stein.

Leonard[1.1.1.1.2.5w], b. in 1782, and baptized at Muddy Creek Reformed Congregation in 1797.

Samuel[1.1.1.1.2.6w], b. about 1784.

Rachel[1.1.1.1.2.7w], b. about 1786, and m. ____ Melchior.

Elisabetha[1.1.1.1.2.8w], b. about 1788, and m. ____ Cronister.

****

Peter Dester/Tester

Peter[1x] resided in Lebanon County, Bethel Township, Pennsylvania, in 1756, when he is listed as poor on the tax list. He may have been the Petter Descher who arrived at Philadelphia in 1751, or the Peter Dester, that arrived in Georgia in 1734. On Nov. 15, 1781, Ulrich Arner served as a substitute for Peter Dester in the 6th Class, 1st Battalion, of the Northampton County Militia. He m. Anna Barbara, and they were residing in Bethel Township on Feb. 3, 1784, when they were sponsors to a baptism of their granddaughter. They had the following children (alternate surname spellings Trouster/Dester/Descher/Teschler):

Eva Elisabeth[1.1x], b. on Mar. 14, 1756 (58), baptized at St. Jacob's Kimmerling's Reformed Church in Lebanon (by Reverend Henry William Stoy, pastor there from Jan. to Apr. 1756) on Apr. 4, 1756 (58), and sponsored by Anthony Kelcker and Elizabeth Kimmerlin.

Jacob[1.2x], b. on Nov. 1, 1759, baptized at St. Jacob's Kimmerling's on Apr. 5, 1760, and sponsored by Jacob and Elizabeth Conrad.

Johann Georg[1.3x], b. about 1761.

Eva Elisabeth Tester

Eva Elisabeth[1.1x] m. Johan Jacob, son of Jacob and Barbara Keller. He was b. on Feb. 15, 1753, baptized at Trinity Tulpehocken Lutheran Church, in Lebanon County, Jackson Township on Mar. 25, 1753 (sponsors were Jacob Lehman and Anna Margaretha Kitzmueller), and d. in Centre County, Potter Township, Pennsylvania, on Mar. 6, 1828. Jacob served in the Revolutionary War, and was discharged at Lebanon on Nov. 2, 1777, after two months of service. They moved to Centre County in 1806, and purchased the Red Mill property. They had the following children in Lebanon County, Bethel Township:

Johan Jacob[1.1.1x], b. on Feb. 20, 1779, baptized at Kimmerling's on Mar. 14, 1779, and sponsored by Casper and Barbara Schop.

John[1.1.2x], b. on Jan. 27, 1781, and d. on Nov. 15, 1871.

Barbara[1.1.3x], b. on Dec. 28, 1783, baptized at Kimmerling's on Feb. 3, 1784, and sponsored by Peter and Barbara Dester.

Elisabeth[1.1.4x], b. on Mar. 11, 1785.

Margaret[1.1.5x], b. on Apr. 26, 1787.

Christian[1.1.6x], b. in Oct. 1789.

Peter[1.1.7x], b. in Jan. 1791.

Philip[1.1.8x], b. in Dec. 1794.

Johann Jacob Keller

Johan Jacob[1.1.1x] m. Elizabeth Kornman, and d. in Centre County, Potter Township on Sep. 12, 1835. They had the following children:

John[1.1.1.1x], b. in Nov. 1801, and d. in Harris Township on Oct. 11, 1865.

Jacob[1.1.1.2x], b. on Jan. 28, 1803, m. Christina Dinges on Dec. 15, 1826, and d. on Feb. 10, 1848. She was b. on Apr. 22, 1807, and d. on Nov. 25, 1850.

Catherine[1.1.1.3x], b. on Apr. 11, 1804, m. John Stauffer, and d. in Ohio on Dec. 31, 1897. He d. at age 94, on Jan. 15, 1898.

George[1.1.1.4x], b. in May 1806, and d. in Ravenna, Ohio, in Sep. 1865.

Elizabeth$^{1.1.1.5x}$, b. in 1808.
Henry$^{1.1.1.6x}$, b. on Feb. 3, 1811, m. Margaret Schenck, and d. in Boalsburg on Feb. 6, 1884.
David$^{1.1.1.7x}$, b. on Jan. 25, 1818, and resided in Boalsburg.
Daniel$^{1.1.1.8x}$, b. on Aug. 15, 1825, and resided in Warren, Ohio (and possibly Illinois).

Christian Keller

Christian$^{1.1.6x}$ m. Catherine, daughter of Christopher Henney, and d. in Centre County, Potter Township, Pennsylvania, on Aug. 12, 1831. They had the following children:
Christian$^{1.1.6.1x}$, resided in Philadelphia.
William$^{1.1.6.2x}$.
John H.$^{1.1.6.3x}$.
Elizabeth$^{1.1.6.4x}$, m. Amos Alexander.
Catherine$^{1.1.6.5x}$, m. John Boozer.
Lydia$^{1.1.6.6x}$, m. Peter Hoffer.
Rebecca$^{1.1.6.7x}$, m. Watson Pennington, and resided in Illinois.
Sarah$^{1.1.6.8x}$, m. Isaac Pennington.

Peter Keller

Peter$^{1.1.7x}$ m. Barbara, daughter of George Minnich, and d. in Centre County, Potter Township in 1840. His will was written on Mar. 20, 1840, and probated on Mar. 27, 1840. Her will was written on Oct. 7, 1852, and probated on Nov. 10, 1852. They had the following children:
George$^{1.1.7.1x}$; Jacob$^{1.1.7.2x}$; Ann$^{1.1.7.3x}$; Catherine$^{1.1.7.4x}$, b. in 1824; Joseph$^{1.1.7.5x}$; Sarah$^{1.1.7.6x}$; Rebecca$^{1.1.7.7x}$; John$^{1.1.7.8x}$.

Johann Georg Tester

Johann Georg$^{1.3x}$ served in the Revolutionary War in the Lancaster County, Pennsylvania, Militia from 1782 to 1784. Georg m. an unknown woman in Lebanon County, Pennsylvania, sometime prior to Feb. 27, 1787, when he and his wife sponsored the baptism of Johann Georg, son of Cornelius Grun, at Tabor First Reformed Church in Lebanon (Johann Georg Grun's birth was on June 7, 1786). By 1789, he and his brother, Jacob, had moved to Shenandoah County, Columbia Furnace, Virginia, where they appeared as delinquent on the tax list. Sometime between 1811 and 1815, George moved to Fairfield County,

Greenfield Township, Ohio, and in the mid-1820s moved to Madison Township, where he d. about 1827. George had the following children:

George$^{1.3.1x}$, b. in Lebanon County, Pennsylvania, in 1786.

Elizabeth$^{1.3.2x}$, b. in Shenandoah County, Virginia, in 1796, and m. William Shope.

Jacob$^{1.3.3x}$, b. in 1798.

Sarah$^{1.3.4x}$, b. in 1800.

Rebecca$^{1.3.5x}$, b. in 1803.

Margaret$^{1.3.6x}$, b. in 1806, m. John C. Mollenhour in Hocking County, Ohio, on Sep. 27, 1828, and d. in Labette County, Kansas, on Aug. 8, 1889. They may have had a son, Lewis J., who m. Sarah A. Lemon in Hocking County, Ohio, on Mar. 27, 1856.

George Tester

George$^{1.3.1x}$ m. Esther Kernbel in Fairfield County, Ohio, on June 23, 1818 (possibly Nancy Nittel/Kernbel by 1833), and resided in Auglaize County, Moulton Township, Ohio, in 1850. Esther d. before 1850. They had the following children (all b. in Fairfield County except the last):

George$^{1.3.1.1x}$, b. in Greenfield Township in 1823, and m. Ann.

John$^{1.3.1.2x}$, b. on Dec. 27, 1826, and m. Esther Elizabeth Coleman in Auglaize County, Ohio, on Apr. 1, 1855 and Elizabeth Hutson in Auglaize County on Nov. 15, 1860. John d. in Auglaize County on Feb. 22, 1903.

Mary Ann$^{1.3.1.3x}$, b. about 1828, and m. John Bigler in Auglaize County on Sep. 23, 1849.

William$^{1.3.1.4x}$, b. about 1830, and m. Rachel Denny in Auglaize County on Oct. 9, 1853 and Ann Dust in Auglaize County on May 18, 1856.

Jacob$^{1.3.1.5x}$, b. in Madison Township on Mar. 8, 1833, m. Catherine Walter in Auglaize County on Apr. 7, 1854, and d. in Auglaize County (his death certificate says he was b. in Hocking County to Jacob and Nancy (Vittel/Nittel) Tester).

Frederick$^{1.3.1.6x}$, b. in 1837, and m. Rebecca J. Robinson in Auglaize County on June 12, 1858.

Sarah$^{1.3.1.7x}$, b. in 1838, and m. George Martin Wust in Auglaize County on Oct. 13, 1856.

Joseph$^{1.3.1.8x}$, b. in Auglaize County, Moulton Township, Ohio, in 1840.

Jacob Tester

Jacob$^{1.3.3x}$ m. Borial Naggle in Fairfield County, Ohio, on Aug. 10, 1823, Sally Walter in Allen County on Oct. 3, 1841 (the husband is not named, but Jacob is the only male of age), and Mary Prence in Allen County, Ohio, on June 29, 1848. Jacob d. in Mercer County, Dublin Township, Ohio, on Oct. 19, 1878. Jacob and Borial had the following children:

Catherine$^{1.3.3.1x}$, b. in Fairfield County, Greenfield Township on Jan. 26, 1824, and m. Samuel Shope.

Frederick$^{1.3.3.2x}$, b. in 1824, and m. Sarah Jane Umstead in Allen County, Ohio, on May 20, 1847.

David$^{1.3.3.3x}$, b. about 1826, and m. Elizabeth Clutter in Allen County, Ohio, on Aug. 4, 1847.

Margaret$^{1.3.3.4x}$, b. in 1827, and m. Peter Lehman in Allen County on Oct. 17, 1850.

George W.$^{1.3.3.5x}$, b. in Hocking County, Falls Township, Ohio, in 1829, m. Sophia Spangler in Allen County, Ohio, on June 19, 1851, and d. in Henry County, Ohio.

John$^{1.3.3.6x}$, b. in Allen County, German Township, Ohio, on June 13, 1832, m. Magdalena Blosser in Allen County, Ohio, on Dec. 27, 1855, and d. in Mercer County, Dublin Township, Ohio, on Dec. 15, 1893. She was b. on Apr. 26, 1837, and d. in Dublin Township on Sep. 16, 1903.

Louisa$^{1.3.3.7x}$, b. about 1834, and m. Harrison Houaman in Allen County on Mar. 3, 1859. She did not appear on the 1850 census.

William M.$^{1.3.3.8x}$, b. in 1836, and m. Levina Adams in Mercer County on Mar. 8, 1864.

Elizabeth$^{1.3.3.9x}$, b. in 1838, and m. Cornelius Shofe in Allen County on July 12, 1866.

Jacob$^{1.3.3.10x}$, b. in 1840, and m. Maria Berryhill in Allen County on Nov. 3, 1864.

Esterline$^{1.3.3.11x}$, b. about 1841, and m. William Bowsher in Allen County on Jan. 23, 1861. She did not appear on the 1850 census.

Samuel$^{1.3.3.12x}$, b. in 1842, and m. Elizabeth Nancy Hume in Allen County, Ohio, on Mar. 5, 1863.

Mary M.$^{1.3.3.13x}$, b. in German Township in 1845.

Sarah Tester

Sarah$^{1.3.4x}$ m. Stephen Clutter in Fairfield County, Ohio, on Nov. 4, 1821, and d. in Allen or Mercer County, Ohio. Stephen was b. in Virginia in 1799, and may have first m. Elizabeth East. They resided in Mercer County, Black Creek Township, Ohio, in 1850. Stephen and Sarah had the following children:

Samuel$^{1.3.4.1x}$, b. in Fairfield County, Madison Township on Mar. 4, 1822, and m. Ann Elizabeth Pfeifer (b. 1827).

Elizabeth$^{1.3.4.2x}$, b. about 1825, and m. David Tester in Allen County, Ohio, on Aug. 4, 1847.

Amos$^{1.3.4.3x}$, b. in 1826 m. (Charlotte Huggins in Allen County, Ohio, on Aug. 30, 1840?1850) and Maria Elizabeth Nichols in Mercer County, Ohio, on Jan. 18, 1849. Maria Elizabeth was b. in 1831.

Stephen$^{1.3.4.4x}$, b. in 1827, and m. Esther Welsch in Mercer County, Ohio, on Nov. 26, 1857 and Thurza Welsch in Mercer County on Jan. 17, 1861.

Catherine$^{1.3.4.5x}$, b. about 1829, and m. Joshua W. Frazee in Mercer County, Ohio, on Dec. 18, 1849.

Nancy Jane$^{1.3.4.6x}$, b. in 1836, and m. Jacob Border in Mercer County on Apr. 20, 1856.

George F.$^{1.3.4.7x}$, b. in 1836, and m. Marana McMillen in Allen County, Ohio, on Sep. 4, 1856.

De Blenard$^{1.3.4.8x}$, b. about 1838, and m. Mary Ellen Woollett in Allen County, Ohio, on Sep. 30, 1860.

Sarah$^{1.3.4.9x}$, b. in 1840.

Rebecca Tester

Rebecca$^{1.3.5x}$ m. William Knittle in Fairfield County, Ohio, in 1823, and d. in Allen County, Auglaize Township, Ohio, in 1883. He was b. in Pennsylvania in 1799. They had the following children:

George$^{1.3.5.1x}$, b. about 1824, and m. Margaret Walters in Allen County on Sep. 17, 1843.

Jacob$^{1.3.5.2x}$, b. in 1827, and m. Malinda Dilsaver in Allen County, Ohio, on Nov. 11, 1851, and Eliza Hamilton in Allen County on Aug. 25, 1853.

Catherine$^{1.3.5.3x}$, b. about 1833, and m. Jonathan Barrick in Allen County on Nov. 2, 1854. She has not been confirmed as a daughter.

Samuel$^{1.3.5.4x}$, b. about 1835, and m. Ann Hains in Allen County on Aug. 7, 1855. He has not been confirmed as a son.

Sarah$^{1.3.5.5x}$, b. about 1843, and m. Abner Carr in Allen County, Ohio, on Aug. 21, 1864. She has not been confirmed as a daughter.

****

Isaac Weidmann

Isaac^{1z} had the following son:
Mathias Martin$^{1.1z}$, b. in Karlsruhe, Durlach, Baden in 1677.

Mathias Martin Weidman

Mathias Martin$^{1.1z}$ had the following children:
Matthias Martin$^{1.1.1z}$, b. in Karlsruhe, Durlach, Baden in 1699 (?).
Christoph$^{1.1.2z}$, b. about 1702. He has not been proven as a son.
Jacob Heinrich$^{1.1.3z}$, b. about 1710. He has not been proven as a son.

Matthias Martin Weidmann/Wittman

Matthias Martin m. Maria Catharina. He resided at Warwick in Jan. 1735, and d. there in 1743. By Mar. 1745, Martin's widow, Maria Catharina, had m. John Lane, and his son, Johan Matthias, was his only minor child. Martin and Maria Catharina had the following children:
Matthias Martin$^{1.1.1.1z}$, b. about 1712.
Johannes$^{1.1.1.2z}$, b. in Karlesruhe, Durlach in 1718.
Maria Elisabetha$^{1.1.1.3z}$, b. in 1719, and m. Johan Adam Haushalter in Warwick on Oct. 17, 1743.
Johan Georg$^{1.1.1.4z}$, b. about 1723, and m. Anna Barbara Haushalter in Warwick on Jan. 1, 1744.
Maria Catarina$^{1.1.1.5z}$, b. about 1725, and m. Johan Herman Lehn in Warwick on Apr. 8, 1744.
Matthias Sebastian$^{1.1.1.6z}$, b. in 1727.
Magdalena$^{1.1.1.7z}$, b. about 1733, and m. Adam Heisner at Moden Creek on Jan. 5, 1755.
Johan Matthias$^{1.1.1.8z}$, b. on May 5, 1735, baptized at Warwick on May 26, 1735, and sponsored by Johan Jacob Eub and Johannes Lutz. Adam Haushalter (his brother in law) was appointed his guardian in Mar. 1745.

Matthias Martin Weidmann

Martin$^{1.1.1.1z}$ m. Margaretha between 1735 and Sep. 1741. He immigrated to Philadelphia with Christoph Weidman in 1733. He received a land warrant in Cocalico Township on Oct. 26, 1745. His will was probated there on June 6, 1766. They had the following children:

Christopher$^{1.1.1.1z}$, b. in 1731 (1725 Durlach), and d. in Lancaster County in 1770.

Maria Elisabeth$^{1.1.1.1.2z}$, b. in Nov. 1733, baptized at Muddy Creek Lutheran on Nov. 14, 1733, and sponsored by Matthias and Maria Catharina Weidman. She m. Adam Haker.

Wendell$^{1.1.1.1.3z}$, b. about 1735 (1730 Durlach).

Johan Jacob$^{1.1.1.1.4z}$, b. on Mar. 12, 1736, baptized at Muddy Creek on Apr. 18, 1736, and sponsored by Johan Jacob and Magdalena Hagie.

Maria Margaretha$^{1.1.1.1.5z}$, b. on Nov. 5, 1738, baptized at Muddy Creek on Nov. 12, 1738, and sponsored by Johan Georg and Margaretha Albert. She m. George Haker.

Maria Barbara$^{1.1.1.1.6z}$, b. on Feb. 8, 1741, baptized at Muddy Creek on Feb. 11, 1741, and sponsored by Baltzar and Maria Barbara Suss. She m. Bernard Gardner in Brickerville Church on Dec. 14, 1758.

Catharina$^{1.1.1.1.7z}$, b. in 1743, and m. George Wacher.

Johannes Weidmann

Johannes$^{1.1.1.2z}$ m. Margaretha Haushalter in Cocalico on July 6, 1741, and resided in Warwick in 1751. They had the following children in Berks County, Tulpehocken Township, Pennsylvania:

Johannes$^{1.1.1.2.1z}$, b. in 1742.

Maria Margaretha$^{1.1.1.2.2z}$, b. in 1744.

Catharina$^{1.1.1.2.3z}$, b. in 1745.

Heinrich$^{1.1.1.2.4z}$, b. in 1753.

Elisabetha$^{1.1.1.2.5z}$, baptized at Berks County, Reading, Trinity Lutheran Church on Oct. 6, 1754.

Johan Georg Wittmann/George Whitman

Johan Georg$^{1.1.1.4z}$ m. Anna Barbara Hausshalter in Lancaster County, Warwick, Pennsylvania, on Jan. 1, 1744, and was in Warwick on Sep. 21, 1747. He may be the George Whiteman/Whitman who came to Hampshire County, Virginia, 1776, but substantial proof for this connection has not been found. On Nov. 19, 1776, George of Virginia purchased 55 acres on South Branch, and 90 acres on Luneys Creek of South Branch Mannor. George was paid for military service at Hampshire County, Romney, in 1775, and d. on Luneys Creek sometime between 1784 and 1786. George of Hampshire County, Virginia, had the following children:

John, b. in 1750.

Mary, b. about 1761, and m. Peter Jones.
Ezekiel about 1766, and m. Dorcas, daughter of John Williams.

John Whitman

John m. Sarah. He served in the Revolutionary War, and was pensioned in Campbell County, Tennessee on Sep. 10, 1832, age 82 or 83. He was a drummer in Captain Heth's Company, Hampshire County Militia. He enlisted in Hampshire County, Virginia, as a Private in Captain Swearingen's Company, 8th Virginia Regiment, and marched to the mouth of Big Beaver (30 miles below Fort Pitt), and assisted in building Fort McIntosh. Then he marched to the head of the Muskingum River, and helped to build Fort Laurens under General McIntosh. After 4 months of service, he reenlisted in Captain Bedinger's Virginia Company under General Steuben and Marquis de Laffayette. He was discharged because of illness on Jan. 28, 1782, having served 9 months. John d. on Dec. 15, 1845, aged 95 years, and is buried in Indian Creek Baptist cemetery (moved to Cumberland View Baptist cemetery). Whitman Hollow is named for him. He was a resident of Campbell County in 1822. They had the following children:

Jacob, b. on Feb. 22, 1781, m. Sarah Agee (September 19, 1783-April 14, 1866), and d. in Campbell County on May 1, 1858. He is buried in Indian Creek Baptist cemetery.

John, b. in 1785, and d. in Tennessee in 1860. He is buried in Indian Creek Baptist cemetery.

Matthias Sebastian Weidmann

Matthias Sebastian$^{1.1.1.6z}$ m. Elisabeth Mumma, and had the following son:

Henry$^{1.1.1.6.1z}$, b. in York County, Pennsylvania, in 1757.

Christoph Wittmann (Weidman)

Christoph$^{1.1.2z}$ m. Anna Barbara. He immigrated to Philadelphia (now Montgomery) County, Falckner Swamp, Pennsylvania, in 1733, with Matthias Weidmann. On Mar. 26, 1747, he (said to be of Philadelphia County) moved to Lancaster County, Cocalico Township, Pennsylvania, and purchased 356 acres from William Bird. On Apr. 1, 1747, he sold 220 acres to John Ruble. He resided in Warwick Township in 1754, and his will was probated in Manheim Township on Feb. 18, 1765. He had the following children:

Johannes$^{1.1.2.1z}$, b. about 1723.

Adam$^{1.1.2.2z}$, b. about 1725, and m. Catarina Gansert at Muddy Creek on June 2, 1747.

Christoph$^{1.1.2.3z}$, b. about 1727.

Johan Heinrich$^{1.1.2.4z}$, b. about 1731, and m. Catarina Bassler at Warwick on Jan. 1, 1752.

Georg Michael$^{1.1.2.5z}$, b. on July 13, 1733, baptized at Falckner Schwamp on Sep. 3, 1733, and sponsored by Georg Michael and Maria Barbara Meck. He m. Catharina Schneider in Lancaster County on June 9, 1759, and resided in Cocalico Township in 1769/70.

Magdalena$^{1.1.2.6z}$ m. Ludwig Janler. This may be the same Magdalena who m. Adam Heisner at Moden Creek on Jan. 5, 1755.

Rosina$^{1.1.2.7z}$, m. Dietrich Kramer.

Regina$^{1.1.2.8z}$, m. William Klirtz.

Christoph Witman

Christoph$^{1.1.2.3z}$ m. Mary Adams in Lancaster County, Cocalico Township, Pennsylvania, on June 20, 1748 and Barbara prior to 1753. He received 110 acres in Cocalico from his parents on Jan. 22, 1754, and he was a cordwainer in Berks County, Reading Township, Pennsylvania, on June 9, 1753 and Jan. 19, 1754. His will was written at Reading on Apr. 29, 1778, and probated on May 20, 1778. Christopher had the following children:

John$^{1.1.2.3.1z}$, received a house in Reading.

William$^{1.1.2.3.2z}$.

Jurg$^{1.1.2.3.3z}$, b. at Reading on June 30, 1754, and received £350 from his father. His mother was Barbara.

Abraham$^{1.1.2.3.4z}$, received shoemaker tools from his father.

Catharina$^{1.1.2.3.5z}$, under 18 in 1778.

Jacob$^{1.1.2.3.6z}$.

Daniel$^{1.1.2.3.7z}$.

Jacob Heinrich Weidmann

Jacob$^{1.1.3z}$ Heinrich m. Eva Friedrica Volk in Karlsruhe, Graben, Neudorf, Baden on Jan. 30, 1731. They immigrated to Pennsylvania in 1736, and Jacob Heinrich d. sometime prior to Mar. 21, 1740, when Johannes Weidtmann and Eva Weidtmann, widow of Heinrich Jacob Weidtmann, sponsored the baptism of Johan Jacob, son of Jacob Balmer of Warwick. After Jacob's death, Eva m. Johan Michael Haagmeyer in Conestoga on Aug. 4, 1741. Jacob and Eva had the following children in Baden:

Maria Salome$^{1.1.3.1z}$, b. in 1731.
Matthias$^{1.1.3.2z}$, b. in 1735 (age 6 months at immigration).

****

INDEX

-A-
Aberli, 96
Ache, 46
Adams, 140, 145
Adelsperger, 27
Agee, 144
Albert, 55, 117, 128, 143
Albright, 100
Alexander, 58, 138
Alkire, 109
Allen, 64, 118
Allmon, 25
Anaschuetz, 124
Andrew, 16
Andrews, 75
Angst, 120
Arnold, 23
Askins, 32
Atchison, 53

-B-
Bader, 24
Baecker, 48
Baer, 73, 74
Baird, 17
Baker, 33, 64, 100, 101
Balmer, 66, 145
Balthis, 76
Bar, 96
Barb, 9
Barker, 39, 107
Barkley, 116
Barnes, 34
Barr, 25
Barrick, 141
Barth, 2
Bartholomew, 87
Bashore, 130
Bassler, 145
Batdorf, 70, 71
Baughman, 64
Bauman, 54, 55
Baur, 98
Baxter, 117, 118
Bayer, 44
Beale, 75, 80
Bear, 46
Becker, 98, 102
Beeman, 53
Beemer, 77
Beery, 27, 30, 31, 35
Beierstorfer, 133
Bender, 73, 82
Bennet, 60
Bennett, 55, 77
Bently, 77
Berger, 119
Bernhard, 124
Berridge, 60
Berryhill, 140
Bible, 13
Biehlmajer, 1, 2, 3, 4, 5
Bigler, 139
Bille, 13
Binder, 96
Binkley, 118
Bird, 144
Bitscher, 131
Bixler, 64
Blaser, 100
Blazer, 74
Bleymeyer, 67
Blosser, 26, 140
Boley, 54
Bolton, 108
Boozer, 138
Border, 141
Bower, 134
Bowers, 8, 134
Bowing, 111
Bowman, 14, 15, 22, 78
Bowsher, 140
Boyd, 117
Boyer, 36, 81
Brake, 101
Bram, 97
Braner, 15
Branner, 14
Brecht, 99
Breimer, 130
Brendel, 85
Brenneman, 31
Brennemon, 60
Brenner, 5, 7, 13
Bright, 104
Brook, 52
Brown, 22, 37, 76
Bruchbach, 40
Brumbach, 72
Brunstetter, 55, 56
Buhlmann, 99
Burns, 111
Burriff, 24
Buswell, 15
Byers, 79

-C-
Cahon, 21
Cairn, 79
Call, 132
Capler, 4
Carins, 73
Carn, 75, 79, 81, 82,

86
Carness, 82
Carns, 55
Carr, 31, 117, 141
Carroll, 76
Case, 53
Casey, 55
Cassel, 56
Chalfant, 86
Cherryholmes, 120
Chrisman, 10
Church, 52
Clapper, 33
Clapsaddle, 55
Clark, 103
Cline, 9
Clor, 6
Clutter, 140
Cochran, 75, 79, 105
Coleman, 139
Collins, 15, 46
Colwell, 31
Condren, 63
Conrad, 33, 70, 137
Cook, 8, 15, 109
Coole, 13
Corly, 132
Counts, 59
Cowden, 52
Cowgill, 84
Craig, 79
Craigen, 110
Crall, 131
Cramer, 62
Craver, 54
Crick, 66
Crim, 49
Crites, 117
Cronister, 136
Crooks, 39
Croy, 49

Culbertson, 57
Cummings, 126
Cupp, 23
Curn, 85
Cutler, 39
Cutright, 109

-D-
Dacherta, 8
Dailey, 72, 74
Dalzell, 108
Daub, 70
Davis, 12, 108
Dean, 22, 77
Decker, 131
Dehaas, 129
Dehoff, 4
Deininger, 111
Denny, 139
Derr, 38
Descher, 136
Dester, 136, 137
Devore, 133
Diefendoerfer, 48
Diefendorffer, 135, 136
Dieffendorfer, 135
Dieffendorffer, 95
Dietz, 99
Diffenderfer, 135
Dillsaver, 133
Dilsaver, 141
Dinges, 137
Ditzler, 46, 71
Donner, 97, 98
Dornman, 113
Dreiner, 130
Dubbs, 71
Dubs, 97
Dull, 60, 62
Dups, 70

Durr, 114
Dust, 139

-E-
Earhart, 17
East, 140
Eastman, 54
Eates, 82
Ebert, 5
Eblin, 77
Eger, 17
Ehrhard, 8
Ehrhardt, 6, 7, 8, 10, 11, 12, 13, 14, 15, 16, 17, 18, 19, 20, 25, 26
Eichelberger, 100, 113
Eichelborner, 102
Eilbert, 54
Elder, 90
Eley, 75
Ellis, 70
Elsasser, 92
Elsbet, 96
Ely, 134
Emmons, 133
Emory, 59
Empich, 121
Emrick, 52
Enders, 75
Endress, 97
Engel, 36, 37
Engelman, 43
Engen, 79
Engle, 22, 116
Ensign, 24
Ergebrecht, 39
Ernst, 114
Eub, 142
Evans, 108

Everett, 38
Evers, 52
Every, 19
Ewing, 84
Eyd, 95
Eyermann, 134

-F-
Fadley, 119
Faeg, 102
Fant, 31
Farier, 25
Faroute, 107, 108
Fast, 11
Feezer, 41
Feg, 102, 125, 127
Fenney, 17
Fiant, 60
Field, 68
Fields, 61
Fierin, 56
Fifer, 134
Fink, 29, 47
Firnssler, 135
Fishburn, 105
Fitsmire, 80
Fitzmoyer, 15
Flamerfelt, 105
Fleming, 23
Flick, 53
Flockirth, 70
Foos, 54
Forest, 32
Fought, 26, 28
Fowler, 54
Fox, 38
Francis, 113
Francois, 75, 91
Frank, 88
Franklin, 56
Frantz, 113

Frazee, 141
Frazier, 25
Freshwater, 33
Frey, 88
Friend, 129
Friener, 21
Fries, 21
Friesner, 10, 20, 21, 22, 24, 25, 26, 27, 28, 30, 31, 32, 33, 34, 35, 36, 37, 38, 39, 40, 47, 50
Fritz, 32, 42
Frock, 119
Fry, 80
Fuesser, 40, 41, 42, 43, 44, 45, 46, 69
Fugli, 97
Funk, 72, 96

-G-
Gallagher, 40
Gansert, 85, 145
Gardner, 143
Garletts, 116
Garvey, 55
Gebhard, 99
Gehr, 50
Geil, 32
Geisselman, 92
Gentzel, 130
Gentzler, 130
Geyer, 61
Gibs, 14
Giesy, 93
Gift, 130
Gilkison, 74
Gittinger, 129
Glatfelter, 119
Grabill, 76
Graffin, 101

Granfern, 111
Grau, 6
Graves, 39
Gray, 49, 64, 136
Greene, 104, 106
Griffith, 46, 106
Grim, 47
Grimm, 20, 21, 47, 48, 49, 50, 51, 95, 135
Grob, 96
Groff, 49
Groover, 75
Gross, 29, 57
Groves, 76
Gruber, 84
Gruenwald, 42
Grun, 138
Gunckel, 71
Gunthard, 97
Gut, 11

-H-
Haagmeyer, 145
Haas, 124, 130
Hadasser, 55
Haess, 135
Hage, 96
Hager, 67
Hagie, 143
Hains, 141
Haker, 143
Haley, 47
Haller, 85
Hallstein, 125
Halteman, 132
Halterman, 132
Hamilton, 22, 32, 77, 141
Hammaker, 64
Hammer, 27

Hanby, 33
Handt, 97
Hanley, 59
Hanna, 107
Harmon, 22, 38
Harper, 109
Harrison, 7, 49, 50
Harruff, 47, 52, 53, 54, 55, 56, 57, 58, 59, 60, 61, 62, 63, 64, 68, 106
Hart, 133
Hartleroad, 53
Hartman, 36
Harvey, 14
Hasel, 1
Hassinger, 130
Hat, 51
Hathaway, 19
Hauckler, 1
Hauendupler, 132
Haupt, 97
Haushalter, 64, 65, 66, 67, 142, 143
Hausholder, 65
Hausshalter, 143
Hautz, 41
Hay, 6
Haynes, 76
Heberle, 99
Hedge, 17
Heed, 49
Heft, 31
Heilman, 89
Heilmann, 88, 89
Heironimus, 83
Heisner, 142, 145
Heitz, 123
Hell, 123
Hendricks, 33, 77
Henkel, 9

Henney, 138
Henrici, 123
Herbach, 92
Herbert, 97
Herbine, 13
Herrbein, 13
Herring, 118, 133
Herschberger, 57
Hertzog, 3
Hess, 59, 62, 68, 69
Heth, 144
Heyd, 37
Heylmann, 88, 89
Hidlebough, 11
Higgins, 61
Hile, 60
Hilton, 40
Hinds, 79
Hineman, 77
Hines, 77
Hinsgardner, 8
Hinton, 58
Hish, 22
Hite, 34, 37
Hobble, 132
Hodgson, 40
Hoff, 80
Hoffer, 138
Hoffert, 34, 35
Hoffman, 80
Hogmire, 101
Holker, 75
Holloway, 62
Holtzdorn, 5
Holtzender, 5
Hoof, 50
Hooft, 50
Hoover, 4, 78
Hopper, 110
Horauff, 52
Hotsinpiller, 72

Houaman, 140
Houltz, 69
Householder, 126
Houtz, 70
Hover, 72, 73
Huber, 96, 97
Huddle, 38
Huffman, 56
Hufford, 31, 39, 40
Huggins, 141
Hughs, 101
Hull, 55
Hume, 140
Hummel, 53
Huni, 97
Hunsaker, 39
Hunter, 18
Hupp, 9
Huprecht, 97
Hutsell, 12
Hutson, 139
Hutzell, 117
Huver, 76

-I-
Imboden, 89
Inhoff, 31
Ireland, 33

-J-
Janler, 145
Jauler, 117
Jefferson, 110
Job, 131
Jonas, 66
Jones, 32
Jopp, 85
Joyce, 62
Julius, 63
Junker, 120
Justice, 57

-K-

Kackley, 78
Kain, 86
Kapp, 101, 111
Karn, 80
Kauffman, 24
Kearn, 79, 86
Keckler, 35
Keifer, 63
Kelcker, 136
Keller, 23, 56, 137, 138
Kemerer, 25
Kemper, 25
Kerby, 12
Kern, 6, 71, 72, 74, 75, 76, 77, 78, 79, 80, 81, 82, 83, 84, 85, 86
Kernbel, 139
Kershner, 128
Kerwood, 27
Kiber, 51
Kiger, 23
Kimmerlin, 136
Kindar, 130
Kindle, 128
King, 29, 59
Kipp, 7
Kips, 7, 8, 9
Kiracoff, 118
Kirkpatrick, 24
Kirschner, 103
Kissinger, 129
Kistler, 54
Kitzmueller, 137
Klein, 47, 53, 114
Klemmer, 67
Kline, 52
Klinger, 28
Kniesz, 89

Knight, 28
Knop, 8
Koch, 21
Koehler, 51
Koenig, 45
Kohr, 99
Kolb, 16
Konig, 123
Konkel, 27
Koppenhefer, 129
Kraft, 135
Kreig, 29
Krill, 43
Krim, 20, 50
Kueble, 70
Kuhborts, 87
Kull, 36, 37
Kuntz, 43
Kunzli, 96
Kurtz, 123

-L-

Landis, 9
Lane, 142
Lang, 48, 97, 98, 135
Langohr, 3
Laubsher, 70
Lawrence, 54
Leagle, 57
Lehman, 137, 140
Lehn, 142
Leib, 46, 123
Leichthaminer, 69
Leonard, 55
Leonhardt, 92
Lessly, 95
Letner, 23
Levarrance, 81, 82
Leviston, 17
Lew, 73
Lewis, 72

Light, 84
Linder, 63
Lindis, 93
Lindley, 107
Lindy, 94
Lint, 116
Lintermayer, 1
Linxweiler, 124
Lippin, 124
Little, 54
Lodowick, 54
Loesh, 101
Lohr, 43
Longacre, 2
Lotman, 93
Louck, 37
Ludwick, 54, 55
Lussi, 96
Lutz, 26, 142

-M-

McBride, 118
McClintock, 64
McCollister, 109
McCrea, 106
McCullaugh, 52
McDonald, 32
McDowell, 94, 107
McFadden, 26
McGlaughlin, 18
Mack, 73
Macklin, 21, 25
McMillen, 141
McNamee, 11
Marricle, 84
Martin, 69
Mason, 77
Massey, 101
Matheny, 24
Mattoon, 68
Mauk, 107

Maurer, 87, 88, 89, 113
May, 13
Mayer, 2
Meck, 145
Meitz, 97
Melchior, 136
Mell, 54
Meucle, 37
Meyer, 124
Mier, 80
Miesse, 23
Mikesell, 107
Miller, 6, 7, 8, 11, 23, 26, 27, 30, 31, 37, 51, 68, 73, 74, 78, 83, 90, 91, 92, 99, 104, 115, 119, 134
Minnich, 71, 94, 138
Mizener, 64
Mollenhour, 139
Moore, 23, 57, 105
Morain, 24
Morgan, 36
Morse, 54
Moser, 75, 80, 91, 92, 93, 94
Moss, 111
Mowery, 63
Moyer, 74, 82
Mueller, 14, 15, 48, 49, 70, 94, 95, 124, 125, 126, 128, 135
Mullenbarger, 7
Muller, 6, 84, 97
Murdoch, 7
Murphy, 29
Musser, 21
Myers, 14, 82

-N-

Naggle, 134, 140
Neely, 133
Neff, 47, 60, 78, 95, 96, 97, 98, 99, 100, 101, 102, 103, 104, 105, 106, 107, 108, 109, 110, 111
Neunkirchen, 123
Nevill, 71
Newton, 64
Nicholas, 109
Nichols, 141
Nittel, 139
Nitts, 114
Noble, 83
Nunniviller, 33

-O-

Obold, 65
Oehrle, 52
Ohlinger, 9
Oldridge, 58
Olinger, 8
Oliver, 20
Orebaugh, 14
Osborne, 106
Osewalt, 63
Overlander, 54

-P-

Painter, 11, 72, 73, 74
Palmer, 35
Patton, 22, 54, 116
Pelz, 8
Pence, 82
Pennington, 138
Peterman, 114
Peters, 77
Peterson, 114
Pfeifer, 141
Pfiefer, 134
Philip, 4
Phillippi, 100
Phillips, 68, 126
Pirkey, 78
Plecker, 14
Pope, 73
Powers, 58
Prence, 140
Price, 8
Pritchard, 32, 79
Pup, 75
Putnam, 61

-R-

Radebach, 56
Ragan, 16
Ramler, 87, 129
Rattermann, 97
Rawlins, 132
Ream, 41
Reed, 103
Reedy, 75
Reemer, 24
Reid, 84
Reidt, 127, 128, 129
Reiger, 70
Rein, 21
Reis, 102
Renkhert, 98
Reuben, 40
Reuter, 88
Reynolds, 11
Rheim, 41
Rhinehart, 35
Richards, 78
Richardson, 17, 59
Ridenouer, 8, 14
Rider, 36
Riegor, 52
Rietmuller, 1

Rife, 36
Riffle, 19
Riner, 130
Ringger, 96, 97
Rittenouer, 77
Roberts, 58
Robertson, 80
Robinson, 139
Roby, 37
Rod, 131
Rodes, 73
Roebuck, 61, 62
Roemer, 128
Roerbaugh, 63
Roeslin, 120
Roller, 8, 14
Roof, 54
Rooks, 29
Rorak, 54
Rosenberger, 78, 84
Ross, 62, 105
Roth, 36, 37, 131
Royer, 70
Ruble, 144
Rudisiler, 97
Rudolph, 78, 98
Ruff, 35
Rugh, 21
Ruhl, 4
Rumple, 118
Rupp, 60
Rush, 79, 81
Russell, 33, 104, 105
Russer, 96
Ryan, 76

-S-

Sailor, 106
Salomonmuller, 111
Salzgeber, 130
Santmann, 96
Sattelthaler, 113
Saur, 98
Savage, 75, 126
Scarff, 15
Schaack, 112, 120, 121
Schaak, 111, 113, 120, 122
Schaeffer, 99, 127
Schall, 113
Schally, 112, 113
Schantzen, 121
Schaque, 122
Schaub, 85
Schaup, 85
Scheck, 114
Schellenberger, 2
Schenck, 1, 2, 5, 138
Scherber, 99
Schick, 113
Schiffler, 123
Schiller, 114
Schindel, 80, 81
Schlauch, 135
Schmidt, 1, 3, 5, 12
Schneder, 49
Schneebeli, 96, 97
Schneider, 90, 102, 123, 145
Schnoeder, 49, 95
Schoch, 2, 111
Schock, 2, 88, 111, 112, 113, 114, 121, 122
Schoeffer, 98
Schoeneberger, 113
Scholl, 36, 37
Schop, 137
Schopp, 130, 131, 133
Schoster, 50
Schreck, 5
Schry, 131
Schryock, 77
Schueck, 115
Schuetz, 25, 51
Schup, 131
Schutz, 102
Schwab, 99
Schwengel, 128
Schwifer, 98
Schwingel, 66, 88, 113, 123, 124, 125, 127, 128, 129, 130
Schwingell, 122
Schwytzer, 96
Schyker, 48
Scribner, 18, 19
See, 101
Seider, 56
Seister, 128
Seitz, 34, 38
Sell, 42, 44
Seltzer, 98
Sessler, 96
Seymour, 103
Shaak, 122
Shack, 111
Shafer, 5
Shaffer, 18, 54, 93
Shake, 1, 114
Shaup, 85, 86
Shaver, 50
Sheck, 114
Sheek, 114
Shepherd, 83
Sherer, 4
Shick, 114
Shields, 39
Shilt, 43
Shock, 115, 116, 117, 118, 119, 120, 134
Shoemaker, 38

Shofe, 140
Shook, 110
Shooke, 114
Shop, 131
Shope, 118, 130, 131, 132, 133, 134, 139, 140
Showalter, 13
Shreiner, 2
Shrum, 78
Shuck, 114
Shufflebarger, 12
Shuk, 114
Shultz, 114, 115
Shumaker, 32
Shuy, 46
Shyman, 33
Simpson, 40, 115
Sipe, 17
Sisco, 55
Smallwood, 76
Smith, 18, 20, 38, 46, 68, 101, 114, 119, 128
Smootz, 78
Snavely, 71
Snell, 36
Snider, 38
Southard, 58
Spangler, 140
Spear, 34
Spieker, 89
Spitler, 24
Spitzer, 50
Spohr, 131, 132
Spotz, 130
Sprecher, 112
Sprinckel, 90
Springer, 7, 10
Spyker, 128
Stanley, 76

Staubus, 16
Staudemeyer, 14
Stauedemeyer, 15
Stauffer, 137
Stautenmayer, 26
Stecher, 121
Steele, 77
Stein, 42, 48, 121, 134, 135, 136
Steinbruckel, 96
Steinel, 85
Steinle, 85
Stephens, 74
Stevens, 79
Stevson, 32
Stewart, 27
Stickles, 17
Stihli, 39
Stinebach, 72
Stivison, 29
Stock, 130
Stoever, 89
Stokes, 58
Stolp, 20
Stoltz, 97, 131
Stonebreaker, 124, 126
Stoneburner, 34
Stose, 59
Stoutmire, 14, 15
Stover, 100
Strahler, 93
Strait, 61
Strasser, 97
Strettell, 91
Strine, 59
Stroeher, 120
Strohl, 29
Stroll, 3, 37
Strother, 76
Stuckey, 22, 30, 33, 133

Studabaker, 19, 38
Stull, 24
Stump, 100, 103
Stupp, 111
Suss, 143
Suter, 96
Swartz, 26, 30, 31, 33, 36
Swearingen, 144
Swern, 74
Swigert, 21
Swingle, 125, 127
Swisher, 23
Syfert, 31
Syler, 75
Syphert, 32

-T-

Tanner, 107
Tapscot, 17
Taylor, 12
Teeter, 61
Teschler, 136
Tester, 118, 132, 134, 136, 137, 138, 139, 140, 141
Theiss, 126, 128
Thom, 103
Thomas, 2, 27, 33, 125
Thompson, 17, 79, 132
Thorn, 103
Tice, 127
Towell, 31
Travel, 105
Tritt, 85
Trouster, 136
Trumboe, 7
Tuping, 101

Turk, 79
Turner, 33
Tussing, 9, 101
Tyson, 91

-U-
Umstead, 140
Underwood, 62
Usteri, 96

-V-
Van Bibber, 132
Van Horn, 120
Vanorsdal, 73
Vittel, 139
Voelkle, 69
Vogel, 3
Voland, 8
Volk, 145
Vollenweid, 97

-W-
Wacher, 143
Waggoner, 63
Wagner, 94
Wagoner, 118
Walb, 70
Walker, 117
Wallrick, 119
Walsch, 63
Walter, 139, 140
Walters, 141
Walther, 47
Ward, 133
Warner, 21, 25
Watson, 59
Weaver, 23, 28, 77
Weber, 70, 82
Weidman, 65, 143
Weidmann, 142, 143, 144, 145

Weidtmann, 145
Weigel, 5
Weil, 23
Weiman, 100
Weimer, 114
Weir, 65, 128
Weiser, 128
Weiss, 91, 94, 95, 97
Weitmann, 128
Wellburn, 58
Weller, 16
Wells, 114
Welsch, 141
Welton, 101
Welty, 27
Werndt, 95
Werner, 124
Werns, 70, 95
Westenbarger, 31
Weybrecht, 3
White, 66
Whiteman, 143
Whitman, 143, 144
Wiley, 58
Williams, 36, 60, 144
Willoughby, 33
Wilson, 24, 75, 76, 104, 106, 109, 110
Wimsett, 58
Winter, 71
Wirtz, 96
Wise, 14
Wiseman, 111
Witman, 145
Wittman, 65, 142
Wittmann, 144
Witzell, 81
Wolf, 4, 32, 52, 132
Wolfersperger, 100
Wolff, 94
Wolfinger, 40

Wollmer, 92
Woods, 109
Woollett, 141
Wortman, 92
Wright, 27, 72
Wust, 139

-Y-
Yahn, 61
Yantis, 32
Yoacum, 103
Yoakham, 101
Yost, 40

-Z-
Zehring, 113
Zeick, 37
Zeitz, 30
Zeller, 30, 129
Zellers, 28
Zerckel, 8
Ziegler, 121, 122
Zimmerman, 96
Zinn, 57
Zirkel, 9
Zyberman, 96

www.ingramcontent.com/pod-product-compliance
Lightning Source LLC
Chambersburg PA
CBHW062226080426
42734CB00010B/2038